LIVING *the* WORD

Scripture Reflections and Commentaries
for Sundays and Holy Days

Dianne Bergant, C.S.A. and
Rev. James A. Wallace, C.Ss.R.

DECEMBER 2, 2012 THROUGH NOVEMBER 24, 2013   YEAR C

LIVING *the* WORD

Scripture Reflections and Commentaries
for Sundays and Holy Days

Vol. 28 December 2, 2012—November 24, 2013

Published annually

Individual copy: $14.95
(2-9 copies: $10.95 per copy;
10-24 copies: $9.95 per copy;
25-99 copies: $8.95 per copy;
100 or more copies: $6.95 per copy)

Editor: Alan J. Hommerding
Copy Editor: Marcia T. Lucey
Typesetter: Tejal Patel
Cover Design: Jane Pitz and Tejal Patel
Director of Publications: Mary Beth Kunde-Anderson

In accordance with c. 827, with the material having been found free from any doctrinal or moral error, permission to publish is granted on June 11, 2012, by the Very Reverend John F. Canary, Vicar General of the Archdiocese of Chicago.

Copyright © 2012 by World Library Publications,
the music and liturgy division of J. S. Paluch Company, Inc.
3708 River Road, Suite 400, Franklin Park, IL 60131-2158
800 566-6150 • fax 888 957-3291
wlpcs@jspaluch.com • wlpmusic.com
All rights reserved.

Printed in the United States of America
WLP 006774 • (ISSN) 1079-4670 • (ISBN) 978-1-58459-518-2

Our renewed liturgy has generated a great deal of interest in sacred scripture. In turn, a richer appreciation of the readings for Mass has done much for participation in our liturgical celebrations. *Living the Word* is designed to help facilitate this twofold deepening of the Christian life. It is our hope that individuals, homilists, catechumens, candidates, discussion groups, religious education classes, and similar gatherings will all benefit from the commentaries and reflections found on these pages.

The readings for each Sunday, holy day, and major celebration from December 2012 through November 2013, Year C of the Lectionary cycle, are presented here, along with a brief passage intended to suggest a focus or approach to consider while reading them. Following the readings is a commentary that provides a context for understanding them, incorporating both biblical scholarship and the Church's age-old wisdom. A reflection section develops the initial focus and ties it together with the commentary. The discussion questions and suggestions for responses that follow offer help in moving from reflection to action, inviting those who use this volume to go about truly "living the word."

Whether reflecting on the scriptures in a group setting or individually, it is best to do so in the context of prayer. Consider creating an atmosphere that will foster prayerful reflection when you are using this book. In a quiet space, perhaps with lit candles and simple seasonal decoration (incense or soft music may also be appropriate), begin with a prayer and read aloud the scriptures for that day, even if you are alone. Groups can encourage members to focus on one word or idea that speaks to them from each reading. Participants might want to share these ideas with one another before continuing.

After listening to the readings, ask yourself how they have changed you, enlightened you, moved you. Proceed to the commentary, reflection, and response. Use the discussion questions to shape your conversation or as a springboard for your own questions. How does the brief "Responding to the Word" reflection invite you to "live the word" in your relationship with God, with family and friends, at work, school, or church, or in the broader community?

Having started with prayer, perhaps once you have spent time in reflection or discussion it will be appropriate to lift up someone or something in a prayer that is related to the readings or your reflections. Pray spontaneously as you think about the texts' meaning for you, or invite people in the group to offer prayers informally.

Finally, what action will you take this week that grows out of your prayerful reflection on this week's scriptures? You may propose your own prayer for help to do something in response to the readings or simply stand and pray the Lord's Prayer. If you are in a group, offer one another a sign of peace before departing. If alone, extend yourself to another in a gesture of peace later in the day or week, in person, by phone, or by offering a simple prayer.

Repeating this pattern over time can help your prayerful reflection to deepen your appreciation for and commitment to God's word every day of your life.

Table of Contents

Prayers Before Reading Scripture

Lord Jesus,
we give you praise.
Speak to us as we read your word,
and send your Spirit into our hearts.
Guide us today and each day in your service,
for you are our way, our truth, our life.
Lord Jesus, we love you:
keep us in your love for ever and ever. *Amen!*

or

Blessed are you, Lord God,
king of all creation:
you have taught us by your word.
Open our hearts to your Spirit,
and lead us on the paths of Christ your Son.
All praise and glory be yours for ever. *Amen!*

or

Lord, open our hearts:
let your Spirit speak to us
as we read your word. *Amen!*

or

Lord Jesus,
to whom shall we go?
You have the words of eternal life.

Speak, Lord,
your servants are listening:
here we are, Lord,
ready to do your will. *Amen!*

Prayers After Reading Scripture

Blessed are you, Lord God,
maker of heaven and earth,
ruler of the universe:
you have sent your Holy Spirit
to teach your truth to your holy people.
We praise you for letting us read your word today.

Grant that we may continue to think and pray
over the words we have read,
and to share your thoughts with others
throughout this day.

Loving God, we praise you
and thank you in Jesus' name. *Amen!*

or

God of all graciousness, we thank you
for speaking to us today
through your holy word. *Amen!*

The seasons of Advent and Christmas together provide glimpses into the mystery of God's saving action in the ordinariness of human life. During Advent we see the marvel of God's prodigious love unfolding in a particular place through a specific family. Prophetic promises assure the anxious people that God's earlier promises will be fulfilled through a descendant of David. This promise of a brighter future is repeated in the picture sketched of the chosen city of Jerusalem. Throughout these seasons, God's choice narrows from focus on a nation, then on the central city of that nation, and finally on the actual village where the promised one will be born. Salvation dawns in a particular place, at a particular time, and thereby completely transforms human history.

Excerpts from the Epistles chart the ways we should live in this transformed reality. Christian virtue should be a witness to all, for that is how God is made manifest. Basic to all Christian living, of course, is love. Rooted in God's love for us, our love for others makes us righteous before God. We are also called to forgiveness, patience, and meekness. It is really in the various Gospel stories that the meaning of the seasons unfolds. The Advent stories are anticipatory; the Christmas accounts announce fulfillment. Together they move from focus on an expansive cosmic sphere to the events that took place just before the actual appearance of God in human flesh, from the birth to the baptism and ministry of Jesus, to the final and glorious coming of the Son of Man.

The seasons' mosaic of readings shows that this is a time for us to reflect on the wondrous fact that God in Christ has entered the events of human existence and from there has called us to live lives rooted in that same Christ. It is through this unique human reality that we come to know God and it is to other human beings that we are sent to proclaim what we know. God came once in the flesh and became so much a part of our existence that never again will human life be bereft of the divine. While God's working may be depicted in descriptions that employ vibrant imagery, the events described were real events with historical significance. This profound reality contains a threefold message for us all: 1) Something definitive has happened in history and it is the marvelous work of God, 2) the appearance of the long-awaited Messiah has brought blessing to all nations, and 3) those open to this mystery form a community that lives by its demands and shows itself as the place where God has pitched a tent to dwell among us.

December 2, 2012

FIRST SUNDAY OF ADVENT

Today's Focus: God of Promise.

The God revealed in Advent is a God who will keep any promises made. The fulfillment of God's promises, already begun in the first coming of Christ, continues to unfold in our world when people of faith and hope live into and out of their relationship with the living God, revealed in Jesus Christ.

FIRST READING
Jeremiah 33:14–16

The days are coming, says the LORD, when I will fulfill the promise I made to the house of Israel and Judah. In those days, in that time, I will raise up for David a just shoot; he shall do what is right and just in the land. In those days Judah shall be safe and Jerusalem shall dwell secure; this is what they shall call her: "The LORD our justice."

PSALM RESPONSE
Psalm 25:1b

To you, O Lord, I lift my soul.

SECOND READING
1 Thessalonians 3:12 — 4:2

Brothers and sisters: May the Lord make you increase and abound in love for one another and for all, just as we have for you, so as to strengthen your hearts, to be blameless in holiness before our God and Father at the coming of our Lord Jesus with all his holy ones. Amen.

Finally, brothers and sisters, we earnestly ask and exhort you in the Lord Jesus that, as you received from us how you should conduct yourselves to please God—and as you are conducting yourselves —you do so even more. For you know what instructions we gave you through the Lord Jesus.

GOSPEL
Luke 21:25–28, 34–36

Jesus said to his disciples: "There will be signs in the sun, the moon, and the stars, and on earth nations will be in dismay, per-plexed by the roaring of the sea and the waves. People will die of fright in anticipation of what is coming upon the world, for the pow-ers of the heavens will be shaken. And then they will see the Son of Man coming in a cloud with power and great glory. But when these signs begin to happen, stand erect and raise your heads because your redemption is at hand.

"Beware that your hearts do not become drowsy from carousing and drunkenness and the anxieties of daily life, and that day catch you by surprise like a trap. For that day will assault everyone who lives on the face of the earth. Be vigilant at all times and pray that you have the strength to escape the tribulations that are imminent and to stand before the Son of Man."

Jeremiah's words announce a future wherein God's promise of restoration will be fulfilled. A shoot, a sign of new life springing from previous life, will be raised up for the Davidic house. Jerusalem, the city whose name means "foundation of peace," is here called "The LORD our justice." Thus, the foundation of this peace is justice, and the basis of the justice is the quality of commitment to the Lord. This oracle opens with an announcement that God will deliver the people to safety, and it concludes with the people rooting their salvation in the righteousness of God.

Paul expresses his desire for the spiritual growth of the Thessalonians. His exhortation contains a tone of urgency, encouraging the believers to continue to live righteous lives. He does not ask that their love increase, but that their capacity for growth be expanded so that they can fill it with love. This love should be both communal (for one another) and universal (for all). It breaks all ethnocentric bounds and, like the love that Paul himself possesses, it resembles the inclusive love of God. Paul implies that the coming time of fulfillment should be an incentive to righteous living.

Jesus speaks of cosmic disturbances and the distress on earth that these disturbances will cause. His cosmic turmoil calls to mind the primordial chaos out of which God brought order (see Genesis 1:1–10), and the destruction at the time of Noah out of which God brought order anew (see Genesis 7:12; 9:9–11). In the case described in this passage, the disturbances are probably less predictions of actual historical events than they are metaphorical images portraying the end of one age and the birth of another. For those who faithfully await the revelation of God, this will not be a time of punishment, but of fulfillment. Since the exact time of the revelation is unknown, the fundamental exhortation is: Beware! Take heed! Be alert! Don't be caught by surprise!

✤ *Reflecting on the Word*

In Thornton Wilder's play *The Skin of our Teeth*, Mrs. Antrobus tells her husband, George, that she didn't marry him because he was perfect, that she didn't even marry him because she loved him; she married him because he gave her a promise. And she gave one to him. And over the years, as their children were growing up, that mutual promise protected all of them, moving them into the future together.

A promise can open up into an unexpected future, marked by new life. God's promises spoken in today's first reading offered hope to a people who had little reason to hope. The hope of a restored Jerusalem, of a descendent of David who would do what is right and just—such promises began to be fulfilled in the person of Jesus of Nazareth.

With Jesus a new age began that promised to bring the old order of chaos and destruction to an end. With his birth a new power entered the world, making it possible to live in love, and allowing men and women to "increase and abound in love for each other and for all," as Paul writes to the Thessalonians. Total fulfillment of God's promises remains in the future.

But beginnings offer hope. A new church year calls on us to live as a people of hope in what God can do in our own day. Advent invites us to renew our relationship with the promises of God made visible in the person of Jesus Christ.

❖ Consider/Discuss:

- Do you think of God as a promise keeper?
- Do you see Jesus as beginning the fulfillment of God's promises?
- What hopes do you have for this new year of grace?

❖ Responding to the Word

Lord, awaken us to your love and grant us your salvation, so we might bring new life to our world by what we say and do. Bless this new year of grace, and may our call to holiness alert the world to your transforming power.

December 8, 2012

IMMACULATE CONCEPTION OF THE BLESSED VIRGIN MARY

Today's Focus: God's Passionate Love for Us

How do we explain the gift of salvation given to us in Jesus Christ? What explains God creating humankind? Even more, what prompted God to recreate humankind in Christ, when such disarray had been—and continues to be—made of creation?

FIRST READING
Genesis 3:9–15, 20

After the man, Adam, had eaten of the tree, the LORD God called to the man and asked him, "Where are you?" He answered, "I heard you in the garden; but I was afraid, because I was naked, so I hid myself." Then he asked, "Who told you that you were naked? You have eaten, then, from the tree of which I had forbidden you to eat!" The man replied, "The woman whom you put here with me—she gave me fruit from the tree, and so I ate it." The LORD God then asked the woman, "Why did you do such a thing?" The woman answered, "The serpent tricked me into it, so I ate it."

Then the LORD God said to the serpent:
"Because you have done this, you shall be banned
      from all the animals
      and from all the wild creatures;
on your belly shall you crawl,
      and dirt shall you eat
      all the days of your life.
I will put enmity between you and the woman,
      and between your offspring and hers;
he will strike at your head,
      while you strike at his heel."
The man called his wife Eve, because she became the mother of all the living.

PSALM RESPONSE
Psalm 98:1a

Sing to the Lord a new song, for he has done marvelous deeds.

SECOND READING
Ephesians 1: 3–6, 11–12

Brothers and sisters: Blessed be the God and Father of our Lord Jesus Christ, who has blessed us in Christ with every spiritual blessing in the heavens, as he chose us in him, before the foundation of the world, to be holy and without blemish before him. In love he destined us for adoption to himself through Jesus Christ, in accord with the favor of his will, for the praise of the glory of his grace that he granted us in the beloved.

In him we were also chosen, destined in accord with the purpose of the One who accomplishes all things according to the intention of his will, so that we might exist for the praise of his glory, we who first hoped in Christ.

GOSPEL
Luke 1:26–38

The angel Gabriel was sent from God to a town of Galilee called Nazareth, to a virgin betrothed to a man named Joseph, of the house of David, and the virgin's name was Mary. And coming to her, he said, "Hail, full of grace! The Lord is with you." But she was greatly troubled at what was said and pondered what sort of greeting this might be. Then the angel said to her, "Do not be afraid, Mary, for you have found favor with God. Behold, you will conceive in your womb and bear a son, and you shall name him Jesus. He will be great and will be called Son of the Most High, and the Lord God will give him the throne of David his father, and he will rule over the house of Jacob forever, and of his kingdom there will be no end." But Mary said to the angel, "How can this be, since I have no relations with a man?" And the angel said to her in reply, "The Holy Spirit will come upon you, and the power of the Most High will overshadow you. Therefore the child to be born will be called holy, the Son of God. And behold, Elizabeth, your relative, has also conceived a son in her old age, and this is the sixth month for her who was called barren; for nothing will be impossible for God." Mary said, "Behold, I am the handmaid of the Lord. May it be done to me according to your word." Then the angel departed from her.

❖ Understanding the Word

Contrary to the Marian interpretation captured in many depictions of the Immaculate Conception, the Genesis story states that it is the offspring of the woman who will have his heel on the serpent's head, not the woman herself. This part of the story is really about the antagonism that will always exist between human beings and the forces of evil. Human beings will always have to battle temptation. However, this feast that celebrates Mary assures us that, regardless of the cunning nature of temptation, good will ultimately triumph.

Paul insists that the blessing of God comes to us through the agency of Christ. The blessings themselves are distinctively of a spiritual, even cosmic, nature. First is election in Christ. Though Paul suggests a kind of primordial predestination, there is no sense here that some are predestined for salvation and others are not. The point is that salvation in Christ is not an afterthought; it was in God's plan from the beginning. The salvation ordained by God through Christ is the cause and not the consequence of righteousness. Adoption, redemption, forgiveness of sin, and the gifts of wisdom and insight are all pure grace, gifts from God, bestowed on us through Christ.

Mary's Immaculate Conception sets her apart so that she might miraculously conceive Jesus, the event described in today's Gospel reading. The opening angelic greeting, "Hail, full of grace! The Lord is with you," emphatically states her extraordinary dignity. She is here invited to be the vehicle of salvation for God's people. As in other stories of angelic appearances to women (Hagar, in Genesis 16:7–16; the mother of Samson, Judges 13:2–7), Mary interacts directly with God's messenger, without the mediation of her father or intended husband. She is not only free of patriarchal restraints; her words show that hers is a free response to God. The expectations of the past are now being fulfilled; God's plan is being accomplished through Mary.

❖ Reflecting on the Word

Behold our mothers: Eve, mother of all the living, and Mary, mother of the Lord and of all his disciples. These two women reflect conflicting human urges: to stretch out our hand to seize what promises to make us godlike, or to bow our heads humbly before the living God, offering ourselves in service.

The two narratives are instructive. In Genesis , after their disobedience, Adam and Eve begin a life of finger-pointing and blame, of regret and recrimination, choosing a world where Eden can no longer be entered. In today's Gospel, after fear and confusion have given way to acceptance and assent to God's word, Mary goes forth in joy to assist her life-bearing cousin Elizabeth.

In Romans, St. Paul complements these images with those of the old Adam and the new Adam, Christ. God's will was set aside by the former, but embraced by the latter. While our baptism empowers us to live in Christ, this can be set aside. A choice is before us: to live as autonomous, self-centered children of Adam, or as adopted, obedient children of God in the risen Lord.

Various forces threaten to separate us from yielding to the divine plan that we be holy and blameless in God's sight, both in our identity as church and as individual disciples of the Lord. But this feast reminds us of the power of God's grace to transform us, just as it did a frightened young woman into the brave singer of the *Magnificat*, the God-bearer of our Lord and Savior, Jesus Christ.

- Do you think this feast only speaks about Mary and what was done for her so she could be the mother of Jesus?
- Do you see yourself as being "graced"? Are you "blessed in Christ, with every spiritual blessing in the heavens"?

❖ *Responding to the Word*

Loving and generous God, you have blessed us from our beginning and destined us to give you praise and glory for all eternity. May we live lives of holiness now and come to the full enjoyment of eternal life. We ask this in the name of Jesus and through the intercession of our Mother Mary.

December 9, 2012

SECOND SUNDAY OF ADVENT

Today's Focus: Dressing Up

From Baruch shouting out to Jerusalem to get ready for her returning children, to John the Baptist calling all to prepare a highway for the Lord, to Paul praying for an increase of love and knowledge for his beloved Philippians—a sense of occasion marks today's readings, challenging us to respond to God's call.

**FIRST
READING**
Baruch 5:1–9

Jerusalem, take off your robe of mourning and misery;
    put on the splendor of glory from God forever:
wrapped in the cloak of justice from God,
    bear on your head the mitre
    that displays the glory of the eternal name.
For God will show all the earth your splendor:
    you will be named by God forever
    the peace of justice, the glory of God's worship.

Up, Jerusalem! stand upon the heights;
    look to the east and see your children
gathered from the east and the west
    at the word of the Holy One,
    rejoicing that they are remembered by God.
Led away on foot by their enemies they left you:
    but God will bring them back to you
    borne aloft in glory as on royal thrones.
For God has commanded
    that every lofty mountain be made low,
and that the age-old depths and gorges
    be filled to level ground,
    that Israel may advance secure in the glory of God.
The forests and every fragrant kind of tree
    have overshadowed Israel at God's command;
for God is leading Israel in joy
    by the light of his glory,
    with his mercy and justice for company.

**PSALM
RESPONSE**
Psalm 126:3

The Lord has done great things for us; we are filled with joy.

Brothers and sisters: I pray always with joy in my every prayer for all of you, because of your partnership for the gospel from the first day until now. I am confident of this, that the one who began a good work in you will continue to complete it until the day of Christ Jesus. God is my witness, how I long for all of you with the affection of Christ Jesus. And this is my prayer: that your love may increase ever more and more in knowledge and every kind of perception, to discern what is of value, so that you may be pure and blameless for the day of Christ, filled with the fruit of righteousness that comes through Jesus Christ for the glory and praise of God.

GOSPEL
Luke 3:1-6

In the fifteenth year of the reign of Tiberius Caesar, when Pontius Pilate was governor of Judea, and Herod was tetrarch of Galilee, and his brother Philip tetrarch of the region of Ituraea and Trachonitis, and Lysanias was tetrarch of Abilene, during the high priesthood of Annas and Caiaphas, the word of God came to John the son of Zechariah in the desert. John went throughout the whole region of the Jordan, proclaiming a baptism of repentance for the forgiveness of sins, as it is written in the book of the words of the prophet Isaiah:

> A *voice of one crying out in the desert*:
> "Prepare the way of the Lord,
>   make straight his paths.
> Every valley shall be filled
>   and every mountain and hill shall be made low.
> The winding roads shall be made straight,
>   and the rough ways made smooth,
> and all flesh shall see the salvation of God."

✛ Understanding the Word

Jerusalem is portrayed as a grieving mother. Her sorrow is for her children carried off and scattered both east and west. Since this meant the loss of any future, Jerusalem faced extinction. This is why she is clothed in the traditional garments of mourning. The prophet directs the city to "Take off your robe of mourning and misery!" Transformed by the glory of God, Jerusalem is told to stand on the heights and witness a reversal of fortune: the captives will return rejoicing; led away on foot, they will be carried back on royal thrones. The splendor that God bestows upon Jerusalem will be revealed to all the earth.

The affection that Paul has for the Philippians flows from his appreciation of their faithfulness to the righteousness that God is accomplishing in them. Although Paul brought the good news of the gospel to these people, he acknowledges that it was really God who made it take root in their hearts, and it is God who will oversee its maturation until it is brought to completion at the day of Christ Jesus. Paul prays that their mutual love will increase, and that they will be pure and blameless for the coming day of Christ.

John the Baptist is a most fascinating figure. He comes from a priestly family (see Luke 1:5), yet he is found in the desert, a place that calls to mind the wandering of the people in the wilderness as they moved out of Egyptian bondage. His activity occurred in the region of the Jordan, the gateway to the Promised Land, the very river crossed by the people as they entered the land. Thus crossing became a symbol of their entrance into a new life. All of this somehow marks John as an agent of momentous transformation. Just as both the Exodus and the return from exile involved a desert crossing, so the end-times renewal proclaimed by John begins in the desert.

❖ Reflecting on the Word

Getting "dressed up" does not seem to happen so much these days. No matter where you go, garb tends to be casual—funerals and weddings excepted (usually!). Jeans have replaced the suit, T-shirts and crew necks stand in for the traditional shirt and tie, and sneakers sub for dress shoes. Gone are most occasions when getting dressed up was *de rigueur.*

Today's readings are as much a "dress-up" call as a wake-up call. Baruch calls on Jerusalem to dress up, replacing her robe of mourning and misery and putting on the splendor of glory: the cloak of justice and the headgear of glory. Her children are returning from exile, "borne aloft in glory on royal thrones." God will see to arranging the rest of creation: mountains made low, gorges filled in, fragrant trees filling the air with their scent.

And John the Baptist is calling on the children of Israel to dress up their inner selves by undergoing a baptism of repentance, receiving God's forgiveness of their sins, and thereby providing God a highway into their hearts, a straight path with no obstacles impeding God's entry in glory. Then, God will dress them with salvation and fullness of life.

Paul's words bring it home. Advent is a time to prepare for the great feast of God's incarnate love. God, made visible in Jesus Christ, at work in us since the day we were baptized in Christ, continues to come today, bringing God's work one step closer to completion.

❖ Consider/Discuss

- How will you "dress up" for the coming feast? What needs to be taken off? What needs to be put on?
- What are you doing this Advent that invites the Lord to come in splendor? What needs to be filled in? What needs to be straightened?

❖ Responding to the Word

God who comes, help us hear your call to prepare for you to come into our lives. May this holy season set our hearts afire with the desire to put on the garments of truth and loving kindness so your light and love may come more fully into our world.

December 16, 2012

THIRD SUNDAY OF ADVENT

Today's Focus: St. Paul's Five-Step Program

Every year the Third Sunday of Advent calls us to live in joy. St. Paul's insistent words ring out: "Rejoice in the Lord always. I shall say it again: rejoice." He then provides us with a program that just might be instrumental in helping us to attain this elusive goal.

FIRST READING
Zephaniah 3: 14–18a

Shout for joy, O daughter Zion!
    Sing joyfully, O Israel!
Be glad and exult with all your heart,
    O daughter Jerusalem!
The LORD has removed the judgment against you,
    he has turned away your enemies;
the King of Israel, the LORD, is in your midst,
    you have no further misfortune to fear.
On that day, it shall be said to Jerusalem:
    Fear not, O Zion, be not discouraged!
The LORD, your God, is in your midst,
    a mighty savior;
he will rejoice over you with gladness,
    and renew you in his love,
he will sing joyfully because of you,
    as one sings at festivals.

PSALM RESPONSE
Isaiah 12:6

Cry out with joy and gladness: for among you is the great and Holy One of Israel.

SECOND READING
Philippians 4: 4–7

Brothers and sisters: Rejoice in the Lord always. I shall say it again: rejoice! Your kindness should be known to all. The Lord is near. Have no anxiety at all, but in everything, by prayer and petition, with thanksgiving, make your requests known to God. Then the peace of God that surpasses all understanding will guard your hearts and minds in Christ Jesus.

GOSPEL
Luke 3:10–18

The crowds asked John the Baptist, "What should we do?" He said to them in reply, "Whoever has two cloaks should share with the person who has none. And whoever has food should do likewise." Even tax collectors came to be baptized and they said to him, "Teacher, what should we do?" He answered them, "Stop collecting more than what is prescribed." Soldiers also asked him, "And what is it that we should do?" He told them, "Do not practice extortion, do not falsely accuse anyone, and be satisfied with your wages."

Now the people were filled with expectation, and all were asking in their hearts whether John might be the Christ. John answered them all, saying, "I am baptizing you with water, but one mightier than I is coming. I am not worthy to loosen the thongs of his sandals. He will baptize you with the Holy Spirit and fire. His winnowing fan is in his hand to clear his threshing floor and to gather the wheat into his barn, but the chaff he will burn with unquenchable fire." Exhorting them in many other ways, he preached good news to the people.

❖❖❖ Understanding the Word

Zephaniah's oracle of salvation directs the people to "Shout! . . . Sing! . . . Be glad and exult!" The reason for this rejoicing is their deliverance from enemies. The misfortune they endured may have been punishment for their sins, but God has removed that judgment and now dwells in their midst as King of Israel and as a mighty savior. "On that day" is an allusion to the day of the Lord, a time in the future when the justice of God will be executed throughout the world. This passage describes the tenderness God has for this restored people and the joy that their restoration evokes in God.

The joy that Paul advocates is not merely the happiness that comes from enjoyment of life. It is joy in the Lord, joy that is grounded in faith in Jesus Christ. Paul calls the believers to live lives of kindness, of gentle forbearance, of willingness to forego retaliation. Such genuine Christian behavior should be visible to all. "The Lord is near" is an end-of-time watchword, acclaiming the future coming of the Lord to set all things right. If the people have lived righteously, the Lord will come to them as a compassionate savior rather than as a severe judge. Finally, the fruit of such righteousness is peace.

The Gospel reading recounts instructions given by John the Baptist to those who came out to see and hear him and to be baptized. In response to their question "What should we do?" he challenges them to carry out their daily responsibilities with concern for others, honesty, and integrity. The people were looking for the Christ, the "anointed one." Lest they mistake him for this Christ, John contrasts himself with the one who is to come, insisting that he is not worthy to undo the sandals of that long-awaited one. John's baptism with water was a ritual of repentance and cleansing. The Christ's baptism of the Spirit will purge and transform our very souls.

St. Paul's letters always offer practical advice, flowing from whatever particular teaching he offers. Today's second reading contains a series of suggestions on how to live joyfully in Christ. They can be heard as independent statements. But consider Paul's words as offering a program for "rejoicing in the Lord always."

First, he advises, "let your kindness be known to all." This advice reminds me of a bumper sticker: "Commit random acts of kindness." In today's Gospel, John the Baptist's call for repentance offers some concrete forms of living kindly. "If you have two cloaks, share one with someone who has none," he says to the crowds. He then advises tax collectors not to use their office to gouge the people, and he advises soldiers not to bully or blackmail.

Paul's second "step" calls us to keep aware that the Lord is near. Our God does not abandon us, even though we have times we might not feel God's presence. Remember the words of the risen Lord: "I will be with you always, even to the end of time" (Matthew 28:20).

Paul's third word advises us how to keep aware of Christ by turning to him whenever anxiety threatens to overwhelm us, and uniting our prayers with his as we make our requests known to the Father. When this is done, steps four and five follow, when peace will "guard your hearts and minds," and out of this peace joy will flow joy as a gift of the Spirit.

✤ Consider/Discuss

- When have you known joy in your life? Is it the same as happiness?
- Are you able to make your requests known to God?
- Have you asked for the gift of joy from the Holy Spirit?

✤ *Responding to the Word*

God who created all things and who sent Jesus to be with us until the end of our days, hear my prayer this day that I may know the joy of the risen Lord. Give me an awareness that the Lord is indeed near, and send the peace that surpasses all understanding into my heart.

December 23, 2012

FOURTH SUNDAY OF ADVENT

Today's Focus: The Touch of God

The meeting of Elizabeth and Mary must have included their greeting each other with a "holy kiss," as Paul advises the community in his Letter to the Romans. Their mutual joy in what God was doing in and through them to bring salvation to the world invites us to look for how God touches our lives, bringing new life.

FIRST READING
Micah 5:1–4a

Thus says the LORD:
  You, Bethlehem-Ephrathah,
    too small to be among the clans of Judah,
  from you shall come forth for me
    one who is to be ruler in Israel;
  whose origin is from of old,
    from ancient times.
Therefore the Lord will give them up, until the time
    when she who is to give birth has borne,
and the rest of his kindred shall return
    to the children of Israel.
He shall stand firm and shepherd his flock
    by the strength of the LORD,
    in the majestic name of the LORD, his God;
and they shall remain, for now his greatness
    shall reach to the ends of the earth;
    he shall be peace.

PSALM RESPONSE
Psalm 80:4

Lord, make us turn to you; let us see your face and we shall be saved.

SECOND READING
Hebrews 10: 5–10

Brothers and sisters: When Christ came into the world, he said:
  "Sacrifice and offering you did not desire,
    but a body you prepared for me;
  in holocausts and sin offerings you took no delight.
  Then I said, 'As is written of me in the scroll,
  behold, I come to do your will, O God.' "

First he says,
  "Sacrifices and offerings, holocausts and sin offerings,
    you neither desired nor delighted in."
These are offered according to the law. Then he says,
  "Behold, I come to do your will."
He takes away the first to establish the second.

By this "will," we have been consecrated through the offering of the body of Jesus Christ once for all.

Mary set out and traveled to the hill country in haste to a town of Judah, where she entered the house of Zechariah and greeted Elizabeth. When Elizabeth heard Mary's greeting, the infant leaped in her womb, and Elizabeth, filled with the Holy Spirit, cried out in a loud voice and said, "Blessed are you among women, and blessed is the fruit of your womb. And how does this happen to me, that the mother of my Lord should come to me? For at the moment the sound of your greeting reached my ears, the infant in my womb leaped for joy. Blessed are you who believed that what was spoken to you by the Lord would be fulfilled."

❖ Understanding the Word

Micah's prophecy states that salvation will come from an insignificant village rather than from the royal city; the power of the ruler comes from God; and a time of trial will be followed by a time of security and peace. Since Bethlehem was the place of David's origin, the reference is rich in early royal importance that is quite distinct from any association with Jerusalem, the dynastic capital of the present reigning royal family. The new ruler promised will be called forth for God and strengthened by God. His rule will be like that of a shepherd who leads, protects, and provides for those in his care.

The passage from Hebrews contains a contrast between the ancient sacrificial ritual and the sacrifice of Christ. Though compliance to the will of God is clearly stated, the specific focus is Christ's offering of his body. The author argues that Christ annuls the first kind of sacrifice (external adherence to law) in order to establish the second (internal obedience). By freely offering his body in sacrifice, Christ identifies his own will with the will of God. We are sanctified through this same sacrifice, not through any sacrifice required by law. For it was through his human body, a body like ours, that he demonstrated his obedience.

In the Gospel passage, Elizabeth is filled with the Holy Spirit and proclaims her faith in the child that Mary is carrying. Elizabeth realizes that she is in the presence of God, and so she rejoices. It is as if Mary is the ark and the child within her is the glory of God. In response to this wondrous experience, Elizabeth exalts first Mary and then her child. She does not pronounce a blessing over them. Instead, she recognizes the blessedness that they possess and she praises it. This blessedness is derived from the dignity of the child, a dignity that Elizabeth acknowledges by referring to him as her Lord (*kýrios*).

Marge Piercy's poem "The Tao of Touch" reminds us of the power of touch. A person can die either without touch or because of touch. There is the touch of love that brings healing and joy, and those blows that shatter bones and relationships. Today's Gospel recalls how God's touch transformed the lives of two women—and the world.

I have a carved wooden statue of Mary gently resting her two hands along Elizabeth's belly as their two foreheads touch. You can imagine tears, laughter, and words springing from pure joy. Elizabeth must have gasped as the life in her womb exuberantly kicked up his heels in greeting.

Not only her body but her words of blessing gave witness to creation's joy: "Blessed are you among women, and blessed is the fruit of your womb," Elizabeth cried. "Blessed are you who believed that what was spoken by the Lord would be fulfilled," she sang. Scripture says the Holy Spirit filled Elizabeth, that Spirit whose gifts include joy, wisdom, and peace, that Spirit who had brought into being the child now growing in her cousin's womb.

Advent's fourth Sunday always takes us into the company of Jesus' kin, putting the spotlight either on Mary, Joseph, or Elizabeth. We enter the stories surrounding the birth of Jesus, God's Son, who came into the lives of ordinary people and transformed them, making them part of God's plan for the salvation of the world. This loving plan continues to be worked out in and through us.

❖ Consider/Discuss

- How do you imagine this meeting between Mary and Elizabeth?
- What helps you to enter the joy Luke presents in this short scene?
- How can this moment help you to enter the joy appropriate to Christmas?

❖ *Responding to the Word*

Beloved God and Father of our Lord Jesus Christ, help us in these final hours of Advent to set aside anything that prevents us from entering into the joy befitting the birth of your Son. Send us that same Spirit that came upon Elizabeth, filling her heart and soul with such great joy.

December 25, 2012

NATIVITY OF THE LORD: MASS DURING THE DAY

Today's Focus: God's Word Made Flesh

When radio or TV announcers say, "We have just received word . . ." or "Word has just come in . . ." we stop to listen. Something unexpected, something important has happened. In a way that defies adequate comprehension, much less celebration, Christmas celebrates the Word that waits to be received and to come into our lives.

FIRST READING
Isaiah 52:7–10

How beautiful upon the mountains
    are the feet of him who brings glad tidings,
announcing peace, bearing good news,
    announcing salvation, and saying to Zion,
    "Your God is King!"

Hark! Your sentinels raise a cry,
    together they shout for joy,
for they see directly, before their eyes,
    the LORD restoring Zion.
Break out together in song,
    O ruins of Jerusalem!
For the LORD comforts his people,
    he redeems Jerusalem.
The LORD has bared his holy arm
    in the sight of all the nations;
all the ends of the earth will behold
    the salvation of our God.

PSALM RESPONSE
Psalm 98:3c

All the ends of the earth have seen the saving power of God.

SECOND READING
Hebrews 1:1–6

Brothers and sisters: In times past, God spoke in partial and various ways to our ancestors through the prophets; in these last days, he has spoken to us through the Son, whom he made heir of all things and through whom he created the universe, who is the refulgence of his glory, the very imprint of his being, and who sustains all things by his mighty word. When he had accomplished purification from sins, he took his seat at the right hand of the Majesty on high, as far superior to the angels as the name he has inherited is more excellent than theirs.

For to which of the angels did God ever say:
You are my son; this day I have begotten you?
Or again:
I will be a father to him, and he shall be a son to me?
And again, when he leads the firstborn into the world, he says:
Let all the angels of God worship him.

In the shorter form of the reading, the passages in brackets are omitted.

GOSPEL
John 1:1–18
or 1:1–5, 9–14

In the beginning was the Word,
    and the Word was with God,
    and the Word was God.
He was in the beginning with God.
All things came to be through him,
    and without him nothing came to be.
What came to be through him was life,
    and this life was the light of the human race;
the light shines in the darkness,
    and the darkness has not overcome it.

[A man named John was sent from God. He came for testimony, to testify to the light, so that all might believe through him. He was not the light, but came to testify to the light.] The true light, which enlightens everyone, was coming into the world.

He was in the world,
    and the world came to be through him,
    but the world did not know him.
He came to what was his own,
    but his own people did not accept him.

But to those who did accept him he gave power to become children of God, to those who believe in his name, who were born not by natural generation nor by human choice nor by a man's decision but of God.

And the Word became flesh
    and made his dwelling among us,
    and we saw his glory,
    the glory as of the Father's only Son,
    full of grace and truth.

[John testified to him and cried out, saying, "This was he of whom I said, 'The one who is coming after me ranks ahead of me because he existed before me.' " From his fullness we have all received, grace in place of grace, because while the law was given through Moses, grace and truth came through Jesus Christ. No one has ever seen God. The only Son, God, who is at the Father's side, has revealed him.]

Isaiah announces the good news of salvation in various ways. First, the moment of proclamation resembles a messenger who swiftly runs to announce that exile and displacement are over. Zion's God has been victorious over their enemies and is coming to dwell among the people. In a second picture, the arm of God is bared, revealing the source of the divine power. This demonstration of strength reminds the people of the might of their protector. Just as the messenger heralds peace and salvation to Zion, so the deliverance of the city heralds the mighty power of God to the ends of the earth.

The passage from Hebrews acclaims Christ as the agent of revelation, creation, and salvation. As a reflection of God's glory and an exact representation of God's being, Christ could rightly be called the revelation of God. As Son of God, Christ is the heir of all things and the agent through whom the world was made and through whom it continues to be sustained. Besides preeminence, this assertion suggests preexistence. Since it was through Wisdom that God created, and Wisdom is the pure emanation of the glory of God, the author concludes that Christ is also the Wisdom of God.

The Gospel of John characterizes Christ as the preexistent Word. Furthermore, like Wisdom, the Word was actively involved in creation. Finally, the Word is the true light that comes into the world. This Word resided in some primordial place, but now has entered human history. Though several translations state that the Word "made his dwelling among us," a better reading of the Greek might be "tented." It calls to mind the tabernacle in the wilderness where God dwelt or tented among the people (Exodus 40:34) as well as the tradition about Wisdom establishing her tent in the midst of the people (Sirach 24:8). The Word of God, who is also the holiness and the wisdom of God, now dwells in our midst.

❖ Reflecting on the Word

Some friends living in Kingston, New York used to see their grandchildren only when they traveled down to Virginia or over to Connecticut. These visits were occasional, but nowhere near the frequency that doting grandparents desired. What a blessing Skype has become for them, allowing them to visit not only by voice, but by sight. Yet there is one thing better: being there in the flesh.

Today's readings give us a glimpse into the heart of God and God's desire to be with us "in the flesh"; they signal how great God's love was from the start. God's word first brought creation into being. Then God's word entered into a relationship, first with Noah, then with Abraham, and then with Moses and the people of Israel. God's word invited them into an intimate relationship called a covenant. And God kept calling them back again and again from infidelity into intimacy through the words of the prophets.

But all this was not enough. As the author of Hebrews reminds us, "In times past, God spoke in partial and various ways to our ancestors through the prophets; in these last days, he has spoken to us through the Son . . . " (1:1). God said, "Jesus." And in the eagle-soaring words of the John's Gospel: "The Word became flesh and made his dwelling among us, and we saw his glory, the glory as of the Father's only Son full of grace and truth." Beyond only seeing him, the text then proclaims: "From his fullness we have all received, grace in place of grace."

✦ Consider/Discuss

- What do you need this year to absorb more deeply the mystery of the birth of Jesus, the Son of God, the Word made flesh, and what it means for you?
- What do you need this year to absorb more deeply the mystery of the birth of Jesus, the Son of God, the Word made flesh, and what it means for our world?
- Could it be silence? Time for prayer? Talking about this with another person of faith?

✦ Responding to the Word

God of creation, God of compassion, God of all beginnings, help us to begin anew to enter into the mystery of your Word become flesh that this event might penetrate our minds and hearts and transform our lives not only during this season, but for the coming new year of grace.

December 30, 2012

THE HOLY FAMILY OF JESUS, MARY, AND JOSEPH

Today's Focus: Jesus, Family Man

Today's feast invites us to consider how the mystery of the Incarnation, of God becoming flesh in Jesus, has something special to say to families. Jesus was born into and grew up in a family. In becoming part of the human family, Jesus revealed his Father's committed love for the human family.

FIRST READING
Sirach 3:2–6, 12–14

God sets a father in honor over his children;
    a mother's authority he confirms over her sons.
Whoever honors his father atones for sins,
    and preserves himself from them.
When he prays, he is heard;
    he stores up riches who reveres his mother.
Whoever honors his father is gladdened by children,
    and, when he prays, is heard.
Whoever reveres his father will live a long life;
    he who obeys his father brings comfort to his mother.

My son, take care of your father when he is old;
    grieve him not as long as he lives.
Even if his mind fail, be considerate of him;
    revile him not all the days of his life;
kindness to a father will not be forgotten,
    firmly planted against the debt of your sins
    —a house raised in justice to you.

PSALM RESPONSE
Psalm 128:1

Blessed are those who fear the Lord and walk in his ways.

In the shorter form of the reading, the passage in brackets is omitted.

SECOND READING
Colossians 3:12–21 or 3:12–17

Brothers and sisters: Put on, as God's chosen ones, holy and beloved, heartfelt compassion, kindness, humility, gentleness, and patience, bearing with one another and forgiving one another, if one has a grievance against another; as the Lord has forgiven you, so must you also do. And over all these put on love, that is, the bond of perfection. And let the peace of Christ control your hearts, the peace into which you were also called in one body. And be thankful. Let the word of Christ dwell in you richly, as in all wisdom you teach and admonish one another, singing psalms, hymns, and spiritual songs with gratitude in your hearts to God. And whatever you do, in word or in deed, do everything in the name of the Lord Jesus, giving thanks to God the Father through him.

[Wives, be subordinate to your husbands, as is proper in the Lord. Husbands, love your wives, and avoid any bitterness toward them. Children, obey your parents in everything, for this is pleasing to the Lord. Fathers, do not provoke your children, so they may not become discouraged.]

GOSPEL
Luke 2:41–52

Each year Jesus' parents went to Jerusalem for the feast of Passover, and when he was twelve years old, they went up according to festival custom. After they had completed its days, as they were returning, the boy Jesus remained behind in Jerusalem, but his parents did not know it. Thinking that he was in the caravan, they journeyed for a day and looked for him among their relatives and acquaintances, but not finding him, they returned to Jerusalem to look for him. After three days they found him in the temple, sitting in the midst of the teachers, listening to them and asking them questions, and all who heard him were astounded at his understanding and his answers. When his parents saw him, they were astonished, and his mother said to him, "Son, why have you done this to us? Your father and I have been looking for you with great anxiety." And he said to them, "Why were you looking for me? Did you not know that I must be in my Father's house?" But they did not understand what he said to them. He went down with them and came to Nazareth, and was obedient to them; and his mother kept all these things in her heart. And Jesus advanced in wisdom and age and favor before God and man.

❖ *Understanding the Word*

Sirach's instruction on family living provides a glimpse into a way of life that brought happiness in the past. It is meant to encourage similar behavior that will bring the same happiness in the present and the future. Its focus is the respect and obedience that children (both sons and daughters) owe their parents (both mother and father). The final verses exhort the adult son to care for his father in his declining years. The picture portrayed is quite moving. Like all biblical teaching, this instruction on respect and care for one's parents is intended for the adult child, not a minor.

The Colossians are told that they are God's chosen, holy, and beloved people. Therefore, they should act accordingly. All the virtues they are called to live out are relational. Directed toward others, they require unselfish sensitivity. The motivation for such self-sacrifice is the forgiveness that the Christians themselves have received from God. The list continues with an admonition to love, the highest of all virtues. The peace of Christ, which is placed before them, is an inner peace that comes from a right relationship with God and therefore true harmony with others.

Today's Gospel reading provides us with the only glimpse we have into the early years of Jesus. While the key element in the passage is the Christological self-declaration of the young Jesus, the context of the account depicts a very religious family unit and an equally submissive son. Although a popular tradition (found in some religious art) suggests that Jesus was teaching in the temple, the text does not state this. He was merely part of the exchange of ideas. There is no conflict between Jesus' responsibilities of sonship in his relationship with Joseph and Sonship in his union with God, for he is faithful to both. Approaching adulthood, he assumes a public role; after his striking appearance in the temple, he returns to a life of obedience to his parents.

❖ Reflecting on the Word

If you were to choose an adjective to accompany "family," what would it be? Holy? Or is it more likely to be "dysfunctional"? If culture reflects reality, our greatest American playwrights hold up families falling apart as the norm: Eugene O'Neil's Tyrone family, Tennessee Williams' haunted Southern siblings, Arthur Miller's Willie and Linda Loman and sons, and, most recently, the families of Tracy Lett's *August: Osage County* and Jon Rabin Baitz's *Other Desert Cities*. Behold, the American family!

And yet, granting that every family, like every person, is imperfect and on occasion wounds each other in both small and big ways, we do find holiness in families. It is the holiness that we see in Mary, Joseph, and Jesus, who cared for and respected each other, a holiness that witnesses to the power of God's grace at work in hearts open to it.

In today's Gospel we see this gracious care in the worry of parents who could not find their son. We hear it in Mary's anxious words to Jesus, in Jesus' fidelity to his dual parentage—earthly and heavenly—and in the simple statement that "he went down with them and came to Nazareth, and was obedient to them."

As members of the human family, imperfect and even sinful, we too are graced with a capacity for "advancing in wisdom and age and favor before God and one another." Each of us is called to holiness, to a fullness of being made possible by being open to the loving touch of God's grace made visible in the Incarnation.

- Do Mary, Joseph, and Jesus have anything to teach us about what it means to be family?
- What does it mean to be a "holy family"? Is it a matter of doing "holy" actions, or saying "holy" words?

❖ Responding to the Word

Loving Father, you have created all who have ever lived in your image and likeness. Help us to recognize all others as our brothers and sisters and to honor, respect, forgive, and love them as your children. Together, enable us to bring your peace and justice, healing and reconciliation to our world.

January 1, 2013

SOLEMNITY OF MARY, THE HOLY MOTHER OF GOD

Today's Focus: God of Blessing

God's desire to bless us is at the heart of today's scriptures. From the beginning God blessed creation, calling it "very good" (Genesis 1:31). Through Moses God gave words of blessing to Aaron the priest to bless the people. And the fullness of blessing came with the gift of Jesus.

FIRST READING
Numbers 6: 22–27

The LORD said to Moses: "Speak to Aaron and his sons and tell them: This is how you shall bless the Israelites. Say to them:

The LORD bless you and keep you!
The LORD let his face shine upon you, and be gracious to you!
The LORD look upon you kindly and give you peace!

So shall they invoke my name upon the Israelites, and I will bless them."

PSALM RESPONSE
Psalm 67:2a

May God bless us in his mercy.

SECOND READING
Galatians 4:4–7

Brothers and sisters: When the fullness of time had come, God sent his Son, born of a woman, born under the law, to ransom those under the law, so that we might receive adoption as sons. As proof that you are sons, God sent the Spirit of his Son into our hearts, crying out, "Abba, Father!" So you are no longer a slave but a son, and if a son then also an heir, through God.

GOSPEL
Luke 2:16–21

The shepherds went in haste to Bethlehem and found Mary and Joseph, and the infant lying in the manger. When they saw this, they made known the message that had been told them about this child. All who heard it were amazed by what had been told them by the shepherds. And Mary kept all these things, reflecting on them in her heart. Then the shepherds returned, glorifying and praising God for all they had heard and seen, just as it had been told to them.

When eight days were completed for his circumcision, he was named Jesus, the name given him by the angel before he was conceived in the womb.

The blessing found in the reading from Numbers is one of the oldest pieces of poetry in the Bible. It is introduced by a statement that gives the content of the blessing both Mosaic and divine legitimacy. To know God's personal name, YHWH, presumes a kind of intimacy. The blessing itself is crisp and direct. Each line invokes a personal divine action: that God bless with good fortune and keep from harm, look favorably toward and be gracious, look upon and grant peace. Though these invocations might be realized in different things for different people at different times, they all ask for peace.

According to Paul, the goal of Christ's mission was to transform the Galatians from being slaves under the law to being adopted children of God. His attitude toward the law is not as negative as it appears at first glance. Here it is a necessary guardian that carefully watches over minors until they are mature enough to take care of themselves. Though the law is inferior to the Spirit of Christ, it is faithful and trustworthy. However, once the Spirit takes hold of the believer, dependence on the law ends and freedom in the Spirit, the rightful inheritance of the children of God, begins.

The Gospel reading is the same as that of the Christmas Mass at Dawn. However, the circumcision and naming of Jesus are included here. This slight difference shifts the focus of the passage away from the shepherds to the child and his parents. As observant Jews, Mary and Joseph fulfilled all the prescriptions of the law; the child was circumcised as custom dictated. Besides being circumcised, the child was given the name earlier told to Mary, the name Jesus, which means "savior." Now almost everything that the angel had announced has come to pass. Mary will have to wait to see how he will acquire the throne of his father David and rule the house of Jacob forever.

❖ *Reflecting on the Word*

As a boy, I remember our parish priest would visit my grandparents' house. Before he left, my grandmother would always ask his blessing and all of us would kneel to receive it. Another childhood memory sees my mother dipping her finger in a small holy water font that hung on the bedroom wall and sprinkling some of the water over my brothers and me in blessing every night.

We begin the New Year hearing an ancient blessing in today's first reading. What a beautiful way to enter into the new year as we gather, calling on God to bless us, to keep us, to let the divine face shine on us, to look on us kindly and to give us peace. These words tell us who our God is and what God wishes to give us—blessing. In Mary, our mother, we see what it means to live out of God's blessing and bring Christ to the world.

In the fullness of time, God blessed creation with Jesus, our Savior, who came to call us to a freedom that is the true blessing of the adopted children of our Abba (Father)-God. Jesus continues to ask God's blessing on us, standing with us, and blessing us with his peace. Today we ask God to bless our world with the peace that the world cannot achieve on its own. Today we ask Mary, the Holy Mother of God, to pray with us as we join her in reflecting on the One whom the angels named as our Savior.

❖ Consider/Discuss

- What blessing do you ask of God as this new year begins?
- When have you last blessed someone (other than when someone sneezes)? Whose blessing would you ask?

❖ Responding to the Word

God of blessing, look kindly upon our world as we begin this new year of grace. Bless all those who work for peace and drive out from the hearts of all your children any temptation to take up arms against another. Mary, our mother, bless us with peace.

January 6, 2013

EPIPHANY OF THE LORD

Today's Focus: Rise and Shine!

The story of the magi directs our attention to a group of stargazers who looked beyond themselves to the heavens and found reason—or better, encouragement—to leave their comfort zone to discover the Source of all life and light. They encourage us to continue our quest for the One who draws us God-wards.

FIRST READING
Isaiah 60:1–6

Rise up in splendor, Jerusalem! Your light has come,
    the glory of the Lord shines upon you.
See, darkness covers the earth,
    and thick clouds cover the peoples;
but upon you the LORD shines,
    and over you appears his glory.
Nations shall walk by your light,
    and kings by your shining radiance.
Raise your eyes and look about;
    they all gather and come to you:
your sons come from afar,
    and your daughters in the arms of their nurses.

Then you shall be radiant at what you see,
    your heart shall throb and overflow,
for the riches of the sea shall be emptied out before you,
    the wealth of nations shall be brought to you.
Caravans of camels shall fill you,
    dromedaries from Midian and Ephah;
all from Sheba shall come
    bearing gold and frankincense,
    and proclaiming the praises of the LORD.

PSALM RESPONSE
Psalm 72:11

Lord, every nation on earth will adore you.

SECOND READING
Ephesians 3: 2–3a, 5–6

Brothers and sisters: You have heard of the stewardship of God's grace that was given to me for your benefit, namely, that the mystery was made known to me by revelation. It was not made known to people in other generations as it has now been revealed to his holy apostles and prophets by the Spirit: that the Gentiles are coheirs, members of the same body, and copartners in the promise in Christ Jesus through the gospel.

35

GOSPEL

Matthew 2: 1–12

When Jesus was born in Bethlehem of Judea, in the days of King Herod, behold, magi from the east arrived in Jerusalem, saying, "Where is the newborn king of the Jews? We saw his star at its rising and have come to do him homage." When King Herod heard this, he was greatly troubled, and all Jerusalem with him. Assembling all the chief priests and the scribes of the people, he inquired of them where the Christ was to be born. They said to him, "In Bethlehem of Judea, for thus it has been written through the prophet:

And you, Bethlehem, land of Judah,
   are by no means least among the rulers of Judah;
   since from you shall come a ruler,
   who is to shepherd my people Israel."

Then Herod called the magi secretly and ascertained from them the time of the star's appearance. He sent them to Bethlehem and said, "Go and search diligently for the child. When you have found him, bring me word, that I too may go and do him homage." After their audience with the king they set out. And behold, the star that they had seen at its rising preceded them, until it came and stopped over the place where the child was. They were overjoyed at seeing the star, and on entering the house they saw the child with Mary his mother. They prostrated themselves and did him homage. Then they opened their treasures and offered him gifts of gold, frankincense, and myrrh. And having been warned in a dream not to return to Herod, they departed for their country by another way.

❖ Understanding the Word

The city of Jerusalem is told to "Arise!" "Shine!" The illumination into which it emerges is the very light of God; it is the glory of the Lord. Jerusalem is not only delivered from its misfortune by God, it is reestablished as a thriving city. Its dispersed inhabitants return, its destroyed reputation is restored, and its despoiled prosperity is reconstituted. This is not a promise to be fulfilled in the future; Jerusalem's salvation is an accomplished fact. It is happening before its very eyes. The wealth from land and sea pours into the city. Such good fortune is evidence of God's favor.

Paul tells the Ephesians that in Christ the Gentiles are co-heirs, co-members and co-partners with the Jews. Since what qualifies one as an heir is life in the Spirit of Christ and not natural generation into a particular national group, there is no obstacle in the path of Gentile incorporation. The body to which all belong is the body of Christ, not the bloodline of Abraham. The promise in Paul's preaching is the promise of universal salvation through Christ, not that of descendants and prosperity in a particular land. This is a radical insight for a church with Jewish roots and traditions.

The three kings or wise men were probably astrologers who studied the heavenly bodies. Since they believed that astral marvels frequently accompanied the birth of great kings, it is understandable that they would go straight to the Judean king. Lest we think the story is a fanciful fabrication, the Gospel writer situates the events squarely in time and place: the reign of Herod, Bethlehem and Jerusalem.

The astrologers read the astral signs, they recognized the true identity of the child, and they understood a message in a dream that told them to return home another way. Their openness brought them to the child, and they did not go away disappointed. This child draws Jew and Gentile alike.

✦ Reflecting on the Word

Early on in Tennessee William's play *The Glass Menagerie*, the always pushing and prodding mother, Amanda, comes into the living room and awakens her sleeping son, Tom, by shouting at his stretched-out figure on the pull-out couch, "Rise and shine! Rise and shine!" An irritated Tom yells back, "I'll rise, Mother, but I won't shine."

By the end of the Christmas season, many of us may have similar feelings. Winter doldrums, whether or not accompanied by freezing weather and power-threatening snowstorms, often motivate little more than a slow-motion arising with little emanating radiance.

But the light of this crowning feast of the Christmas season does not depend on us. Light comes to us, as it did to the magi and to the shepherds in the fields, and as it did to Bethlehem, to Nazareth, and eventually to Jerusalem, Samaria, and from there out to the ends of the earth. The Light comes to us as gift, as grace. This Light enables Jews and Gentiles, men and women of North America, South America, Europe, Africa, Asia, Oceania, and the Middle East to look at each other and recognize brothers and sisters rather than strangers, aliens, even enemies.

The feast of the Epiphany expresses God's will that all creation come to know the God revealed in Jesus Christ, who continues to shine forth in light and love. The promise of the feast is that all of us are capable of absorbing and reflecting this light so that the whole earth may be delivered from its darkness.

✦ Consider/Discuss

- Do you see yourself as a reflector of God's light, someone with a capacity to provide an epiphany for others?
- What helps or hinders you from recognizing all men and women as your brothers and sisters, beloved of God?

✦ Responding to the Word

Lord Jesus, you continue to come into the world as light that pushes back the darkness. Continue to enlighten our minds and hearts, opening them to receive you in whatever way you come to us. Help us to find you in our daily lives by removing whatever prevents our seeing your light.

January 13, 2013

BAPTISM OF THE LORD

Today's Focus: Baptized for Mission

We end the Christmas season, appropriately, with a song. It is a song attributed to an anonymous figure called the Servant from the book of the prophet Isaiah. In today's first reading, and alluded to in the Gospel, this song speaks of Jesus' special mission: pleasing the Father and establishing justice on the earth.

FIRST READING
Isaiah 42:1–4, 6–7

Thus says the LORD:
Here is my servant whom I uphold,
   my chosen one with whom I am pleased,
upon whom I have put my spirit;
   he shall bring forth justice to the nations,
not crying out, not shouting,
   not making his voice heard in the street.
A bruised reed he shall not break,
   and a smoldering wick he shall not quench,
until he establishes justice on the earth;
   the coastlands will wait for his teaching.

I, the LORD, have called you for the victory of justice,
   I have grasped you by the hand;
I formed you, and set you
   as a covenant of the people,
   a light for the nations,
to open the eyes of the blind,
   to bring out prisoners from confinement,
   and from the dungeon, those who live in darkness.

PSALM RESPONSE
Psalm 29:11b

The Lord will bless his people with peace.

SECOND READING
Acts 10:34–38

Peter proceeded to speak to those gathered in the house of Cornelius, saying: "In truth, I see that God shows no partiality. Rather, in every nation whoever fears him and acts uprightly is acceptable to him. You know the word that he sent to the Israelites as he proclaimed peace through Jesus Christ, who is Lord of all, what has happened all over Judea, beginning in Galilee after the baptism that John preached, how God anointed Jesus of Nazareth with the Holy Spirit and power. He went about doing good and healing all those oppressed by the devil, for God was with him."

GOSPEL
Luke 3:15–16,
21–22

The people were filled with expectation, and all were asking in their hearts whether John might be the Christ. John answered them all, saying, "I am baptizing you with water, but one mightier than I is coming. I am not worthy to loosen the thongs of his sandals. He will baptize you with the Holy Spirit and fire."

After all the people had been baptized and Jesus also had been baptized and was praying, heaven was opened and the Holy Spirit descended upon him in bodily form like a dove. And a voice came from heaven, "You are my beloved Son; with you I am well pleased."

❖ *Understanding the Word*

The passage from Isaiah, known as one of the Servant Songs, describes a mysterious figure who acts as a pious agent of God's compassionate care. The servant in this song has received the spirit of the Lord in order to bring forth justice to the nations. This justice is not harsh and exacting, but gentle and understanding, a source of consolation. The servant is also called by God to be a light to the nations. This passage describes the deliverance of the whole world, not simply the rescue of Israel from its particular bondage. The universalism here cannot be denied.

Cornelius was a recently converted Roman centurion. Normally, an observant Jew like Peter would not enter the home of a Gentile. It was a newly gained insight from God that changed Peter's view of those who did not have Jewish ancestry. He realized that "God shows no partiality." All are acceptable to God, Jew and Gentile alike. Peter, who knew the historical Jesus intimately and should have understood the implications of the message that he preached and the example that he gave, did not at first understand the radical nature of this gospel. But now he could testify that it is truly "good news of peace."

Lest the people mistake him for the Christ, John contrasts his ministry with that of Jesus. John's baptism with water was a ritual of repentance and cleansing; the Christ's baptism of the Spirit and fire will transform and purge. John further admits that the Christ is far superior to him. He insists that he is not worthy to undo the sandals of that long-awaited one. Still Jesus submitted himself to John's baptism. The voice from heaven and the descent of the Spirit confirm Jesus' unique identity. This episode has been considered by many as the event of divine commissioning of Jesus. As God's beloved Son he will baptize with the Spirit, thus bringing about the regeneration of the world.

39

For many people, the end of the Christmas season carries a touch of sadness. Joy gives way to January. The liturgy, however, turns our attention to the work that lies at the heart of the mystery of the Incarnation. This feast of the Lord's baptism is the final feast of the Christmas season, serving as a bridge from Christmastime to Ordinary Time. It presents Jesus as God's "beloved Son." His baptism placed Jesus on the road of his mission: to reveal the Father and to begin to bring about the kingdom of God in the world.

Our first reading helps us understand Jesus' mission in light of an unknown Old Testament figure called the Servant. The book of the prophet Isaiah contains four poems called the Servant Songs: 42:1–7; 49:1–7; 50:4–11; 52:13 — 53:12. These songs speak of a servant on whom God has poured God's spirit to be God's agent in the world and bring justice to the nations. The Christian community hears these songs in light of Jesus. St. Paul likewise quoted an early hymn (Philippians 2:5–11), singing of Jesus as one who emptied himself, taking the form of a slave, becoming obedient even unto death on a cross.

Our baptism brought us into the Body of Christ, setting us on the path of continuing Jesus' mission. When the Holy Spirit came upon us, we became God's beloved children in Christ and the mission of Christ, which is the mission of the church, became our mission.

✤ Consider/Discuss

- Do you connect your baptism with your work in the world?
- What can you do, as part of the church, to bring God's justice to the world?

✤ Responding to the Word

Good Father, you have sent the Holy Spirit upon your people to serve the world by working to bring about the victory of justice. Give us the strength to persevere in this work and do not allow our zeal to break any bruised reed or quench any smoldering wick. Let us do our work in gentleness, kindness, and peace.

Time and again during this period of Ordinary Time, we catch a glimpse of the future, a hint of what lies ahead for Jesus and for those who are his disciples. During this time of the liturgical year, themes from the Gospel readings usually set the direction of our prayerful considerations. During these first Sundays of the year we read how Jesus began his own ministry and then called disciples to further the reign of God that he had inaugurated. Disciples are empowered to do this because they have risen with Christ to a new way of living. So empowered, they can accomplish the impossible.

Jesus' ministry begins on an ambiguous note. On the one hand, he seems to be thrust into the public sphere before he is ready. Then, when he does reveal himself, his claims are met with mixed reactions. This is followed by an account of the call of the first disciples. The manner in which Jesus' ministry is received should have alerted the disciples to the reception that they could expect. Their initial instruction includes a lesson on the paradox that the reign of God will uncover, chief among which is love of one's enemies. Deeply rooted attitudes from which flow acts of righteousness are clearly preferred to mere external works that have no interior grounding.

In the corresponding first readings we find pictures from the Old Testament that depict renewed communities of Israelites as well as sketches of individuals called to serve God in very special ways. Each reading in its own way shows that God calls specific individuals through whom God will constitute or reconstitute a community of believers.

The seriousness of this call can at times be quite overwhelming. The task before those called is nothing less than the establishment of the reign of God. Once these individuals have been chosen and have accepted their election, the preached message begins to unfold. At the heart of the message is the call to trust in God. This is followed by the very challenging injunction to love one's enemies.

The Epistles from these first Sundays in Ordinary Time are taken from Paul's First Letter to the Corinthians. Here too the theme of community can be found. Paul's notion of community is remarkably vivid in this description. He uses images that both underscore the unity that is essential and the diversity that is unavoidable. He is not willing to relinquish one for the sake of the other. In his eyes, to do so would violate God's intent. Not only are we all members of the one body, but for the body to be healthy, the members must be bound together by love.

January 20, 2013

SECOND SUNDAY IN ORDINARY TIME

Today's Focus: Our Extravagant Bridegroom

We find many titles for Jesus in the Gospels: Lord, Messiah, Son of David, and, his own preferred title, the Son of Man. One paid less attention, although worthy of it, is Jesus the Bridegroom. As a guest at Cana, Jesus signals he is the Bridegroom we have been longing for.

FIRST READING
Isaiah 62:1–5

For Zion's sake I will not be silent,
　for Jerusalem's sake I will not be quiet,
until her vindication shines forth like the dawn
　and her victory like a burning torch.

Nations shall behold your vindication,
　and all the kings your glory;
you shall be called by a new name
　pronounced by the mouth of the Lord.
You shall be a glorious crown in the hand of the Lord,
　a royal diadem held by your God.
No more shall people call you "Forsaken,"
　or your land "Desolate,"
but you shall be called "My Delight,"
　and your land "Espoused."
For the Lord delights in you
　and makes your land his spouse.
As a young man marries a virgin,
　your Builder shall marry you;
and as a bridegroom rejoices in his bride
　so shall your God rejoice in you.

PSALM RESPONSE
Psalm 96:3

Proclaim his marvelous deeds to all the nations.

SECOND READING
1 Corinthians 12: 4–11

Brothers and sisters: There are different kinds of spiritual gifts but the same Spirit; there are different forms of service but the same Lord; there are different workings but the same God who produces all of them in everyone. To each individual the manifestation of the Spirit is given for some benefit. To one is given through the Spirit the expression of wisdom; to another, the expression of knowledge according to the same Spirit; to another, faith by the same Spirit; to another, gifts of healing by the one Spirit; to another, mighty deeds; to another, prophecy; to another, discernment of spirits; to another, varieties of tongues; to another, interpretation of tongues. But one and the same Spirit produces all of these, distributing them individually to each person as he wishes.

GOSPEL
John 2:1–11
There was a wedding at Cana in Galilee, and the mother of Jesus was there. Jesus and his disciples were also invited to the wedding. When the wine ran short, the mother of Jesus said to him, "They have no wine." And Jesus said to her, "Woman, how does your concern affect me? My hour has not yet come." His mother said to the servers, "Do whatever he tells you." Now there were six stone water jars there for Jewish ceremonial washings, each holding twenty to thirty gallons. Jesus told them, "Fill the jars with water." So they filled them to the brim. Then he told them, "Draw some out now and take it to the headwaiter." So they took it. And when the headwaiter tasted the water that had become wine, without knowing where it came from—although the servers who had drawn the water knew—, the headwaiter called the bridegroom and said to him, "Everyone serves good wine first, and then when people have drunk freely, an inferior one; but you have kept the good wine until now." Jesus did this as the beginning of his signs at Cana in Galilee and so revealed his glory, and his disciples began to believe in him.

❖ Understanding the Word

According to Isaiah, the vindication that is in store for Jerusalem is more than a restoration. The city is promised a new name, and this implies a new creation. One of the best ways of portraying God's passionate love and the depths of the intimacy that God desires is with marriage imagery. Within the context of such intimacy, the consequence of betrayal of God's love is characterized as "forsaken" or "barren." The people who were once forsaken are now the delight of the Lord; the land that once was barren is now newly espoused.

Paul launches into a discourse on the varieties of functions within the Christian community. He speaks of gifts, ministries, and works. "Gifts" here refers to operations of the Spirit, notably speaking in tongues and prophesying, gifts that were usually operative during worship. Ministry was service within the community. Works were feats of great energy or divine power. Since all of these gifts or ministries or works were manifestations of the Spirit, no one was to be considered superior to another. Further, they were not given for the self-aggrandizement of the one who received them. All were given for the benefit of the entire community.

According to John, Jesus' hour is the time when he will be manifested in all his glory. The culmination of this hour will take place when he is lifted up on the cross. However, throughout his ministry there will be times when aspects of this glory will be manifested. The miracle of changing water into wine at the wedding feast at Cana is one such time. The miracles of Jesus were never mere exhibitions of supernatural power. They were always revelations of the inbreaking of the reign of God. Evidently the hour of his glorification had arrived. In this first sign, Jesus transformed a Jewish ceremonial into a celebration for the end of time. His glory was manifested to his disciples and they believed in him. The establishment of the reign of God had begun.

Weddings of the famous have become known for their extravagance. Syndicated radio host Diane Rehm once recalled how she and her husband had gone to two weddings over a few months, each costing over twenty thousand dollars, and neither marriage lasted a year. It seems that as expenses have increased, longevity has decreased. Even so, our faith holds up one marriage whose extravagance is located in its fidelity: Christ's love for his bride, the church.

One of the less remembered titles Jesus applies to himself in the Gospels is the bridegroom. When asked why his disciples do not fast, he replies that as long as the bridegroom is present, there is no fasting. It is a time for celebration. Jesus remains the bridegroom the Father sent to woo God's people. The generous and extravagant abundance of the bridegroom comes across in today's miracle at Cana. Even though he has said his hour—that is, the hour when he reveals the extravagant love of God—has not yet come, still Jesus yields to his mother's request to remedy the embarrassment of a wedding without wine.

The moral: when the Bridegroom comes, there will be endless joy. Ordinary Time begins with this marvelous story, proclaiming that God's generosity cannot be overestimated. We see it in the gifts St. Paul mentions in his letter to the fractious Corinthians, gifts that continue to be given. Such abundance and variety of gifts reflect God's extravagant love for us. Such gifts are given for the good of all.

❖❖ Consider/Discuss

- What does the image of Jesus the Bridegroom say about your relationship with him?
- What gifts of a generous God do you see in your own life and in those around you?

❖❖ *Responding to the Word*

Lord Jesus, you remain the bridegroom come to reveal your Father's extravagant love. In union with many of the saints, we dare to call you the spouse of our souls. May we revel in your passionate love shown on the cross, and reveal that love to those most in need of it.

January 27, 2013

THIRD SUNDAY IN ORDINARY TIME

Today's Focus: God's Word Enlivens the Spirit

"Word" is a static reality, merely sitting there, waiting for someone to breathe life into it. But, in today's readings, "word" is something that brings life to mind and heart, soul and body.

FIRST READING
Nehemiah 8: 2–4a, 5–6, 8–10

Ezra the priest brought the law before the assembly, which consisted of men, women, and those children old enough to understand. Standing at one end of the open place that was before the Water Gate, he read out of the book from daybreak till midday, in the presence of the men, the women, and those children old enough to understand; and all the people listened attentively to the book of the law. Ezra the scribe stood on a wooden platform that had been made for the occasion. He opened the scroll so that all the people might see it—for he was standing higher up than any of the people—; and, as he opened it, all the people rose. Ezra blessed the LORD, the great God, and all the people, their hands raised high, answered, "Amen, amen!" Then they bowed down and prostrated themselves before the LORD, their faces to the ground. Ezra read plainly from the book of the law of God, interpreting it so that all could understand what was read. Then Nehemiah, that is, His Excellency, and Ezra the priest-scribe and the Levites who were instructing the people said to all the people: "Today is holy to the LORD your God. Do not be sad, and do not weep"—for all the people were weeping as they heard the words of the law. He said further: "Go, eat rich foods and drink sweet drinks, and allot portions to those who had nothing prepared; for today is holy to our LORD. Do not be saddened this day, for rejoicing in the LORD must be your strength!"

PSALM RESPONSE
John 6:63c

Your words, Lord, are Spirit and life.

SECOND READING
1 Corinthians 12:12–30 or 12:12–14, 27

Brothers and sisters: As a body is one though it has many parts, and all the parts of the body, though many, are one body, so also Christ. For in one Spirit we were all baptized into one body, whether Jews or Greeks, slaves or free persons, and we were all given to drink of one Spirit.

Now the body is not a single part, but many. [If a foot should say, "Because I am not a hand I do not belong to the body," it does not for this reason belong any less to the body. Or if an ear should say, "Because I am not an eye I do not belong to the body," it does not for this reason belong any less to the body. If the whole body were an eye, where would the hearing be? If the whole body were hearing, where would the sense of smell be? But as it is, God placed the parts, each one of them, in the body as he intended. If they were all one part, where would the body be? But as it is, there are many parts, yet one body. The eye cannot say to the hand, "I do not need you," nor again the head to the feet, "I do not need you." Indeed, the parts of the body that seem to be weaker are all the more necessary, and those parts of the body that we consider less honorable we surround with greater honor, and our less presentable parts are treated with greater propriety, whereas our more presentable parts do not need this. But God has so constructed the body as to give greater honor to a part that is without it, so that there may be no division in the body, but that the parts may have the same concern for one another. If one part suffers, all the parts suffer with it; if one part is honored, all the parts share its joy.]

Now you are Christ's body, and individually parts of it. [Some people God has designated in the church to be, first, apostles; second, prophets; third, teachers; then, mighty deeds; then gifts of healing, assistance, administration, and varieties of tongues. Are all apostles? Are all prophets? Are all teachers? Do all work mighty deeds? Do all have gifts of healing? Do all speak in tongues? Do all interpret?]

GOSPEL
Luke 1:1–4; 4:14–21

Since many have undertaken to compile a narrative of the events that have been fulfilled among us, just as those who were eyewitnesses from the beginning and ministers of the word have handed them down to us, I too have decided, after investigating everything accurately anew, to write it down in an orderly sequence for you, most excellent Theophilus, so that you may realize the certainty of the teachings you have received.

Jesus returned to Galilee in the power of the Spirit, and news of him spread throughout the whole region. He taught in their synagogues and was praised by all.

He came to Nazareth, where he had grown up, and went according to his custom into the synagogue on the sabbath day. He stood up to read and was handed a scroll of the prophet Isaiah. He unrolled the scroll and found the passage where it was written:

> The Spirit of the Lord is upon me,
>   because he has anointed me
>   to bring glad tidings to the poor.
> He has sent me to proclaim liberty to captives
>   and recovery of sight to the blind,
>   to let the oppressed go free,
>   and to proclaim a year acceptable to the Lord.

Rolling up the scroll, he handed it back to the attendant and sat down, and the eyes of all in the synagogue looked intently at him. He said to them, "Today this Scripture passage is fulfilled in your hearing."

❖ *Understanding the Word*

Ezra was the religious leader of the Jewish community that had recently returned from the Babylonian exile. Nehemiah led the people back and then supervised the rebuilding of the walls of Jerusalem. During a liturgical event, Ezra, acting in his capacity as priest, opens the scroll and interprets the law for those present. For their part, the people stand in respect for the words that they hear. His reading is more liturgical than historical, with some of the details of the narrative meant for future generations that will read the account as part of their own liturgical recommitment to the law.

Paul continues his instruction on the diversity found within the community by using the analogy of the body. In the body, each part has its own unique function, but all parts work for the good of the whole. This figure of speech characterizes several aspects of the ideal Christian community. It portrays unity in diversity; it underscores the absence of competition among members, since no one activity is elevated above the others; it underscores the interdependence that exists within the community. The unity within the community is based on common baptism. Cultural and gender differences will remain, but they will not determine one's membership within the community.

The author of the Gospel reading claims that, though not an eyewitness to the events that he recounts, his reports are part of the authoritative tradition of the church and therefore can be trusted. He then tells how Jesus returned to Nazareth, his hometown, and attended the synagogue service there. After reading a passage from Isaiah, Jesus made a bold claim: "Today this Scripture passage is fulfilled in your hearing." In this way he announced that he was the one filled with the Spirit as spoken of by the prophet; he was the one who would inaugurate the hoped-for year of deliverance; he was the one who would launch the long-awaited era of fulfillment.

Sometimes the Sunday scripture readings pass by barely noticed. The words read don't get inside, perhaps because we are preoccupied or worrying over something. But every so often the reader and the words read become one in a way that enters into our heart. One such moment is recorded in today's first reading.

This scene took place over five hundred years before the time of Jesus. The reader was Ezra the priest, who was standing up on a platform in an open place in the city of Jerusalem. The magnificent temple built by Solomon had been destroyed in 587 BC and the people had been taken off into exile in Babylon. In 538 they had been allowed to return, and now, for the first time, they were gathered to hear their priest Ezra read to them the book of the law, the Torah. This book taught them how God had saved them and how God wanted them to live. The people listened for hours, tears running down their faces, as Ezra read and explained to them the meaning of the words for their lives. These words fell upon the hearts of the listeners, penetrating the thick and hardened covering that exile had created, eventually causing their tears to flow. The word of God had done its work, bringing them back to life.

Sometimes rebirth happens gently, as we heard today; at other times, God's word functions as shock therapy.

❖❖ Consider/Discuss

- Can you remember a time when God's word penetrated your being?
- Do you give God's word any opportunity to make its home in you?
- Have you ever celebrated God's word speaking to you by going to "eat rich foods and drink sweet drinks"?

❖❖ *Responding to the Word*

Lord God, you have given us your revealed word as spiritual food to nourish your people, and to strengthen your church as the Body of your Son Jesus Christ. May we recognize and partake of this food when we gather at the table of the Word.

February 3, 2013

FOURTH SUNDAY IN ORDINARY TIME

Today's Focus: God's Word Expands the Heart

God's word not only enlivens but is also a two-edged sword provoking opposition. Spoken by prophets, past and present, it challenges treasured ways of thinking, relating, and acting. God's word often prunes what works against life so greater fruitfulness can result. It will achieve the end for which it was sent.

FIRST READING
Jeremiah 1:4–5, 17–19

The word of the LORD came to me, saying:
Before I formed you in the womb I knew you,
  before you were born I dedicated you,
  a prophet to the nations I appointed you.

But do you gird your loins;
  stand up and tell them
  all that I command you.
Be not crushed on their account,
  as though I would leave you crushed before them;
for it is I this day
  who have made you a fortified city,
a pillar of iron, a wall of brass,
  against the whole land:
against Judah's kings and princes,
  against its priests and people.
They will fight against you but not prevail over you,
  for I am with you to deliver you, says the LORD.

PSALM RESPONSE
Psalm 71:15ab

I will sing of your salvation.

SECOND READING
1 Corinthians 12:31 — 13:13 or 13:4–13

In the shorter form of the reading, the passages in brackets are omitted.
Brothers and sisters: [Strive eagerly for the greatest spiritual gifts. But I shall show you a still more excellent way.

If I speak in human and angelic tongues, but do not have love, I am a resounding gong or a clashing cymbal. And if I have the gift of prophecy, and comprehend all mysteries and all knowledge; if I have all faith so as to move mountains, but do not have love, I am nothing. If I give away everything I own, and if I hand my body over so that I may boast, but do not have love, I gain nothing.]

Love is patient, love is kind. It is not jealous, it is not pompous, it is not inflated, it is not rude, it does not seek its own interests, it is not quick-tempered, it does not brood over injury, it does not rejoice over wrongdoing but rejoices with the truth. It bears all things, believes all things, hopes all things, endures all things.

49

Love never fails. If there are prophecies, they will be brought to nothing; if tongues, they will cease; if knowledge, it will be brought to nothing. For we know partially and we prophesy partially, but when the perfect comes, the partial will pass away. When I was a child, I used to talk as a child, think as a child, reason as a child; when I became a man, I put aside childish things. At present we see indistinctly, as in a mirror, but then face to face. At present I know partially; then I shall know fully, as I am fully known. So faith, hope, love remain, these three; but the greatest of these is love.

GOSPEL
Luke 4:21–30

Jesus began speaking in the synagogue, saying: "Today this Scripture passage is fulfilled in your hearing." And all spoke highly of him and were amazed at the gracious words that came from his mouth. They also asked, "Isn't this the son of Joseph?" He said to them, "Surely you will quote me this proverb, 'Physician, cure yourself,' and say, 'Do here in your native place the things that we heard were done in Capernaum.' " And he said, "Amen, I say to you, no prophet is accepted in his own native place. Indeed, I tell you, there were many widows in Israel in the days of Elijah when the sky was closed for three and a half years and a severe famine spread over the entire land. It was to none of these that Elijah was sent, but only to a widow in Zarephath in the land of Sidon. Again, there were many lepers in Israel during the time of Elisha the prophet; yet not one of them was cleansed, but only Naaman the Syrian."

When the people in the synagogue heard this, they were all filled with fury. They rose up, drove him out of the town, and led him to the brow of the hill on which their town had been built, to hurl him down headlong. But Jesus passed through the midst of them and went away.

❖ Understanding the Word

Having assured him of his prophetic call, God prepares Jeremiah for the fate that lies ahead of him. God will fortify the prophet as one would fortify a city. While the metaphor connotes extraordinary defense, it implies the possibility of massive assault. Jeremiah's assailants will be the very people to whom he is sent to prophesy. They will include both the Jerusalem establishment and the people of the land. That is why he must prepare himself for battle. However, the passage ends with words of encouragement. His adversaries will not prevail against the prophet, because the Lord will be with him.

Paul's praise of love is one of the best-known biblical passages. Last Sunday, Paul insisted that all gifts bestowed upon individuals by the Spirit function for the building up of the community. Today he concentrates on love, the "more excellent way." He then contrasts life in this world with life in the next. Despite all of the gifts we receive from God, they are only partially realized here. The fragmentary nature of this life is compared to seeing but a reflection, while the perfect nature of the next life is like looking at someone face to face.

The scripture to which Jesus refers in this reading is a passage from Isaiah read as part of last Sunday's Gospel (Isaiah 61:1–2). It announces the ultimate age of fulfillment. It provides a glimpse into the kind of messiah that Jesus will be, namely one who will refashion society for the sake of the oppressed. Here Jesus insists that God even goes beyond the confines of Israel into the territory of the Gentiles. This filled the people in the synagogue with fury. To think that the prophetic promise of fulfillment would be extended to the Gentiles was, in their estimation, pure blasphemy. In indignation, they rose up against Jesus. They drove him outside the city limits and sought to cast him down, but he escaped unscathed.

❖ Reflecting on the Word

When Jesus went to his hometown synagogue on the Sabbath, after his time in the desert, he read a passage from Isaiah 61 (see last week's Gospel), outlining a three-fold ministry of preaching the good news to the poor, bringing liberation to the oppressed and captives, and, above all, giving "recovery of sight to the blind"—a phrase from one of the Servant Songs (Isaiah 42:1–9) that presented a servant who came for *all* the nations.

Some have said the sudden switch from amazement at Jesus' gracious words to a murderous hostility was due to Luke conflating several incidents. But a good argument has been made that it is Jesus extending the boundaries of God's love to the Gentiles, those outside the covenant, that so enrages his hometown listeners, a group very similar to the present-day settlers in Israel. Then, Jesus pours oil on the flames by noting that two revered prophets of Israel, Elijah and Elisha, helped, even cured Gentiles rather than their own people.

During Israel's history, God worked through the prophets—from Elijah to Isaiah to Jeremiah to Jesus—to expand the boundaries of the hearts of God's people to include the poor, the weak, and the Gentiles. We hear God's word attempting to penetrate our own hearts in St. Paul's call to cultivate love: a call to patience and kindness, not being rude or self-seeking, but enduring all things. God's word often calls for a dying so that more life can flood into and out from us.

❖ Consider/Discuss

- How has God's word confronted you and called you to change?
- What quality from St. Paul's meditation on love do you find most difficult to live?

❖ Responding to the Word

Your word, O Lord, is not always easy to receive. Sometimes it calls us to surrender what we most want to cling to, to take up what we most want to run from, and to live outside of where we are most comfortable. Give us courage to hear your word and to live it with fidelity.

February 10, 2013

FIFTH SUNDAY IN ORDINARY TIME

Today's Focus: In the Presence of the Holy One

To be in the presence of the Holy One is an awesome experience. Today's readings direct our attention to three men who have had this experience: Isaiah, Paul, and Simon Peter. Their experiences can be instructive for us, when we find ourselves in the presence of the Holy One.

FIRST READING
Isaiah 6:1–2a, 3–8

In the year King Uzziah died, I saw the Lord seated on a high and lofty throne, with the train of his garment filling the temple. Seraphim were stationed above.

They cried one to the other, "Holy, holy, holy is the LORD of hosts! All the earth is filled with his glory!" At the sound of that cry, the frame of the door shook and the house was filled with smoke.

Then I said, "Woe is me, I am doomed! For I am a man of unclean lips, living among a people of unclean lips; yet my eyes have seen the King, the LORD of hosts!" Then one of the seraphim flew to me, holding an ember that he had taken with tongs from the altar.

He touched my mouth with it, and said, "See, now that this has touched your lips, your wickedness is removed, your sin purged."

Then I heard the voice of the Lord saying, "Whom shall I send? Who will go for us?" "Here I am," I said; "send me!"

PSALM RESPONSE
Psalm 138:1c

In the sight of the angels I will sing your praises, Lord.

SECOND READING
1 Corinthians 15:1–11 or 15:3–8, 11

In the shorter form of the reading, the passages in brackets are omitted.
[I am reminding you,] brothers and sisters,[of the gospel I preached to you, which you indeed received and in which you also stand. Through it you are also being saved, if you hold fast to the word I preached to you, unless you believed in vain. For] I handed on to you as of first importance what I also received: that Christ died for our sins in accordance with the Scriptures; that he was buried; that he was raised on the third day in accordance with the Scriptures; that he appeared to Cephas, then to the Twelve. After that, he appeared to more than five hundred brothers at once, most of whom are still living, though some have fallen asleep. After that he appeared to James, then to all the apostles. Last of all, as to one born abnormally, he appeared to me. [For I am the least of the apostles, not fit to be called an apostle, because I persecuted the church of God. But by the grace of God I am what I am, and his grace to me has not been ineffective. Indeed, I have toiled harder than all of them; not I, however, but the grace of God that is with me.] Therefore, whether it be I or they, so we preach and so you believed.

GOSPEL
Luke 5:1–11

While the crowd was pressing in on Jesus and listening to the word of God, he was standing by the Lake of Gennesaret. He saw two boats there alongside the lake; the fishermen had disembarked and were washing their nets. Getting into one of the boats, the one belonging to Simon, he asked him to put out a short distance from the shore. Then he sat down and taught the crowds from the boat. After he had finished speaking, he said to Simon, "Put out into deep water and lower your nets for a catch." Simon said in reply, "Master, we have worked hard all night and have caught nothing, but at your command I will lower the nets." When they had done this, they caught a great number of fish and their nets were tearing. They signaled to their partners in the other boat to come to help them. They came and filled both boats so that the boats were in danger of sinking. When Simon Peter saw this, he fell at the knees of Jesus and said, "Depart from me, Lord, for I am a sinful man." For astonishment at the catch of fish they had made seized him and all those with him, and likewise James and John, the sons of Zebedee, who were partners of Simon. Jesus said to Simon, "Do not be afraid; from now on you will be catching men." When they brought their boats to the shore, they left everything and followed him.

❖ Understanding the Word

The reading from Isaiah reports a visionary experience the prophet had during a liturgical celebration held in the temple. The God of Israel is depicted as supreme among all other gods, since only the mightiest would be sitting on the heavenly throne. This is a bold idea for a vulnerable nation in the throes of political unrest. The threefold acclamation of praise—Holy! Holy! Holy!—expresses the superlative. There is no god as holy as the God of Israel. It is not by accident that, rather than his eyes or his hands, Isaiah's lips are cleansed. He will, after all, use them to proclaim the word of the Lord.

The reading from Paul contains one of the earliest creedal statements: Christ died, he was buried, he was raised, and he appeared. Paul adds his own name to the list of those who saw the Lord. He likens himself to an aborted fetus, rejected from a womb and not ready for a normal birth. He turns this characterization into a profession of faith. Though once a persecutor, by the grace of God he now toils harder than all the others. His final statement is telling. It makes no difference who preaches the gospel, so long as others hear it and believe.

Simon and those with him in the boat recognize the divine power at work in and through Jesus. Jesus does not provide these fishermen a remarkable catch merely in order to dispel the frustration they experienced after an unsuccessful night of fishing. The miracle became an acted-out prophecy revealing both Jesus' own mysterious authority and the ministry to which the disciples are being called. Jesus declares that a turning point in their lives has been reached. The commission states, From now on . . . ! The astonishment of the fishermen turns to commitment. They leave everything—the incredible catch, their business, the stability of their homes, families, and neighborhoods—and they follow him.

Today we witness three encounters with the Holy One in three different settings, but with three similar responses, both immediate and long-term. Isaiah's vision of God in the temple included angels surrounding God and praising God's glory. His immediate response was fear and unworthiness at seeing the living God. But God's compassionate action of purifying his lips leads Isaiah to offer his service.

For Simon Peter, the experience of the holy came when a stranger walked by as Simon was finishing an unsuccessful night of fishing. Jesus got into his boat, taught the crowds first, then turned to Simon. Something in Jesus' manner must have persuaded Simon to follow his directions. The result was so many fish that the boats almost sank. Simon suddenly knew he was in the presence of the Holy One. Unworthiness and fear flooded his heart, but, as God did with Isaiah, Jesus removed Simon's fear and Simon followed him.

Paul briefly alludes to his own unworthiness to be an apostle, rooted in his experience of the Holy One on the road to Damascus. He witnesses to God's grace at work by preaching what has been handed on to him: that Christ died for our sins, was raised from the dead, and appeared to Paul, the least of all the apostles.

An experience of the holy can come to us in church, in the midst of our work, or even when we are heading in a very different direction than the one God has planned for us. Pray God we will respond to it.

❖ Consider/Discuss

- Are you are open to the presence of the Holy One in worship and in daily life?
- What does it mean to say, "Lord, I am not worthy that you should enter under my roof, but only say the word and my soul shall be healed"?

❖ Responding to the Word

O Holy God, we pray that we may be open to recognizing your holy presence wherever and however you show yourself to us. Do not let fear of our unworthiness prevent us from responding to your invitation to serve you in whatever way you ask.

The readings for the Lenten season offer us an overview of God's workings in human history. They begin with a composite of pictures showing God's loving providence, beginning with Abram through Moses until the return from the Exile. Even though the people had to endure calamity as punishment for their sinfulness, the loving care of God always brought them out of each agonizing experience. Reflecting on events such as these can only elicit sentiments of confidence in and thanksgiving for God's graciousness despite human weakness and infidelity. The Epistles reveal the central role that Jesus plays in this drama of salvation. The Gospel readings continue the theme, highlighting both Jesus' suffering and glory, and our sin against and reconciliation with God. Finally, the Passion of Jesus, as terrifying as it was, uncovers the depth of God's love, the reason for our trust, and the value of Jesus' sacrifice.

Contrary to a popular perception of the meaning of Lent, the focus in the readings is less on human sinfulness and the need for penance than it is on divine graciousness and willingness to offer us another chance despite our unworthiness. Lent reminds us that human selfishness and betrayal are outmatched by God's forgiveness and magnanimity.

The Easter readings demonstrate the extent of this divine care as they recount the unfolding of the power of the Resurrection. The entire Easter season celebrates the membership of those newly initiated. Within the liturgy, the texts read during this time constitute a mystagogical catechesis, which is a formative instruction for the newly baptized. However, their message is not limited to the neophytes (the newly initiated); it is also meant for all of us believers.

Scene after scene in the Easter Epistles describes the glorious effects of Jesus' own post-Resurrection transformation. Awed by these marvels, we are prompted to praise and thank God. The psalms for this season offer themselves as wonderful vehicles for doing just that. The Gospel readings provide us with another perspective of the Risen Lord. He is not merely content to savor his victory; rather, he wants us all to enjoy a share in his triumph. To this end he assures his followers of the reality of his resurrection, and then he prepares them to spread the news of the power of the Resurrection throughout the entire world. Finally, the readings from Acts of the Apostles demonstrate the wonders that can be accomplished by weak and struggling human beings when they listen to the words of Jesus, commit themselves to following their direction, and open themselves to the prompting of the Spirit. These narratives merely sketch the beginnings. The rest is up to those of us who hear the Good News.

February 17, 2013

FIRST SUNDAY OF LENT

Today's Focus: Pledging Allegiance

Today's opening prayer asks God to help us "grow in understanding of the riches hidden in Christ and by worthy conduct pursue their effects." All three readings deal with professing faith in the living God. We move toward pledging our allegiance of faith on Easter.

FIRST READING
Deuteronomy 26:
4–10

Moses spoke to the people, saying: "The priest shall receive the basket from you and shall set it in front of the altar of the LORD, your God. Then you shall declare before the LORD, your God, 'My father was a wandering Aramean who went down to Egypt with a small household and lived there as an alien. But there he became a nation great, strong, and numerous. When the Egyptians mal-treated and oppressed us, imposing hard labor upon us, we cried to the LORD, the God of our fathers, and he heard our cry and saw our affliction, our toil, and our oppression. He brought us out of Egypt with his strong hand and outstretched arm, with terrifying power, with signs and wonders; and bringing us into this country, he gave us this land flowing with milk and honey. Therefore, I have now brought you the firstfruits of the products of the soil which you, O LORD, have given me.' And having set them before the Lord, your God, you shall bow down in his presence."

PSALM RESPONSE
Psalm 91:15b

Be with me, Lord, when I am in trouble.

SECOND READING
Romans 10:
8–13

Brothers and sisters: What does Scripture say?
The word is near you,
in your mouth and in your heart
—that is, the word of faith that we preach—, for, if you confess with your mouth that Jesus is Lord and believe in your heart that God raised him from the dead, you will be saved. For one believes with the heart and so is justified, and one confesses with the mouth and so is saved. For the Scripture says,
No one who believes in him will be put to shame.
For there is no distinction between Jew and Greek; the same Lord is Lord of all, enriching all who call upon him. For "everyone who calls on the name of the Lord will be saved."

GOSPEL
Luke 4:1–13

Filled with the Holy Spirit, Jesus returned from the Jordan and was led by the Spirit into the desert for forty days, to be tempted by the devil. He ate nothing during those days, and when they were over he was hungry. The devil said to him, "If you are the Son of God, command this stone to become bread." Jesus answered him, "It is written, *One does not live on bread alone.*"

Then he took him up and showed him all the kingdoms of the world in a single instant. The devil said to him, "I shall give to you all this power and glory; for it has been handed over to me, and I may give it to whomever I wish. All this will be yours, if you worship me." Jesus said to him in reply, "It is written:

You shall worship the Lord, your God,
and him alone shall you serve."

Then he led him to Jerusalem, made him stand on the parapet of the temple, and said to him, "If you are the Son of God, throw yourself down from here, for it is written:

He will command his angels concerning you, to guard you,
and:

With their hands they will support you,
lest you dash your foot against a stone."

Jesus said to him in reply, "It also says,

You shall not put the Lord, your God, to the test."

When the devil had finished every temptation, he departed from him for a time.

❖ Understanding the Word

The reading from Deuteronomy contains one of the most important creedal statements found in the Pentateuch. This profession of faith was part of the Israelite celebration of First Fruits. The cultic ritual described here consisted of both action (the offering of the basket containing the produce) and the recitation of the saving acts of God on behalf of the people. This passage describes Moses instructing the Israelites for future observances of this festival. Since these directives come from Moses, the spokesperson of God, they have Mosaic and therefore divine legitimacy.

The essence of Paul's preaching is twofold: the centrality of Christ in the drama of salvation, and the need to accept the gospel in order to open oneself to Christ's saving power. To call Jesus Lord had ramifications in both Jewish and Greek circles. In the Jewish tradition, it identified Jesus with the one true God. In a Greek culture, it claimed that Jesus—and no other political lord or master—was the one to whom whole-hearted allegiance belonged. Finally, it is faith in Jesus, not membership in the chosen people of Israel, that justifies and saves.

The account of Jesus' temptations in the wilderness states that Jesus was under the influence of the Holy Spirit. In each temptation Jesus is challenged to prove that he is the Son of God. The temptation to produce bread recalls Israel's hunger in the wilderness and God's graciousness in supplying the people with manna. In the second temptation, Jesus rejects the devil's offer to turn over control of the world to him. The last test was an attempt to force God to protect Jesus. In each instance Jesus rejects the temptation and refers to a passage from Deuteronomy. Three times the devil tempts Jesus; three times Jesus proves his allegiance to God. He never directly addresses the question of his divine sonship, but he always shows himself to be faithful, whereas Israel was not.

✢ Reflecting on the Word

Lent's journey will take us to the celebration of the paschal mystery of Easter. During these forty days we are invited into a space of sensory deprivation when we gather for worship: no flowers on the altar, no music for its own sake but only to accompany our singing, and no colorful banners that might distract us from the task at hand: to prepare our minds and hearts to renew our baptismal promises during the celebration.

We will be asked both to renounce Satan and all his perks and promises and to place our wholehearted trust in God who created us, in the Son who redeemed us, and in the Spirit who dwells within us and enlightens us. Lent is a serious season but not necessarily a somber one; it is the waiting room for Easter joy. One Lenten Preface (the priest's prayer before the Holy, Holy, Holy) even speaks of it as a season that is a gracious gift from God, making us joyful because we are purified to celebrate the Easter mysteries.

Just as Jesus was tempted throughout his ministry to turn aside from his mission, his followers will be, too. The three temptations speak to our own experience when we seek self-gratification rather than the glory of God.

God's word today calls us to make God our true nourishment, our true wealth, our faithful source of strength, and the solid foundation of our trust. Paul's bold proclamation to the Romans extends to us: the Lord enriches all who call upon him. All who call on him will be saved.

✢ Consider/Discuss

- Where do you want to find yourself at the end of this Lenten journey?
- What temptation lures you to turn aside from having God and Christ at the center of your life?

✢ Responding to the Word

Lord Jesus, as you had the help of the Spirit to turn aside from the temptations that came to you during the time in the desert and the years of your ministry, help us to turn to this same Spirit to help us in our efforts to grow in faith, hope, and charity this Lent.

February 24, 2013

SECOND SUNDAY OF LENT

Today's Focus: The Glory Yet to Come

Every Lent takes us first into the desert to witness Jesus being tested and tempted; then, on the Second Sunday, we go up the mountain with Peter, James, and John to witness the Transfiguration and its accompanying vision. This event takes us more deeply into God's unfolding plan for Jesus—and us.

FIRST READING
Genesis 15: 5–12, 17–18

The Lord God took Abram outside and said, "Look up at the sky and count the stars, if you can. Just so," he added, "shall your descendants be." Abram put his faith in the LORD, who credited it to him as an act of righteousness.

He then said to him, "I am the LORD who brought you from Ur of the Chaldeans to give you this land as a possession." "O Lord GOD," he asked, "how am I to know that I shall possess it?" He answered him, "Bring me a three-year-old heifer, a three-year-old she-goat, a three-year-old ram, a turtledove, and a young pigeon." Abram brought him all these, split them in two, and placed each half opposite the other; but the birds he did not cut up. Birds of prey swooped down on the carcasses, but Abram stayed with them. As the sun was about to set, a trance fell upon Abram, and a deep, terrifying darkness enveloped him.

When the sun had set and it was dark, there appeared a smoking fire pot and a flaming torch, which passed between those pieces. It was on that occasion that the LORD made a covenant with Abram, saying: "To your descendants I give this land, from the Wadi of Egypt to the Great River, the Euphrates."

PSALM RESPONSE
Psalm 27:1a

The Lord is my light and my salvation.

In the shorter form of the reading, the passage in brackets is omitted.

SECOND READING
Philippians 3: 17 — 4:1 or 3:20 — 4:1

[Join with others in being imitators of me, brothers and sisters, and observe those who thus conduct themselves according to the model you have in us. For many, as I have often told you and now tell you even in tears, conduct themselves as enemies of the cross of Christ. Their end is destruction. Their God is their stomach; their glory is in their "shame." Their minds are occupied with earthly things. But] our citizenship is in heaven, and from it we also await a savior, the Lord Jesus Christ. He will change our lowly body to conform with his glorified body by the power that enables him also to bring all things into subjection to himself.

Therefore, my brothers and sisters, whom I love and long for, my joy and crown, in this way stand firm in the Lord.

Jesus took Peter, John, and James and went up the mountain to pray. While he was praying his face changed in appearance and his clothing became dazzling white. And behold, two men were conversing with him, Moses and Elijah, who appeared in glory and spoke of his exodus that he was going to accomplish in Jerusalem. Peter and his companions had been overcome by sleep, but becoming fully awake, they saw his glory and the two men standing with him. As they were about to part from him, Peter said to Jesus, "Master, it is good that we are here; let us make three tents, one for you, one for Moses, and one for Elijah." But he did not know what he was saying. While he was still speaking, a cloud came and cast a shadow over them, and they became frightened when they entered the cloud. Then from the cloud came a voice that said, "This is my chosen Son; listen to him." After the voice had spoken, Jesus was found alone. They fell silent and did not at that time tell anyone what they had seen.

❖ Understanding the Word

Two promises are made to Abram: a multitude of descendants, and a vast expanse of land to be given to those descendants. Abram's response of faith is credited to him as righteousness. The passage also contains a divine self-identification similar to the one that introduces the Decalogue. The ritual known as "cutting the covenant" is performed. It is a dramatized curse in which the covenant partners promise that if either partner transgresses the prescriptions of the covenant, the other can inflict the fate of the animals on the violator. The harshness of the penalty signals the seriousness of this covenant-making.

In his exhortation to the Philippians, Paul compares the fate of the true believers with that of opponents of the gospel. It is not clear who these opponents were. Perhaps they were Gnostics (who believed they'd been given a "special knowledge")—Christians who believed that they had already passed into a spiritualized form of existence and could live in this world unscathed by its temptations. True believers, on the other hand, were really aliens in this earthly place. Their citizenship was in heaven. Unlike the enemies of the cross, they knew that they would have to embrace that cross, and then, with Christ's coming, they would be transformed into his glory.

At the time of his transfiguration Jesus is joined by Moses and Elijah, who represent Israel's law and the prophets. The exodus of which they speak is Jesus' death, resurrection, and ascension, all of the important events in God's plan of salvation. This discussion indicated that Jesus' death was not a tragic mistake, something that he was unable to avoid. Rather, those who represented the entire religious tradition of Israel knew it beforehand. The voice from heaven not only authenticates who Jesus is, but also instructs the disciples to listen to his words, regardless of how challenging or perplexing they might be. It will take the actual unfolding of the events of Jesus' exodus for them to understand its meaning.

God's promises are not empty words carried off by the wind soon after they are uttered. From the beginning God has backed up divine promises with action. We see this today in the story of God sealing the promise to Abraham of many descendants and the gift of the land with the mystifying occurrence of a floating fire pot and flaming torch passing through Abraham's sacrifice. God's words lead to a ratifying action.

In the Gospel God comes to Jesus. At first this is made evident in the change of Jesus' face and clothing. Then the great prophets Moses and Elijah appear, mediators of God's word to the people through both the Torah and prophetic deeds, who speak with Jesus about his coming death in Jerusalem. Finally, as with Israel in the desert, God manifests the divine presence, coming in a cloud and proclaiming Jesus as "chosen Son." "Listen to him," the voice says. Divine word is backed up by divine deed.

This yearly glimpse of glory in the story of the Transfiguration tells us yet again that God recognizes our need for signs and support in our journey of faith. Walking in faith is not all shadows and darkness. Light comes into our lives, sometimes in such unexpected ways that we only become aware of it in retrospect. These moments whisper of God's ongoing presence with us, of promises yet to be fulfilled. Paul speaks of our citizenship even now being in heaven, calling us to "stand firm in the Lord."

✥ *Consider/Discuss*

- Can you remember a moment when the promise of our faith was affirmed by a gracious event, enabling you to recognize God's presence?
- Do you believe that our citizenship is in heaven and that our bodies are destined to being conformed to Christ's glorified body?

✥ *Responding to the Word*

Lord, enlighten the eyes of our hearts, providing a glimpse of the glory promised us because of your saving death and resurrection. As we move toward renewing the promises made at baptism, make our hearts ever more confident in the Father's fidelity and the ongoing strength that comes from the Spirit.

March 3, 2013

THIRD SUNDAY OF LENT (C)

Today's Focus: Seize the Day—Now

Lent is the Church's springtime. It is a time for inner growth, made possible by openness to the Spirit who gives new life. As with the fig tree that wasn't bearing fruit, Jesus uses this season to cultivate and tend his people. Lent is an invitation to action on our part.

FIRST READING
Exodus 3:1–8a, 13–15

Moses was tending the flock of his father-in-law Jethro, the priest of Midian. Leading the flock across the desert, he came to Horeb, the mountain of God. There an angel of the LORD appeared to Moses in fire flaming out of a bush. As he looked on, he was surprised to see that the bush, though on fire, was not consumed. So Moses decided, "I must go over to look at this remarkable sight, and see why the bush is not burned."

When the LORD saw him coming over to look at it more closely, God called out to him from the bush, "Moses! Moses!" He answered, "Here I am." God said, "Come no nearer! Remove the sandals from your feet, for the place where you stand is holy ground. I am the God of your fathers," he continued, "the God of Abraham, the God of Isaac, the God of Jacob." Moses hid his face, for he was afraid to look at God. But the LORD said, "I have witnessed the affliction of my people in Egypt and have heard their cry of complaint against their slave drivers, so I know well what they are suffering. Therefore I have come down to rescue them from the hands of the Egyptians and lead them out of that land into a good and spacious land, a land flowing with milk and honey."

Moses said to God, "But when I go to the Israelites and say to them, 'The God of your fathers has sent me to you,' if they ask me, 'What is his name?' what am I to tell them?" God replied, "I am who am." Then he added, "This is what you shall tell the Israelites: I AM sent me to you."

God spoke further to Moses, "Thus shall you say to the Israelites: The LORD, the God of your fathers, the God of Abraham, the God of Isaac, the God of Jacob, has sent me to you.

"This is my name forever; thus am I to be remembered through all generations."

PSALM RESPONSE
Psalm 103:8a

The Lord is kind and merciful.

SECOND READING
1 Corinthians 10: 1–6, 10–12 I do not want you to be unaware, brothers and sisters, that our ancestors were all under the cloud and all passed through the sea, and all of them were baptized into Moses in the cloud and in the sea. All ate the same spiritual food, and all drank the same spiritual drink, for they drank from a spiritual rock that followed them, and the rock was the Christ. Yet God was not pleased with most of them, for they were struck down in the desert.

These things happened as examples for us, so that we might not desire evil things, as they did. Do not grumble as some of them did, and suffered death by the destroyer. These things happened to them as an example, and they have been written down as a warning to us, upon whom the end of the ages has come. Therefore, whoever thinks he is standing secure should take care not to fall.

GOSPEL
Luke 13:1–9 Some people told Jesus about the Galileans whose blood Pilate had mingled with the blood of their sacrifices. Jesus said to them in reply, "Do you think that because these Galileans suffered in this way they were greater sinners than all other Galileans? By no means! But I tell you, if you do not repent, you will all perish as they did! Or those eighteen people who were killed when the tower at Siloam fell on them—do you think they were more guilty than everyone else who lived in Jerusalem? By no means! But I tell you, if you do not repent, you will all perish as they did!"

And he told them this parable: "There once was a person who had a fig tree planted in his orchard, and when he came in search of fruit on it but found none, he said to the gardener, 'For three years now I have come in search of fruit on this fig tree but have found none. So cut it down. Why should it exhaust the soil?' He said to him in reply, 'Sir, leave it for this year also, and I shall cultivate the ground around it and fertilize it; it may bear fruit in the future. If not you can cut it down.' "

❖ Understanding the Word

The mountain upon which God speaks to Moses is a holy mountain ("Remove your sandals"), because it is a place of divine revelation. The God who speaks is the God worshiped by the ancestors. This same God promises to release the Israelites from Egyptian bondage. The name that God reveals is similar in sound and appearance to a form of the verb "to be." It denotes continuing action and may mean "I AM always." This new name implies God's continuing active involvement. The promise of deliverance identifies the way that God will be with the people: always present to rescue.

Paul warns the Corinthians about over-confidence in their status as Christians. Although Baptism and Eucharist are means of union with God, they do not work automatically. Paul turns to the wilderness events to illustrate this. The miraculous events in the wilderness were of no avail for most of the people of that generation. Likewise, the Corinthians' own calling and initiation into its mysteries was, in itself, no guarantee of salvation. They would have to demonstrate their fidelity again and again. Christian life requires persistent Christian living.

Jesus speaks of the suddenness of recent tragedies and the possible unpreparedness of their victims. He exhorts his hearers to repent lest they suffer the same fate—not that they might be spared such calamity, but that they should be prepared for it. They should be reconciled with God before disaster strikes. He then tells a parable to demonstrate the mercy of God. In it, God is like both the owner and the diligent worker, willing to give time to repent. However, final condemnation is still a real possibility. Jesus teaches that we should always be prepared for sudden death by being reconciled with God at all times. While God might be patient with us, this patience requires that we participate with the opportunities that God provides for our maturing in righteousness. We risk God's judgment if we disregard God's grace.

❖ Reflecting on the Word

Carpe diem was one of the phrases you'd learn if you studied Latin in high school. It means "Seize the day." For a high school student it seemed to offer a permit to act impulsively. Speaking as someone more than fifty years away from that time, it offers an inducement to act wisely—*now*.

Moses is told by a voice from a burning bush that the God of his ancestors wanted him to go back down to Egypt, from which he had fled after murdering an Egyptian. All Moses was given at this encounter was an obscure name for God, and a proposed plan to rescue the Israelite slaves and lead them to a new land. Not a very attractive offer for one peacefully tending sheep, but Moses seized the day, hearing the call to act—*now*.

Jesus calls on his fellow Jews to seize the day by repenting. Life is short. People die tragically without deserving it. Look to your own life, he tells them. God has given you these days, so bear fruit—*now*.

Paul calls on the Corinthian to seize the day. Not just our actions but even our desires can mislead us. So don't be complacent, a word that means sedating your spirit by being overly pleased with yourself. Turn to God—*now*.

Baptism lays a foundation, giving us the Spirit and the virtues of faith, hope, and love. In a month we are going to renew our baptismal promises on Easter, confirming our desire to seize the day, every day, as an opportunity to grow closer to God—*now*.

❖ Consider/Discuss

- Have you "settled in" to being a Catholic? Have you become a "couch Catholic," not overly exerting yourself in living out of your faith?
- This coming week brings us to Lent's mid-point. Is anything happening on the conversion/turn-to-the-Lord front?

❖ Responding to the Word

Lord, teach us to number our days and realize how quickly life passes, days into weeks into months into years. Rouse our spirits and teach us how to work with your Spirit to make fruitful the gifts you have given to us for the good of others. Move us to act wisely.

March 3, 2013

THIRD SUNDAY OF LENT (A)

Today's Focus: Our Thirsty God

Readings from Year A are selected especially for the catechumens preparing to be baptized at the Easter Vigil. We find God providing water for the people Moses had led out to the desert and Jesus offering himself as living water to all thirsting for God. God answers our thirst.

FIRST READING
Exodus 17: 3–7

In those days, in their thirst for water, the people grumbled against Moses, saying, "Why did you ever make us leave Egypt? Was it just to have us die here of thirst with our children and our livestock?" So Moses cried out to the LORD, "What shall I do with this people? A little more and they will stone me!" The LORD answered Moses, "Go over there in front of the people, along with some of the elders of Israel, holding in your hand, as you go, the staff with which you struck the river. I will be standing there in front of you on the rock in Horeb. Strike the rock, and the water will flow from it for the people to drink." This Moses did, in the presence of the elders of Israel. The place was called Massah and Meribah, because the Israelites quarreled there and tested the LORD, saying, "Is the LORD in our midst or not?"

PSALM RESPONSE
Psalm 95:8

If today you hear his voice, harden not your hearts.

SECOND READING
Romans 5: 1–2, 5–8

Brothers and sisters: Since we have been justified by faith, we have peace with God through our Lord Jesus Christ, through whom we have gained access by faith to this grace in which we stand, and we boast in hope of the glory of God.

And hope does not disappoint, because the love of God has been poured out into our hearts through the Holy Spirit who has been given to us. For Christ, while we were still helpless, died at the appointed time for the ungodly. Indeed, only with difficulty does one die for a just person, though perhaps for a good person one might even find courage to die. But God proves his love for us in that while we were still sinners Christ died for us.

GOSPEL
*John 4:5–42 or
4:5–15, 19b–26,
39a, 40–42*

Jesus came to a town of Samaria called Sychar, near the plot of land that Jacob had given to his son Joseph. Jacob's well was there. Jesus, tired from his journey, sat down there at the well. It was about noon.

A woman of Samaria came to draw water. Jesus said to her, "Give me a drink." His disciples had gone into the town to buy food. The Samaritan woman said to him, "How can you, a Jew, ask me, a Samaritan woman, for a drink?"—For Jews use nothing in common with Samaritans.—Jesus answered and said to her, "If you knew the gift of God and who is saying to you, 'Give me a drink,' you would have asked him and he would have given you living water." The woman said to him, "Sir, you do not even have a bucket and the cistern is deep; where then can you get this living water? Are you greater than our father Jacob, who gave us this cistern and drank from it himself with his children and his flocks?" Jesus answered and said to her, "Everyone who drinks this water will be thirsty again; but whoever drinks the water I shall give will never thirst; the water I shall give will become in him a spring of water welling up to eternal life." The woman said to him, "Sir, give me this water, so that I may not be thirsty or have to keep coming here to draw water."

[Jesus said to her, "Go call your husband and come back." The woman answered and said to him, "I do not have a husband." Jesus answered her, "You are right in saying, 'I do not have a husband.' For you have had five husbands, and the one you have now is not your husband. What you have said is true." The woman said to him, "Sir,] I can see that you are a prophet. Our ancestors worshiped on this mountain; but you people say that the place to worship is in Jerusalem." Jesus said to her, "Believe me, woman, the hour is coming when you will worship the Father neither on this mountain nor in Jerusalem. You people worship what you do not understand; we worship what we understand, because salvation is from the Jews. But the hour is coming, and is now here, when true worshipers will worship the Father in Spirit and truth; and indeed the Father seeks such people to worship him. God is Spirit, and those who worship him must worship in Spirit and truth."

The woman said to him, "I know that the Messiah is coming, the one called the Christ; when he comes, he will tell us everything." Jesus said to her, "I am he, the one speaking with you."

[At that moment his disciples returned, and were amazed that he was talking with a woman, but still no one said, "What are you looking for?" or "Why are you talking with her?" The woman left her water jar and went into the town and said to the people, "Come see a man who told me everything I have done. Could he possibly be the Christ?" They went out of the town and came to him. Meanwhile, the disciples urged him, "Rabbi, eat." But he said to them, "I have food to eat of which you do not know." So the disciples said to one another, "Could someone have brought him something to eat?" Jesus said to them, "My food is to do the will of the one who sent me and to finish his work. Do you not say, 'In four months the harvest will be here'? I tell you, look up and see the fields ripe for the harvest. The reaper is already receiving payment and gathering crops for eternal life, so that the sower and reaper can rejoice together. For here the saying is verified that 'One sows and another reaps.' I sent you to reap what you have not worked for; others have done the work, and you are sharing the fruits of their work."]

Many of the Samaritans of that town began to believe in him [because of the word of the woman who testified, "He told me everything I have done."] When the Samaritans came to him, they invited him to stay with them; and he stayed there two days. Many more began to believe in him because of his word, and they said to the woman, "We no longer believe because of your word; for we have heard for ourselves, and we know that this is truly the savior of the world."

❖❖ Understanding the Word

The miracle of water from the rock is God's response to the people's rebellion in the wilderness. Moses' authority is under direct attack. Nonetheless, just as God delivered the people from the bondage of Egypt through the leadership of Moses, so now, again through the actions of Moses, God provides for their needs. Moses is instructed to employ the staff he used to perform the signs and wonders that surrounded the liberation from Egypt. When he strikes the rock, life-giving water flows forth. This is but another example of God's boundless and compassionate love for sinners.

The justification of the Romans is based on the righteousness that originates in God, a righteousness that gives and sustains life, security, and well-being. According to Paul, we have no right to this relationship with God. It has been given to us, won for us by the Lord Jesus Christ. We did not deserve it. We were sinners, alienated from God, when Christ died for us and gained access for us to the grace that places us in right relationship with God. The prodigious quantity of God's graciousness is beyond our comprehension. It is poured out like water, life-giving, enriching, and overflowing.

The living water metaphor about which Jesus and the Samaritan woman converse has a long and rich history in the religious tradition of Israel, where it is seen as a principle of spiritual life. Jesus' unexplained knowledge of the woman's marital situation prompts her to call him a prophet and to launch into another discussion about the proper place to worship God. Here too Jesus moves the conversation away from what is merely perceptible to the level of deep spiritual meaning, from a discussion of the place of worship to one that characterizes the manner of worship. The word of salvation comes to the Samaritan village through a woman, it takes root in the hearts of these despised and marginalized people, and it grows into a great harvest.

❖ Reflecting on the Word

There are a number of thirsty people in our readings today: the Israelites out in the desert, grumbling about the lack of water and wondering why they ever left Egypt; the woman of Samaria, who has gone to the well to draw water for herself and her companion at home; and Jesus, traveling through Samaritan territory with his disciples.

The thirst of the Israelites was physical. Once again disheartened, they were grumbling that Moses had taken them out in the desert to die. It must have gotten serious because we are told that Moses himself feared for his life. God's response is dramatic: "Take your staff, go over to that rock and strike it." And the water flowed.

The nameless woman is shown to be thirsty on several levels. Physically, yes, but her thirst is on far deeper levels—for companionship (five husbands and now living with yet another person!) and for communion with God. Jesus promises her that people will worship God in Spirit and in truth. Indeed, the Father seeks such people.

Is it possible the one most thirsty is God? The Father thirsts for all of us to draw closer, to live fully the life that only God can give, that life celebrated on Easter, made possible by the dying and rising of Jesus. Those to be baptized enter into divine life at baptism, but all believers continue to be satisfied by the life-giving water that is Jesus.

❖ Consider/Discuss

- What are you thirsting for?
- Do you approach God as one who can satisfy your deepest thirst?

❖ Responding to the Word

Risen Lord, you came to bring us life-giving water. Such water poured over us at our baptism. We pray for those who will soon enter into this water and become sons and daughters of the Father, co-heirs with you. Strengthen them, enlighten them, guide them, encourage them, in these final days of preparation.

March 10, 2013

FOURTH SUNDAY OF LENT (C)

Today's Focus: The Greatest Virtue

If there is a perfect parable, it is the story of the prodigal son. This story continues to convert through its portrayal of the father. As you listen to it again, think about what it reveals about our God—and what impact that has on your life.

FIRST READING
Joshua 5:9a, 10–12

The LORD said to Joshua, "Today I have removed the reproach of Egypt from you."

While the Israelites were encamped at Gilgal on the plains of Jericho, they celebrated the Passover on the evening of the fourteenth of the month. On the day after the Passover, they ate of the produce of the land in the form of unleavened cakes and parched grain. On that same day after the Passover, on which they ate of the produce of the land, the manna ceased. No longer was there manna for the Israelites, who that year ate of the yield of the land of Canaan.

PSALM RESPONSE
Psalm 34:9a

Taste and see the goodness of the Lord.

SECOND READING
2 Corinthians 5: 17–21

Brothers and sisters: Whoever is in Christ is a new creation: the old things have passed away; behold, new things have come. And all this is from God, who has reconciled us to himself through Christ and given us the ministry of reconciliation, namely, God was reconciling the world to himself in Christ, not counting their trespasses against them and entrusting to us the message of reconciliation. So we are ambassadors for Christ, as if God were appealing through us. We implore you on behalf of Christ, be reconciled to God. For our sake he made him to be sin who did not know sin, so that we might become the righteousness of God in him.

GOSPEL
Luke 15:1–3,
11–32

Tax collectors and sinners were all drawing near to listen to Jesus, but the Pharisees and scribes began to complain, saying, "This man welcomes sinners and eats with them." So to them Jesus addressed this parable: "A man had two sons, and the younger son said to his father, 'Father give me the share of your estate that should come to me.' So the father divided the property between them. After a few days, the younger son collected all his belongings and set off to a distant country where he squandered his inheritance on a life of dissipation. When he had freely spent everything, a severe famine struck that country, and he found himself in dire need. So he hired himself out to one of the local citizens who sent him to his farm to tend the swine. And he longed to eat his fill of the pods on which the swine fed, but nobody gave him any. Coming to his senses he thought, 'How many of my father's hired workers have more than enough food to eat, but here am I, dying from hunger. I shall get up and go to my father and I shall say to him, "Father, I have sinned against heaven and against you. I no longer deserve to be called your son; treat me as you would treat one of your hired workers." ' So he got up and went back to his father. While he was still a long way off, his father caught sight of him, and was filled with compassion. He ran to his son, embraced him and kissed him. His son said to him, 'Father, I have sinned against heaven and against you; I no longer deserve to be called your son.' But his father ordered his servants, 'Quickly bring the finest robe and put it on him; put a ring on his finger and sandals on his feet. Take the fattened calf and slaughter it. Then let us celebrate with a feast, because this son of mine was dead, and has come to life again; he was lost, and has been found.' Then the celebration began. Now the older son had been out in the field and, on his way back, as he neared the house, he heard the sound of music and dancing. He called one of the servants and asked what this might mean. The servant said to him, 'Your brother has returned and your father has slaughtered the fattened calf because he has him back safe and sound.' He became angry, and when he refused to enter the house, his father came out and pleaded with him. He said to his father in reply, 'Look, all these years I served you and not once did I disobey your orders; yet you never gave me even a young goat to feast on with my friends. But when your son returns who swallowed up your property with prostitutes, for him you slaughter the fattened calf.' He said to him, 'My son, you are here with me always; everything I have is yours. But now we must celebrate and rejoice, because your brother was dead and has come to life again; he was lost and has been found.' "

The first reading recounts the first celebration of Passover in the land. The story suggests that the people have just crossed the Jordan. However, mention of cakes and parched grain implies that they had been settled long enough to produce a harvest. Though the feast identified is Passover, there is no mention of the required lamb. Instead there is a reference to unleavened cakes, suggesting the feast of Unleavened Bread. Whenever Passover was celebrated, it commemorated the Exodus from Egypt. The present story probably grew out of a celebration that combined the festivals of Passover and Unleavened Bread.

Paul focuses on the reconciliation that puts an end to any enmity with God. He uses the notion of a replacement sacrifice in his explanation of how God's reconciliation is accomplished. Though he was innocent, Christ became the sin offering for the guilty. Joined to Christ, believers now share in the righteousness of Christ, and through Christ, in the righteousness of God. Having himself been reconciled with God, Paul becomes the agent through whom God works in the lives of others. All of this God has graciously accomplished for sinners through the magnanimous sacrifice of Christ. This is the good news that Paul preaches.

Jesus singles out two groups of people, tax-collectors and sinners. To eat with such people was thought to somehow share life with them. The Pharisees and scribes, those who dealt with the Law and the things of God, criticized Jesus for the company he kept. Jesus saw this association as opening the reign of God to all. The parable illustrates the mercy that God shows to repentant sinners. It also contrasts God's openness with the closed-mindedness of those who consider themselves faithful. Jesus is really contrasting the compassion of God with the mean-spiritedness of the Pharisees and scribes. Like the elder brother, they lack compassion and they seem to resent the fact that God is merciful toward sinners who repent.

✤ Reflecting on the Word

If somebody were to ask you what your greatest virtue is, what would you say? A virtue is a habit of doing good, according to Thomas Aquinas. A virtue is something you are able to do because you have been graced by God. And being graced means being gifted. So another way of asking this question is: what is the greatest gift you have been given? You might immediately answer, "Love," as St. Paul himself writes in his Letter to the Corinthians (1 Corinthians 12:31 — 13:13).

Now, love has many faces: patience, kindness, and compassion, to name a few. But I would propose that the greatest expression of this gift—and the most difficult one to carry out—is forgiveness. The story of the prodigal son is really the story of a father prodigal in forgiveness for his children. This father speaks to us of our merciful God, always ready to forgive. And this story was Jesus' answer to why he hung out with sinners.

During this season when we are preparing to renew our baptismal promises, we would do well to examine how well we are living out the virtues given to us at baptism; we call them theological virtues: faith, hope, and love. In this season, when we often turn to the sacrament of reconciliation to ask forgiveness from the Father who continues to reconcile the world to himself through Christ, it is also good to ask how are we doing as forgivers, as agents of reconciliation.

✤ Consider/Discuss

- Is there someone who needs your forgiveness?
- Is there someone from whom you need to ask forgiveness?

✤ *Responding to the Word*

Loving Lord, when we look at the cross, we see the love of the Father embodied In your saving death for our salvation. Because of your death and resurrection, we are part of a new creation, reconciled to the Father. Make us your worthy ambassadors, able to embody your merciful love.

March 10, 2013

FOURTH SUNDAY OF LENT (A)

Today's Focus: A Different Kind of Seeing

Sometimes we say, "I see," when we don't. It can allow us to ponder, to buy some time while we consider the issue at hand. But there are other times when we think we see but we really don't and don't know we don't. Today's readings offer instructive examples.

FIRST READING
1 Samuel 16: 1b, 6–7, 10–13a

The Lord said to Samuel: "Fill your horn with oil, and be on your way. I am sending you to Jesse of Bethlehem, for I have chosen my king from among his sons."

As Jesse and his sons came to the sacrifice, Samuel looked at Eliab and thought, "Surely the Lord's anointed is here before him." But the Lord said to Samuel: "Do not judge from his appearance or from his lofty stature, because I have rejected him. Not as man sees does God see, because man sees the appearance but the Lord looks into the heart." In the same way Jesse presented seven sons before Samuel, but Samuel said to Jesse, "The Lord has not chosen any one of these." Then Samuel asked Jesse, "Are these all the sons you have?" Jesse replied, "There is still the youngest, who is tending the sheep." Samuel said to Jesse, "Send for him; we will not begin the sacrificial banquet until he arrives here." Jesse sent and had the young man brought to them. He was ruddy, a youth handsome to behold and making a splendid appearance. The Lord said, "There—anoint him, for this is the one!" Then Samuel, with the horn of oil in hand, anointed David in the presence of his brothers; and from that day on, the spirit of the Lord rushed upon David.

PSALM RESPONSE
Psalm 23:1

The Lord is my shepherd; there is nothing I shall want.

SECOND READING
Ephesians 5: 8–14

Brothers and sisters: You were once darkness, but now you are light in the Lord. Live as children of light, for light produces every kind of goodness and righteousness and truth. Try to learn what is pleasing to the Lord. Take no part in the fruitless works of darkness; rather expose them, for it is shameful even to mention the things done by them in secret; but everything exposed by the light becomes visible, for everything that becomes visible is light. Therefore, it says:

"Awake, O sleeper,
and arise from the dead,
and Christ will give you light."

In the shorter version of the reading, the four passages in brackets are omitted.

GOSPEL
*John 9:1–41 or
9:1, 6–9, 13–17,
34–38*

As Jesus passed by he saw a man blind from birth. [His disciples asked him, "Rabbi, who sinned, this man or his parents, that he was born blind?" Jesus answered, "Neither he nor his parents sinned; it is so that the works of God might be made visible through him. We have to do the works of the one who sent me while it is day. Night is coming when no one can work. While I am in the world, I am the light of the world." When he had said this,] he spat on the ground and made clay with the saliva, and smeared the clay on his eyes, and said to him, "Go wash in the Pool of Siloam"—which means Sent—. So he went and washed, and came back able to see.

His neighbors and those who had seen him earlier as a beggar said, "Isn't this the one who used to sit and beg?" Some said, "It is," but others said, "No, he just looks like him." He said, "I am." [So they said to him, "How were your eyes opened?" He replied, "The man called Jesus made clay and anointed my eyes and told me, 'Go to Siloam and wash.' So I went there and washed and was able to see." And they said to him, "Where is he?" He said, "I don't know."]

They brought the one who was once blind to the Pharisees. Now Jesus had made clay and opened his eyes on a sabbath. So then the Pharisees also asked him how he was able to see. He said to them, "He put clay on my eyes, and I washed, and now I can see." So some of the Pharisees said, "This man is not from God, because he does not keep the sabbath." But others said, "How can a sinful man do such signs?" And there was a division among them. So they said to the blind man again, "What do you have to say about him, since he opened your eyes?" He said, "He is a prophet."

[Now the Jews did not believe that he had been blind and gained his sight until they summoned the parents of the one who had gained his sight. They asked them, "Is this your son, who you say was born blind? How does he now see?" His parents answered and said, "We know that this is our son and that he was born blind. We do not know how he sees now, nor do we know who opened his eyes. Ask him, he is of age; he can speak for himself." His parents said this because they were afraid of the Jews, for the Jews had already agreed that if anyone acknowledged him as the Christ, he would be expelled from the synagogue. For this reason his parents said, "He is of age; question him."

75

So a second time they called the man who had been blind and said to him, "Give God the praise! We know that this man is a sinner." He replied, "If he is a sinner, I do not know. One thing I do know is that I was blind and now I see." So they said to him, "What did he do to you? How did he open your eyes?" He answered them, "I told you already and you did not listen. Why do you want to hear it again? Do you want to become his disciples, too?" They ridiculed him and said, "You are that man's disciple; we are disciples of Moses! We know that God spoke to Moses, but we do not know where this one is from." The man answered and said to them, "This is what is so amazing, that you do not know where he is from, yet he opened my eyes. We know that God does not listen to sinners, but if one is devout and does his will, he listens to him. It is unheard of that anyone ever opened the eyes of a person born blind. If this man were not from God, he would not be able to do anything."] They answered and said to him, "You were born totally in sin, and are you trying to teach us?" Then they threw him out.

When Jesus heard that they had thrown him out, he found him and said, "Do you believe in the Son of Man?" He answered and said, "Who is he, sir, that I may believe in him?" Jesus said to him, "You have seen him, the one speaking with you is he." He said, "I do believe, Lord," and he worshiped him. [Then Jesus said, "I came into this world for judgment, so that those who do not see might see, and those who do see might become blind."

Some of the Pharisees who were with him heard this and said to him, "Surely we are not also blind, are we?" Jesus said to them, "If you were blind, you would have no sin; but now you are saying, 'We see,' so your sin remains."]

❖ Understanding the Word

The search for the new king and the choice and anointing of David open a new chapter in the story of Israel. The anointing of David is a solemn and sacred action that ceremonially sealed God's choosing him. Following the ritual, the spirit of the Lord rushes upon him. This spirit was understood as a principle of dynamic divine action, a force that had visible effects in human history. Those seized by the spirit were thus empowered to act within the community in some unique fashion. This story recounts how it took hold of a future king.

The move from darkness to light is the principal metaphor used in the Letter to the Ephesians to describe the radical change that takes place in the lives of Christians as a result of their commitment to Christ. Christians are not only warned about the works of darkness, but also urged to expose them. This counsel is given as a play on the difference between virtuous behavior that can be plainly seen, because it is done in the light, and shameful behavior that is hidden in the secret of darkness. Christians have entered into a new state of being, which will require a new way of living.

The struggle between darkness and light is a thread that runs throughout the account of the man cured of blindness. Jesus uses this two-part form to underscore the urgency of his ministry. He and his disciples must do God's work while it is yet day, for the night will come when such work will have to cease. Jesus identifies himself as the light of the world. The man who was brought from physical blindness to sight moves from spiritual blindness to religious insight. This is not true of the Pharisees. They are blind to the truth that the newly cured man saw so clearly. The one who was blind now sees, and those who can see are really blind.

❖ Reflecting on the Word

First, there is the seer (a "see-er") who doesn't see. Samuel, God's prophet, was sent to anoint a replacement for King Saul. When his eyes fell on the oldest son of Jesse, Samuel thought he was seeing the next king of Israel. Eliab had some of the same qualities as Saul: tall, striking in appearance. But God was looking at the heart and the divine gaze turned elsewhere—indeed, outside the room, to where the youngest of Jesse's sons was tending sheep. (Ever since Abel, God seemed to be partial to shepherds!)

In the Gospel, the man born blind is the only one who does see clearly, or rather, who comes to see clearly. As with most of us, he comes to a 20/20 spiritual vision gradually. When they first ask him who healed him, he replies forthrightly, "The man called Jesus made clay and anointed my eyes." And when they say Jesus can't be from God and heal on the Sabbath, the cured man asks how Jesus could be a sinner and do what he did; then he calls Jesus a prophet. Later, he says, "If he were not from God, he would not be able to do anything." And, finally, on meeting up with Jesus again, he acknowledges him as Son of Man and as Lord.

On the other side were all these seeing people who do not see Jesus for who he was. To really see Jesus, you need faith. This gift will be generously given—in God's time—to those who seek it.

❖ Consider/Discuss

- How do you see Jesus?
- Are there people who do not see who Jesus is? Have you asked God to give them the sight of faith?

❖ Responding to the Word

Lord Jesus, you are the light that lifts the blindness from the eyes of our heart, mind, and spirit. To see you is to come to faith in you as Lord and Savior. Give this gift of sight to those who do not have it. Grant, Lord, that they may see.

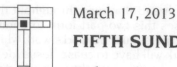

March 17, 2013

FIFTH SUNDAY OF LENT (C)

Today's Focus: An Alternative Strategy

The past can trap us. But it cannot trap God. In Jesus God did something radically new. In him the story took a wondrous turn toward the light. The response to human sinfulness became abundant mercy, not anger, much less destruction, allowing for our ongoing transformation into children of God.

FIRST READING
Isaiah 43:16–21

Thus says the LORD,
  who opens a way in the sea
  and a path in the mighty waters,
who leads out chariots and horsemen,
  a powerful army,
till they lie prostrate together, never to rise,
  snuffed out and quenched like a wick.
Remember not the events of the past,
  the things of long ago consider not;
see, I am doing something new!
  Now it springs forth, do you not perceive it?
In the desert I make a way,
  in the wasteland, rivers.
Wild beasts honor me,
  jackals and ostriches,
for I put water in the desert
  and rivers in the wasteland
  for my chosen people to drink,
the people whom I formed for myself,
  that they might announce my praise.

PSALM RESPONSE
Psalm 126:3

The Lord has done great things for us; we are filled with joy.

SECOND READING
Philippians 3: 8–14

Brothers and sisters: I consider everything as a loss because of the supreme good of knowing Christ Jesus my Lord. For his sake I have accepted the loss of all things and I consider them so much rubbish, that I may gain Christ and be found in him, not having any righteousness of my own based on the law but that which comes through faith in Christ, the righteousness from God, depending on faith to know him and the power of his resurrection and the sharing of his sufferings by being conformed to his death, if somehow I may attain the resurrection from the dead.

It is not that I have already taken hold of it or have already attained perfect maturity, but I continue my pursuit in hope that I may possess it, since I have indeed been taken possession of by Christ Jesus. Brothers and sisters, I for my part do not consider myself to have taken possession. Just one thing: forgetting what lies behind but straining forward to what lies ahead, I continue my pursuit toward the goal, the prize of God's upward calling, in Christ Jesus.

GOSPEL
John 8:1–11

Jesus went to the Mount of Olives. But early in the morning he arrived again in the temple area, and all the people started coming to him, and he sat down and taught them. Then the scribes and the Pharisees brought a woman who had been caught in adultery and made her stand in the middle. They said to him, "Teacher, this woman was caught in the very act of committing adultery. Now in the law, Moses commanded us to stone such women. So what do you say?" They said this to test him, so that they could have some charge to bring against him. Jesus bent down and began to write on the ground with his finger. But when they continued asking him, he straightened up and said to them, "Let the one among you who is without sin be the first to throw a stone at her." Again he bent down and wrote on the ground. And in response, they went away one by one, beginning with the elders. So he was left alone with the woman before him. Then Jesus straightened up and said to her, "Woman, where are they? Has no one condemned you?" She replied, "No one, sir." Then Jesus said, "Neither do I condemn you. Go, and from now on do not sin any more."

✤ Understanding the Word

Isaiah calls the people away from inordinate dependence on the past, a dependence that prevented them from seeing the astonishing new thing that God was accomplishing before their very eyes. The new thing is a new creation, a new reality so overwhelming that the people could never have imagined it by themselves. Surely the God who was victorious in the primordial battle, and who created the magnificently ordered universe out of its wreckage, can create something new from a people who had recently been released from the control of their conquerors. This is the promise of salvation proclaimed by the prophet.

Paul contrasts his relationship with Christ with the life he led and the values he championed before his conversion. Now he wants to be made righteous through union with Christ, and to share in Christ's sufferings in order to attain resurrection from the dead. He knows that profession of faith in Christ does not automatically transport one into a higher realm of being, which is what the Christians known as Gnostics seem to have claimed. It is only by taking on the day-to-day struggle with life in a way that conforms to the example set by Christ that this identification is possible.

The narrative of the woman caught in the act of adultery is really a story of conflict between Jesus and some of the religious authorities of his time. If Jesus said she should be stoned as the law required, he would be appropriating to himself the right to pass a death sentence, a right that belonged to the Romans alone. He would also be acting against his own teachings on mercy and compassion, and he would probably alienate those in the community who already opposed this particular death sentence. If he forgave the guilty woman, he would be disregarding the legitimate sentence under Israel's law, and he would probably alienate those who interpreted the law more literally. Ultimately, Jesus exhorts the woman to sin no more. Compassion and mercy have won out.

Reflecting on the Word

"Where was the guy?" asked some teens, after one of their mothers asked what questions came to their mind when they heard this Gospel story of the woman caught in adultery. Good question. Maybe he had friends among the scribes and Pharisees, who let him get away. These Jewish leaders, supposedly dedicated to the Law of Moses, decided to use the woman to get at Jesus, who came to fulfill the Law.

But Jesus was having none of it. Of course, he knew the Law of Moses and their desire to trap him at this woman's expense. If he said, "Stone her," his reputation as a man who spoke so eloquently of God's mercy would also die. If he said, "Let her go," his credibility as a rabbi would be at stake. And so, Jesus challenges them: "Let the one among you who is without sin be the first to cast a stone at her."

Some say this story doesn't fit in with John's Gospel, that it belongs more to the Luke's world with its particular emphasis on Christ's compassion. But John's Jesus is the Word become flesh, the light come into the darkness, whose glory we have seen. For John, God is love, gracious love. And in this season of God calling us all to draw closer, turning from whatever sin distances us from God, is there a better story that tells whom we shall meet when we do?

❖ Consider/Discuss

- Have you ever been trapped in self-righteousness, making harsh judgments that not only condemned another but imprisoned you?
- When have you known the mercy of God? Who showed it to you?

❖ Responding to the Word

Lord Jesus, if we did not know you, where would we be? What would we be like? What would we become? What would we be seeking, pursuing, hungering for? What would we hope for? You came as a light into the darkness of the world, a light that the darkness has not overcome.

March 17, 2013

FIFTH SUNDAY OF LENT (A)

Today's Focus: Back to Life

The story of Jesus raising Lazarus contains the most basic gospel proclamation: "I am the resurrection and the life." The Father sent his Son so that death would not have the final word. Jesus was the final word, God's Word, spoken once and for all, to overturn the power of death.

FIRST READING
Ezekiel 37: 12–14

Thus says the LORD GOD: O my people, I will open your graves and have you rise from them, and bring you back to the land of Israel. Then you shall know that I am the LORD, when I open your graves and have you rise from them, O my people! I will put my spirit in you that you may live, and I will settle you upon your land; thus you shall know that I am the LORD. I have promised, and I will do it, says the LORD.

PSALM RESPONSE
Psalm 130:7

With the Lord there is mercy and fullness of redemption.

SECOND READING
Romans 8:8–11

Brothers and sisters: Those who are in the flesh cannot please God. But you are not in the flesh; on the contrary, you are in the spirit, if only the Spirit of God dwells in you. Whoever does not have the Spirit of Christ does not belong to him. But if Christ is in you, although the body is dead because of sin, the spirit is alive because of righteousness. If the Spirit of the one who raised Jesus from the dead dwells in you, the one who raised Christ from the dead will give life to your mortal bodies also, through his Spirit dwelling in you.

In the shorter version of the reading, the five passages in brackets are omitted.

GOSPEL
John 11:1–45 or 11:3–7, 17, 20–27, 33b–45

[Now a man was ill, Lazarus from Bethany, the village of Mary and her sister Martha. Mary was the one who had anointed the Lord with perfumed oil and dried his feet with her hair; it was her brother Lazarus who was ill. So] the sisters sent word to him saying, "Master, the one you love is ill." When Jesus heard this he said, "This illness is not to end in death, but is for the glory of God, that the Son of God may be glorified through it." Now Jesus loved Martha and her sister and Lazarus. So when he heard that he was ill, he remained for two days in the place where he was. Then after this he said to his disciples, "Let us go back to Judea." [The disciples said to him, "Rabbi, the Jews were just trying to stone you, and you want to go back there?" Jesus answered, "Are there not twelve hours in a day? If one walks during the day, he does not stumble, because he sees the light of this world. But if one walks at night, he stumbles, because the light is not in him." He said this, and then told them, "Our friend Lazarus is asleep, but

81

I am going to awaken him." So the disciples said to him, "Master, if he is asleep, he will be saved." But Jesus was talking about his death, while they thought that he meant ordinary sleep. So then Jesus said to them clearly, "Lazarus has died. And I am glad for you that I was not there, that you may believe. Let us go to him." So Thomas, called Didymus, said to his fellow disciples, "Let us also go to die with him."]

When Jesus arrived, he found that Lazarus had already been in the tomb for four days. [Now Bethany was near Jerusalem, only about two miles away. And many of the Jews had come to Martha and Mary to comfort them about their brother.] When Martha heard that Jesus was coming, she went to meet him; but Mary sat at home. Martha said to Jesus, "Lord, if you had been here, my brother would not have died. But even now I know that whatever you ask of God, God will give you." Jesus said to her, "Your brother will rise." Martha said to him, "I know he will rise, in the resurrection on the last day." Jesus told her, "I am the resurrection and the life; whoever believes in me, even if he dies, will live, and everyone who lives and believes in me will never die. Do you believe this?" She said to him, "Yes, Lord. I have come to believe that you are the Christ, the Son of God, the one who is coming into the world."

[When she had said this, she went and called her sister Mary secretly, saying, "The teacher is here and is asking for you." As soon as she heard this, she rose quickly and went to him. For Jesus had not yet come into the village, but was still where Martha had met him. So when the Jews who were with her in the house comforting her saw Mary get up quickly and go out, they followed her, presuming that she was going to the tomb to weep there. When Mary came to where Jesus was and saw him, she fell at his feet and said to him, "Lord, if you had been here, my brother would not have died." When] Jesus [saw her weeping and the Jews who had come with her weeping, he] became perturbed and deeply troubled, and said, "Where have you laid him?" They said to him, "Sir, come and see." And Jesus wept. So the Jews said, "See how he loved him." But some of them said, "Could not the one who opened the eyes of the blind man have done something so that this man would not have died?"

So Jesus, perturbed again, came to the tomb. It was a cave, and a stone lay across it. Jesus said, "Take away the stone." Martha, the dead man's sister, said to him, "Lord, by now there will be a stench; he has been dead for four days." Jesus said to her, "Did I not tell you that if you believe you will see the glory of God?" So they took away the stone. And Jesus raised his eyes and said, "Father, I thank you for hearing me. I know that you always hear me; but because of the crowd here I have said this, that they may believe that you sent me."

And when he had said this, he cried out in a loud voice, "Lazarus, come out!" The dead man came out, tied hand and foot with burial bands, and his face was wrapped in a cloth. So Jesus said to them, "Untie him and let him go."

Now many of the Jews who had come to Mary and seen what he had done began to believe in him.

❖ Understanding the Word

Ezekiel uses bodily resuscitation as a metaphor for Israel's reestablishment after its exile in a foreign land. The fact that the metaphor describes reconstitution of the dead does not necessarily mean that the people believed in resurrection. In fact, its improbability may be one of the strongest reasons for employing it, for then God's wondrous power over death itself could be revealed. Resurrection would proclaim that God can bring life out of death, can make the impossible possible. The reconstitution of the bodies is likened to a new creation. Both original creation and this reconstitution are unconditional gifts from a magnanimous God.

Paul contrasts life in the flesh and life in the spirit. By flesh he means human nature in all the limitations that sometimes incline one away from God and the things of God. Life in the spirit is attuned to God and is that dimension of the human being that can be joined to the very Spirit of God. The real point of this passage is the resurrection of those who live a life in the spirit in union with God. Just as Christ conquered death and lives anew, so those joined to Christ will share in his victory and will enjoy new life.

The death of Lazarus became the opportunity for Jesus to identity himself as the Resurrection and the Life. The explanation of this claim is the heart of Jesus' teaching here. Belief in him establishes a bond of life that not even death can sever. This bond will survive physical death and keep believers from an eternal death. A solemn question is posed: "Do you believe?" Martha's answer is immediate and unequivocal: "Yes, Lord!" She may not understand, but she believes. The raising of Lazarus could not be denied, but it could be misunderstood. Jesus is not merely a wonder-worker; he himself has the power of resurrection and he is the source of eternal life.

❖ Reflecting on the Word

For God who spoke through the prophet Ezekiel, the people of Israel, carried off into Babylon, had become dead inside. They had lost hope during the decades spent in exile. So God raised up a prophet, Ezekiel—one of the strangest of the prophets—who not only had strange visions but did strange things. Ezekiel certainly got their attention. In this vision of dry bones lying in the valley, returning to life is a gradual process: first the sinews, then the flesh, then the skin, and, finally, the breath that is the spirit of life. God will bring the people back to life and bring them back home.

The promise of Lent is that God's spirit can bring us back to life, to fullness of life that is available to us because of the saving death and resurrection of Jesus. Addressing her hurt and loss, Jesus says to Martha: "I am the resurrection and the life; whoever believes in me, even if he dies, will live, and everyone who lives and believes in me will never die." Then, the challenging question: "Do you believe this?"

Lent leads us to professing a faith that is life-giving. Do you believe in God the Father almighty? Do you believe in Jesus Christ his only Son, our Lord? Do you believe in the Holy Spirit? Are you ready to answer? The good thing is that we answer as a community, as a body, supporting each other in faith. We hold each other up by our faith.

✦ Consider/Discuss

- Have you ever experienced a time where you felt dried up, all inner life gone, all spirit sapped?
- What does it mean to say: I believe that you, Lord Jesus, are the resurrection and the life? How does it make a difference in your life?

✦ Responding to the Word

Lord Jesus Christ, we approach the end of Lent, preparing to celebrate the new life you will pour into those being baptized. Stir up in them and in all of your people the fire of faith that we might proclaim you as our resurrection and our life at the Easter feast.

March 24, 2013

PALM SUNDAY OF THE PASSION OF THE LORD

Today's Focus: Serving Till His Last Breath

A piece of palm leads us to remember the story of Jesus and his final hours. The one to whom we shout Hosanna as we begin the liturgy is the one who "emptied himself, taking the form of a slave" and who "humbled himself, becoming obedient to the point of death, even death on a cross."

FIRST
READING
Isaiah 50:4–7

The Lord GOD has given me
    a well-trained tongue,
that I might know how to speak to the weary
    a word that will rouse them.
Morning after morning
    he opens my ear that I may hear;
and I have not rebelled,
    have not turned back.
I gave my back to those who beat me,
    my cheeks to those who plucked my beard;
my face I did not shield
    from buffets and spitting.

The Lord GOD is my help,
    therefore I am not disgraced;
I have set my face like flint,
    knowing that I shall not be put to shame.

PSALM
RESPONSE
Psalm 22:2a

My God, my God, why have you abandoned me?

SECOND
READING
Philippians 2:
6–11

Christ Jesus, though he was in the form of God,
    did not regard equality with God
    something to be grasped.
Rather, he emptied himself,
    taking the form of a slave,
    coming in human likeness;
    and found human in appearance,
    he humbled himself,
    becoming obedient to the point of death,
    even death on a cross.

Because of this, God greatly exalted him
    and bestowed on him the name
    which is above every name,
    that at the name of Jesus
    every knee should bend,
    of those in heaven and on earth and under the earth,
    and every tongue confess that
    Jesus Christ is Lord,
    to the glory of God the Father.

In the shorter form of the Passion, the passages in brackets are omitted.

GOSPEL
Luke 22:
14 — 23:56 or
23:1–49

[When the hour came, Jesus took his place at table with the apostles. He said to them, "I have eagerly desired to eat this Passover with you before I suffer, for, I tell you, I shall not eat it again until there is fulfillment in the kingdom of God." Then he took a cup, gave thanks, and said, "Take this and share it among yourselves; for I tell you that from this time on I shall not drink of the fruit of the vine until the kingdom of God comes." Then he took the bread, said the blessing, broke it, and gave it to them, saying, "This is my body, which will be given for you; do this in memory of me." And likewise the cup after they had eaten, saying, "This cup is the new covenant in my blood, which will be shed for you.

"And yet behold, the hand of the one who is to betray me is with me on the table; for the Son of Man indeed goes as it has been determined; but woe to that man by whom he is betrayed." And they began to debate among themselves who among them would do such a deed.

Then an argument broke out among them about which of them should be regarded as the greatest. He said to them, "The kings of the Gentiles lord it over them and those in authority over them are addressed as 'Benefactors'; but among you it shall not be so. Rather, let the greatest among you be as the youngest, and the leader as the servant. For who is greater: the one seated at table or the one who serves? Is it not the one seated at table? I am among you as the one who serves. It is you who have stood by me in my trials; and I confer a kingdom on you, just as my Father has conferred one on me, that you may eat and drink at my table in my kingdom; and you will sit on thrones judging the twelve tribes of Israel.

"Simon, Simon, behold Satan has demanded to sift all of you like wheat, but I have prayed that your own faith may not fail; and once you have turned back, you must strengthen your brothers." He said to him, "Lord, I am prepared to go to prison and to die with you." But he replied, "I tell you, Peter, before the cock crows this day, you will deny three times that you know me."

He said to them, "When I sent you forth without a money bag or a sack or sandals, were you in need of anything?" "No, nothing," they replied. He said to them, "But now one who has a money bag should take it, and likewise a sack, and one who does not have a sword should sell his cloak and buy one. For I tell you that this

Scripture must be fulfilled in me, namely,

He was counted among the wicked;

and indeed what is written about me is coming to fulfillment." Then they said, "Lord, look, there are two swords here." But he replied, "It is enough!"

Then going out, he went, as was his custom, to the Mount of Olives, and the disciples followed him. When he arrived at the place he said to them, "Pray that you may not undergo the test." After withdrawing about a stone's throw from them and kneeling, he prayed, saying, "Father, if you are willing, take this cup away from me; still, not my will but yours be done." And to strengthen him an angel from heaven appeared to him. He was in such agony and he prayed so fervently that his sweat became like drops of blood falling on the ground. When he rose from prayer and returned to his disciples, he found them sleeping from grief. He said to them, "Why are you sleeping? Get up and pray that you may not undergo the test."

While he was still speaking, a crowd approached and in front was one of the Twelve, a man named Judas. He went up to Jesus to kiss him. Jesus said to him, "Judas, are you betraying the Son of Man with a kiss?" His disciples realized what was about to happen, and they asked, "Lord, shall we strike with a sword?" And one of them struck the high priest's servant and cut off his right ear. But Jesus said in reply, "Stop, no more of this!" Then he touched the servant's ear and healed him. And Jesus said to the chief priests and temple guards and elders who had come for him, "Have you come out as against a robber, with swords and clubs? Day after day I was with you in the temple area, and you did not seize me; but this is your hour, the time for the power of darkness."

After arresting him they led him away and took him into the house of the high priest; Peter was following at a distance. They lit a fire in the middle of the courtyard and sat around it, and Peter sat down with them. When a maid saw him seated in the light, she looked intently at him and said, "This man too was with him." But he denied it saying, "Woman, I do not know him." A short while later someone else saw him and said, "You too are one of them"; but Peter answered, "My friend, I am not." About an hour later, still another insisted, "Assuredly, this man too was with him, for he also is a Galilean." But Peter said, "My friend, I do not know what you are talking about." Just as he was saying this, the cock crowed, and the Lord turned and looked at Peter; and Peter remembered the word of the Lord, how he had said to him, "Before the cock crows today, you will deny me three times." He went out and began to weep bitterly. The men who held Jesus in custody were ridiculing and beating him. They blindfolded him and questioned him, saying, "Prophesy! Who is it that struck you?" And they reviled him in saying many other things against him.

When day came the council of elders of the people met, both chief priests and scribes, and they brought him before their Sanhedrin. They said, "If you are the Christ, tell us," but he replied to them, "If I tell you, you will not believe, and if I question, you will not respond. But from this time on the Son of Man will be seated at the right hand of the power of God." They all asked, "Are you then the Son of God?" He replied to them, "You say that I am." Then they said, "What further need have we for testimony? We have heard it from his own mouth."]

Then the whole assembly of them arose and brought him before Pilate. They brought charges against him, saying, "We found this man misleading our people; he opposes the payment of taxes to Caesar and maintains that he is the Christ, a king." Pilate asked him, "Are you the king of the Jews?" He said to him in reply, "You say so." Pilate then addressed the chief priests and the crowds, "I find this man not guilty." But they were adamant and said, "He is inciting the people with his teaching throughout all Judea, from Galilee where he began even to here."

On hearing this Pilate asked if the man was a Galilean; and upon learning that he was under Herod's jurisdiction, he sent him to Herod who was in Jerusalem at that time. Herod was very glad to see Jesus; he had been wanting to see him for a long time, for he had heard about him and had been hoping to see him perform some sign. He questioned him at length, but he gave him no answer. The chief priests and scribes, meanwhile, stood by accusing him harshly. Herod and his soldiers treated him contemptuously and mocked him, and after clothing him in resplendent garb, he sent him back to Pilate. Herod and Pilate became friends that very day, even though they had been enemies formerly. Pilate then summoned the chief priests, the rulers, and the people and said to them, "You brought this man to me and accused him of inciting the people to revolt. I have conducted my investigation in your presence and have not found this man guilty of the charges you have brought against him, nor did Herod, for he sent him back to us. So no capital crime has been committed by him. Therefore I shall have him flogged and then release him."

But all together they shouted out, "Away with this man! Release Barabbas to us."—Now Barabbas had been imprisoned for a rebellion that had taken place in the city and for murder.—Again Pilate addressed them, still wishing to release Jesus, but they continued their shouting, "Crucify him! Crucify him!" Pilate addressed them a third time, "What evil has this man done? I found him guilty of no capital crime. Therefore I shall have him flogged and then release him." With loud shouts, however, they persisted in calling for his crucifixion, and their voices prevailed. The verdict of Pilate was that their demand should be granted. So he released the man who had been imprisoned for rebellion and murder, for whom they asked, and he handed Jesus over to them to deal with as they wished.

As they led him away they took hold of a certain Simon, a Cyrenian, who was coming in from the country; and after laying the cross on him, they made him carry it behind Jesus. A large crowd of people followed Jesus, including many women who mourned and lamented him. Jesus turned to them and said, "Daughters of Jerusalem, do not weep for me; weep instead for yourselves and for your children, for indeed, the days are coming when people will say, 'Blessed are the barren, the wombs that never bore and the breasts that never nursed.' At that time people will say to the mountains, 'Fall upon us!' and to the hills, 'Cover us!' for if these things are done when the wood is green what will happen when it is dry?" Now two others, both criminals, were led away with him to be executed.

When they came to the place called the Skull, they crucified him and the criminals there, one on his right, the other on his left. Then Jesus said, "Father, forgive them, they know not what they do." They divided his garments by casting lots. The people stood by and watched; the rulers, meanwhile, sneered at him and said, "He saved others, let him save himself if he is the chosen one, the Christ of God." Even the soldiers jeered at him. As they approached to offer him wine they called out, "If you are King of the Jews, save yourself." Above him there was an inscription that read, "This is the King of the Jews."

Now one of the criminals hanging there reviled Jesus, saying, "Are you not the Christ? Save yourself and us." The other, however, rebuking him, said in reply, "Have you no fear of God, for you are subject to the same condemnation? And indeed, we have been condemned justly, for the sentence we received corresponds to our crimes, but this man has done nothing criminal." Then he said, "Jesus, remember me when you come into your kingdom." He replied to him, "Amen, I say to you, today you will be with me in Paradise."

It was now about noon and darkness came over the whole land until three in the afternoon because of an eclipse of the sun. Then the veil of the temple was torn down the middle. Jesus cried out in a loud voice, "Father, into your hands I commend my spirit"; and when he had said this he breathed his last.

The centurion who witnessed what had happened glorified God and said, "This man was innocent beyond doubt." When all the people who had gathered for this spectacle saw what had happened, they returned home beating their breasts; but all his acquaintances stood at a distance, including the women who had followed him from Galilee and saw these events.

[Now there was a virtuous and righteous man named Joseph who, though he was a member of the council, had not consented to their plan of action. He came from the Jewish town of Arimathea and was awaiting the kingdom of God. He went to Pilate and asked for the body of Jesus. After he had taken the body down, he wrapped it in a linen cloth and laid him in a rock-hewn tomb in which no one had yet been buried. It was the day of preparation, and the sabbath was about to begin. The women who had come from Galilee with him followed behind, and when they had seen the tomb and the way in which his body was laid in it, they returned and prepared spices and perfumed oils. Then they rested on the sabbath according to the commandment.]

❖ Understanding the Word

A heavy price is exacted of the servant spoken of by Isaiah. He suffers both personal insult and physical attack. In the face of his affliction, he maintains that God is his strength. Such maltreatment was usually interpreted as punishment. However, that is not the case here. This is an innocent victim. Much of the content of this passage resonates with that found in many of the laments. However, there is really no complaint here, just a description of the sufferings that accrue from faithfully carrying out the mission assigned by God. If anything, this passage resembles a declaration of confidence in God's sustaining presence.

Being in the form of God, Christ enjoys a Godlike manner of being. Nonetheless, he did not cling to this or use his exalted status for his own ends. Furthermore, though in the form of God, he chose the form of a servant or slave. This does not mean that he only resembled a human being; he really was one. Having taken on the form of a slave, he made himself obedient. Finally, the exaltation of Christ is as glorious as his humiliation was debasing. Consequently, every knee shall do him homage and every tongue shall proclaim his sovereignty.

The narrative of the Lord's Supper is a classic farewell scene. Its connection with the Passover underscores the supper's end-time significance; mention of "covenant in blood" points to its sacrificial character. The events that take place on the Mount of Olives are the prelude to the rejection and the agony in store for Jesus. Faced with the terrors, he accepts them as the will of God. Throughout this narrative, Jesus is portrayed as the non-violent, innocent victim of the unwarranted hatred and bloodthirsty desires of major sections of both the Jewish and the Roman populations. The execution is reported in a matter-of-fact manner. The culminating event of the redemption of the world is accomplished with dispatch.

That last night could not have been easy. At supper, Jesus knows his end is approaching, with much suffering, after being betrayed by someone he has loved, now sitting at the table. He knows Simon will deny him three times. And he has to face an argument that breaks out among the disciples—again!—over who is the greatest. But Jesus patiently reminds them that service will win them a place in the kingdom. It will take a visit from the Spirit for this message to sink in.

From the cross we see how faithful Jesus himself is to this call to serve all. Only in Luke's Passion does Jesus speak these words we hear this Palm Sunday. His first word is a prayer of forgiveness. Looking around at those mocking him and jeering at him, he prays: "Father, forgive them, they know not what they do." His second word comforts, responding to the request of the thief on his right: "Today you will be with me in Paradise." And his final word, addressed to God, serves us: "Father, into your hands I commend my spirit," teaching us how to die trusting God.

Three times Pilate declares Jesus innocent. This judgment is further reinforced by the Roman centurion saying: "This man was innocent beyond doubt." The word innocent literally means one who does no harm. More than that, until his last breath, Jesus is the savior who does only good, who serves, bringing forgiveness, replacing fear with the promise of paradise, and showing all that God can truly be trusted.

❖ Consider/Discuss

- Which of the three "words" that Jesus speaks from the cross serves you most?
- Does the Passion of Luke call you to serve in any way?

❖ Responding to the Word

Lord, even in your last hours, you teach us to serve those whom God brings into our lives, even those who do not treat us well. May we be quick to forgive, quick to respond to those in great need, and quick to entrust our lives to the Father. May your prayers be ours.

Notes

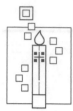

March 31, 2013

EASTER SUNDAY OF THE RESURRECTION OF THE LORD

Today's Focus: A Day to Believe In

Easter draws us into the mystery at the heart of our faith: the celebration of the paschal mystery of the dying and rising of Christ. In Peter's proclamation, Colossians' exhortation, and John's Easter story, we are challenged to respond in faith: Alleluia, I believe.

FIRST READING
Acts 10:34a, 37–43

Peter proceeded to speak and said: "You know what has happened all over Judea, beginning in Galilee after the baptism that John preached, how God anointed Jesus of Nazareth with the Holy Spirit and power. He went about doing good and healing all those oppressed by the devil, for God was with him. We are witnesses of all that he did both in the country of the Jews and in Jerusalem. They put him to death by hanging him on a tree. This man God raised on the third day and granted that he be visible, not to all the people, but to us, the witnesses chosen by God in advance, who ate and drank with him after he rose from the dead. He commissioned us to preach to the people and testify that he is the one appointed by God as judge of the living and the dead. To him all the prophets bear witness, that everyone who believes in him will receive forgiveness of sins through his name.

PSALM RESPONSE
Psalm 118:24

This is the day the Lord has made; let us rejoice and be glad.

SECOND READING
Colossians 3: 1–4

Brothers and sisters: If then you were raised with Christ, seek what is above, where Christ is seated at the right hand of God. Think of what is above, not of what is on earth. For you have died, and your life is hidden with Christ in God. When Christ your life appears, then you too will appear with him in glory.

– or –

1 Corinthians 5: 6b–8

Brothers and sisters: Do you not know that a little yeast leavens all the dough? Clear out the old yeast, so that you may become a fresh batch of dough, inasmuch as you are unleavened. For our paschal lamb, Christ, has been sacrificed. Therefore, let us celebrate the feast, not with the old yeast, the yeast of malice and wickedness, but with the unleavened bread of sincerity and truth.

GOSPEL
John 20:1–9

On the first day of the week, Mary of Magdala came to the tomb early in the morning, while it was still dark, and saw the stone removed from the tomb. So she ran and went to Simon Peter and to the other disciple whom Jesus loved, and told them, "They have taken the Lord from the tomb, and we don't know where they put him." So Peter and the other disciple went out and came to the tomb. They both ran, but the other disciple ran faster than Peter and arrived at the tomb first; he bent down and saw the burial cloths there, but did not go in. When Simon Peter arrived after him, he went into the tomb and saw the burial cloths there, and the cloth that had covered his head, not with the burial cloths but rolled up in a separate place. Then the other disciple also went in, the one who had arrived at the tomb first, and he saw and believed. For they did not yet understand the Scripture that he had to rise from the dead.

❖ Understanding the Word

Peter traces the scope and the spread of the gospel. He states that the power of Jesus' ministry flowed from his having been anointed by God with the Holy Spirit. It was in and through this power that he performed good works. Peter himself was a witness to all of these wonders. Although Jesus' ministry began with his baptism by John, it continues through people like Peter who are commissioned to preach the gospel and to bear witness to it. The power of the Resurrection is open to all who believe in Jesus. This is truly good news to the Gentiles.

The short passage from Colossians contains the fundamental teaching about the Resurrection and the way the death and resurrection of Christ transform the lives of Christians. It contrasts the world above (heaven) and the world below (earth). Having risen from the dead, Christ is now in the realm of heaven. True Christian behavior flows from belief in this reality. Joined with Christ, believers are already with Christ in God. This is not merely a dimension of Christians' future expectation, it is an already-accomplished fact. They have not left this world, but they are summoned to be attentive to the things of another world.

The Gospel reading's reference to darkness rather than the dawn of a new day may be the author's way of incorporating the light/darkness symbolism. The stone had been moved from Jesus' tomb and Mary of Magdala presumed that his body had been taken away. She seems to have entertained no thought of his resurrection. She ran off to tell Peter and "the other disciple," an example of how Jesus' disciples did not understand the scriptures concerning his resurrection. They would need both a Resurrection experience and the opening of their minds to the meaning of the scriptures. Neither Mary, probably Jesus' closest female disciple, nor Peter, the leader of the Christian community, nor "the other disciple" grasped the truth of the Resurrection.

Some biblical scholars (including St. Augustine and our own Sister Dianne Bergant) say neither Mary, Peter, nor the beloved disciple in John's Gospel came to Easter faith on that Easter morning; it only came later after the risen Jesus had appeared to them. All three simply believed the body was gone. Other scholars (such as Francis Moloney and Sister Sandra Schneiders), however, say that the beloved disciple did come to faith, reading the signs about him, notably the presence and placement of the burial cloths.

There is no space to get into this worthy discussion here. Since John's Gospel is a Gospel of "signs," I like to think that the Resurrection was the final sign, and the beloved disciple who was so close to Jesus that he could lean his head on his shoulder at the Last Supper "got it," that he was able to grasp the joyous event without fully understanding it. Love often "sees" what understanding can only later explain.

Whatever was the case on Easter morning, not long after the matter was clear: Jesus was raised by the Father. Belief in the Resurrection then led to the courageous preaching of Peter on Pentecost, then in the house of the Roman centurion Cornelius heard today. That same belief was at the heart of all of Paul's letters and those written in his name. This belief is behind the call today to "seek what is above" where Christ is with the Father. And it is this belief that we are invited to witness to on Easter by renewing our baptismal promises.

✤ Consider/Discuss

- What difference does the resurrection of Jesus mean for your life? How does it change the way you live?
- Does renewing your baptism promises on Easter challenge you in any way?

✤ Responding to the Word

Blessed are you, Father, for raising your beloved Son, Jesus, from the dead and bringing us to faith in his saving death and resurrection. Give us a taste of the joy that filled the hearts of the first disciples and help us to trust in the life that is promised through faith in him.

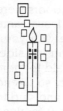

April 7, 2013

SECOND SUNDAY OF EASTER
(OR SUNDAY OF THE DIVINE MERCY)

Today's Focus: Risen Lord, Gift Giver

The risen Lord appeared before his apostles on Easter night, the first time since they ran away from him at his arrest. He came bearing gifts, the gifts flowing from the Resurrection life he now wishes to share with all those who are his disciples. We share in those gifts.

FIRST READING
Acts 5:12–16

Many signs and wonders were done among the people at the hands of the apostles. They were all together in Solomon's portico. None of the others dared to join them, but the people esteemed them. Yet more than ever, believers in the Lord, great numbers of men and women, were added to them. Thus they even carried the sick out into the streets and laid them on cots and mats so that when Peter came by, at least his shadow might fall on one or another of them. A large number of people from the towns in the vicinity of Jerusalem also gathered, bringing the sick and those disturbed by unclean spirits, and they were all cured.

PSALM RESPONSE
Psalm 118:1

Give thanks to the Lord for he is good, his love is everlasting.

SECOND READING
Revelation 1: 9–11a, 12–13, 17–19

I, John, your brother, who share with you the distress, the kingdom, and the endurance we have in Jesus, found myself on the island called Patmos because I proclaimed God's word and gave testimony to Jesus. I was caught up in spirit on the Lord's day and heard behind me a voice as loud as a trumpet, which said, "Write on a scroll what you see." Then I turned to see whose voice it was that spoke to me, and when I turned, I saw seven gold lampstands and in the midst of the lampstands one like a son of man, wearing an ankle-length robe, with a gold sash around his chest.

When I caught sight of him, I fell down at his feet as though dead. He touched me with his right hand and said, "Do not be afraid. I am the first and the last, the one who lives. Once I was dead, but now I am alive forever and ever. I hold the keys to death and the netherworld. Write down, therefore, what you have seen, and what is happening, and what will happen afterwards."

GOSPEL
John 20:19–31
On the evening of that first day of the week, when the doors were locked, where the disciples were, for fear of the Jews, Jesus came and stood in their midst and said to them, "Peace be with you." When he had said this, he showed them his hands and his side. The disciples rejoiced when they saw the Lord. Jesus said to them again, "Peace be with you. As the Father has sent me, so I send you." And when he had said this, he breathed on them and said to them, "Receive the Holy Spirit. Whose sins you forgive are forgiven them, and whose sins you retain are retained."

Thomas, called Didymus, one of the Twelve, was not with them when Jesus came. So the other disciples said to him, "We have seen the Lord." But he said to them, "Unless I see the mark of the nails in his hands and put my finger into the nailmarks and put my hand into his side, I will not believe."

Now a week later his disciples were again inside and Thomas was with them. Jesus came, although the doors were locked, and stood in their midst and said, "Peace be with you." Then he said to Thomas, "Put your finger here and see my hands, and bring your hand and put it into my side, and do not be unbelieving, but believe." Thomas answered and said to him, "My Lord and my God!" Jesus said to him, "Have you come to believe because you have seen me? Blessed are those who have not seen and have believed."

Now Jesus did many other signs in the presence of his disciples that are not written in this book. But these are written that you may come to believe that Jesus is the Christ, the Son of God, and that through this belief you may have life in his name.

❖ *Understanding the Word*

"Signs and wonders" refers to the miracles that the apostles were able to accomplish through the divine power bestowed on them by Jesus. This passage is probably a collection of motifs rather than a coherent summary. It states that some people were afraid to join the community of believers; it then contradicts itself by claiming that great numbers were added to their ranks. Actually, both were probably true. The great accomplishments of the early Christians certainly struck fear in the hearts of some, while at the same time they attracted others. Fear and admiration can and do exist side by side, especially when the power of God is evident.

John is caught up by the Spirit and is commissioned by God as were the prophets of old. The function of his vision is twofold: it clarifies the nature of his task, and it confers divine authority on it. John is gripped with fear, literally frightened to death. The figure in the vision responds with the standard declaration of reassurance: Fear not! Do not be afraid! The figure then identifies himself with the classic divine self-revelation: I am! (*égó eími*). The figure in the vision clearly takes to himself divine characteristics. This vision is not merely for John; it is clearly meant for the churches as well.

It is on the evening of the Resurrection day itself that the Holy Spirit is bestowed on the disciples, who are then commissioned to go forth and declare salvation and judgment. The absent Thomas represents the second generation of Christians, those called to believe through the testimony of others. The faith required of him is, in a way, more demanding than that required of those who actually encountered the risen Lord. Viewed in this way, his doubt might be more understandable. According to Jesus, as profound as was Thomas' ultimate faith, it does not compare with the faith of those who do not enjoy the kind of experience of the Lord described here.

❖ Reflecting on the Word

One of the nicest things about the Easter season is that it has escaped much of the commercialization of Christmas. For most, the urge to shop is not part of this great feast. And when you think of Easter music, hymns and hallelujahs come to mind; there are only a few Easter songs. Is there something about this feast so sacred that even the merchandisers have refrained from exploiting it?

At the same time, today's Gospel reminds us that while we do not get caught up with gift-giving, Easter is still a season to remember the gifts unique to it, those the risen Lord brought when he appeared to the apostles hiding in the upper room behind locked doors. The crippling fear they suffered was released by these gifts.

First, he gives them peace (*shalom*), which stands for all God's blessings that can enrich human life. Then he breathes the Holy Spirit on them—the great gift of the risen Lord, allowing them to offer God's forgiveness to all who seek it. Finally, there is the gift of faith, the ability to believe without seeing, to read the signs God so generously scatters throughout our world. All these gifts are manifestations of the Spirit.

In our first reading we witness the gift of the Spirit found at work in Peter healing the sick and delivering those "disturbed by unclean spirits." And the Spirit is found in the visions given to John the seer in Revelation, so we might have hope in God who has overturned the power of death.

❖ Consider/Discuss

- Have any of the Easter gifts mentioned helped you to see with the eyes of faith?
- Have you known Easter's gifts—peace, forgiveness, healing, and hope—as able to free you from fear?

❖ Responding to the Word

Risen Lord, you continue to come to us when we lock ourselves away from the world out of fear. Breathe upon us and send your Spirit to give us the courage to go forth and bring your gifts to others. We thank you for the gifts of the Easter season.

April 14, 2013

THIRD SUNDAY OF EASTER

Today's Focus: Profile of an Easter People

Being an Easter people, living lives of faith rooted in Jesus our risen Lord, brings both gifts and responsibilities. Last Sunday's readings spoke of the gifts that deliver us from living lives hemmed in by fear. This week God's word highlights what faith empowers us to be.

FIRST READING
Acts 5:27–32, 40b–41

When the captain and the court officers had brought the apostles in and made them stand before the Sanhedrin, the high priest questioned them, "We gave you strict orders, did we not, to stop teaching in that name? Yet you have filled Jerusalem with your teaching and want to bring this man's blood upon us." But Peter and the apostles said in reply, "We must obey God rather than men. The God of our ancestors raised Jesus, though you had him killed by hanging him on a tree. God exalted him at his right hand as leader and savior to grant Israel repentance and forgiveness of sins. We are witnesses of these things, as is the Holy Spirit whom God has given to those who obey him."

The Sanhedrin ordered the apostles to stop speaking in the name of Jesus, and dismissed them. So they left the presence of the Sanhedrin, rejoicing that they had been found worthy to suffer dishonor for the sake of the name.

PSALM RESPONSE
Psalm 30:2a

I will praise you, Lord, for you have rescued me.

SECOND READING
Revelation 5: 11–14

I, John, looked and heard the voices of many angels who surrounded the throne and the living creatures and the elders. They were countless in number, and they cried out in a loud voice:
"Worthy is the Lamb that was slain
to receive power and riches, wisdom and strength,
honor and glory and blessing."

Then I heard every creature in heaven and on earth and under the earth and in the sea, everything in the universe, cry out:
"To the one who sits on the throne and to the Lamb
be blessing and honor, glory and might,
forever and ever."

The four living creatures answered, "Amen," and the elders fell down and worshiped.

GOSPEL
John 21:1–19 or
21:1–14

At that time, Jesus revealed himself again to his disciples at the Sea of Tiberias. He revealed himself in this way. Together were Simon Peter, Thomas called Didymus, Nathanael from Cana in Galilee, Zebedee's sons, and two others of his disciples. Simon Peter said to them, "I am going fishing." They said to him, "We also will come with you." So they went out and got into the boat, but that night they caught nothing. When it was already dawn, Jesus was standing on the shore; but the disciples did not realize that it was Jesus. Jesus said to them, "Children, have you caught anything to eat?" They answered him, "No." So he said to them, "Cast the net over the right side of the boat and you will find something." So they cast it, and were not able to pull it in because of the number of fish. So the disciple whom Jesus loved said to Peter, "It is the Lord." When Simon Peter heard that it was the Lord, he tucked in his garment, for he was lightly clad, and jumped into the sea. The other disciples came in the boat, for they were not far from shore, only about a hundred yards, dragging the net with the fish. When they climbed out on shore, they saw a charcoal fire with fish on it and bread. Jesus said to them, "Bring some of the fish you just caught." So Simon Peter went over and dragged the net ashore full of one hundred fifty-three large fish. Even though there were so many, the net was not torn. Jesus said to them, "Come, have breakfast." And none of the disciples dared to ask him, "Who are you?" because they realized it was the Lord. Jesus came over and took the bread and gave it to them, and in like manner the fish. This was now the third time Jesus was revealed to his disciples after being raised from the dead.

[When they had finished breakfast, Jesus said to Simon Peter, "Simon, son of John, do you love me more than these?" Simon Peter answered him, "Yes, Lord, you know that I love you." Jesus said to him, "Feed my lambs." He then said to Simon Peter a second time, "Simon, son of John, do you love me?" Simon Peter answered him, "Yes, Lord, you know that I love you." Jesus said to him, "Tend my sheep." Jesus said to him the third time, "Simon, son of John, do you love me?" Peter was distressed that Jesus had said to him a third time, "Do you love me?" and he said to him, "Lord, you know everything; you know that I love you." Jesus said to him, "Feed my sheep. Amen, amen, I say to you, when you were younger, you used to dress yourself and go where you wanted; but when you grow old, you will stretch out your hands, and someone else will dress you and lead you where you do not want to go." He said this signifying by what kind of death he would glorify God. And when he had said this, he said to him, "Follow me."]

The court scene depicted in the first reading describes apostles who are courageous witnesses to the resurrection of Jesus and heralds of this wondrous event to the world. They have been so successful that the high priest is concerned that the temper of the people may have changed and the ruling body might be blamed for Jesus' death. Peter then launches into a sermon consisting of the fundamental apostolic proclamation. God has reversed the plans of those who put Jesus to death, raising him from the dead and exalting him in a place of honor at God's own right hand.

The vision that John describes reveals the heavenly throne room, where angels, living creatures, and elders surround the throne of God. The living creatures are reminiscent of the figures that stood guard at the entrance of temples. Twenty-four elders join the four living creatures and the angels in praise. Although the focus is the investiture of the Lamb, the message behind the vision is more specifically theological than Christological. God, not the Lamb, is seated on the throne. Worship of and devotion to Christ must be understood in terms of his relationship with God. To this all cry out, Amen!

Even Jesus' intimate companions did not recognize the risen Lord. Here recognition comes through his actions, not through his words. Only after the disciples pulled in the multitude of fish did they know it was he. Jesus' exchange with Peter has many links with Peter's earlier denial of him. Sobered by that denial, Peter does not now declare that he is capable of being more faithful than the others. Three times Peter denied; three times he is called upon to declare his love. When he does, he is commissioned to assume the role of shepherd in the place of Jesus. He is now a shepherd who can show compassion to those who have failed. As shepherd, he will suffer a fate similar to that which Jesus suffered.

❖ Reflecting on the Word

Each reading today calls us to live out our faith in the risen Lord in a particular way. Acts calls us to be courageous witnesses to Christ the Lord. The apostles have been hauled into court before the high priest and the other religious leaders of the Sanhedrin, the supreme religious council in Jerusalem. Peter argues that the Sanhedrin's command to cease teaching about Jesus must yield to a higher call to witness in the Spirit whom the living God has given to them. In that same spirit, Pope Paul VI reminded us that the modern person listens more willingly to witnesses more than to teachers, and if he or she listens to teachers it is because they are witnesses.

Revelation affirms that the proper response to Easter is to give glory and praise to the Lamb and to God who sits on the throne. Augustine told us that we are an Easter people and alleluia is our song. Each Sunday we gather as worshipers. Worship of the Lamb leads to witness, which then leads to worship.

The final encounter in John's Gospel is between Jesus and Peter. Jesus comes to Peter asking, "Do you love me?" then "Feed my lambs." The witness of the Lord and worshiper of the Lamb is also to be a lover of the Lord's little ones. All three of these activities flow from our baptism. All three are to be done not as solo activities but as part of the body of Christ.

❖ Consider/Discuss

- Do you see your call to be a disciple as including the call to witness, worship, and watch out for the lowly and the least?
- How does your faith community help you to live out your calling?

❖ Responding to the Word

Strengthen us, Jesus, to witness with conviction to our faith in you as Lord and Savior. May the Holy Spirit lead us to praise and honor the Father through you all our days, and find clear expression in caring for your people by working for justice and peace for all.

April 21, 2013

FOURTH SUNDAY OF EASTER

Today's Focus: Good Shepherds Still Needed

The image of the crucified Lord was rarely found in art before the fourth century, but Jesus as the Good Shepherd is found in the catacombs in Rome going back to the early days of the church. Every Easter season our liturgy places this image before us to contemplate.

FIRST READING
Acts 13:14, 43–52

Paul and Barnabas continued on from Perga and reached Antioch in Pisidia. On the sabbath they entered the synagogue and took their seats. Many Jews and worshipers who were converts to Judaism followed Paul and Barnabas, who spoke to them and urged them to remain faithful to the grace of God.

On the following sabbath almost the whole city gathered to hear the word of the Lord. When the Jews saw the crowds, they were filled with jealousy and with violent abuse contradicted what Paul said. Both Paul and Barnabas spoke out boldly and said, "It was necessary that the word of God be spoken to you first, but since you reject it and condemn yourselves as unworthy of eternal life, we now turn to the Gentiles. For so the Lord has commanded us,

I have made you a light to the Gentiles,
that you may be an instrument of salvation
to the ends of the earth."

The Gentiles were delighted when they heard this and glorified the word of the Lord. All who were destined for eternal life came to believe, and the word of the Lord continued to spread through the whole region. The Jews, however, incited the women of prominence who were worshipers and the leading men of the city, stirred up a persecution against Paul and Barnabas, and expelled them from their territory. So they shook the dust from their feet in protest against them, and went to Iconium. The disciples were filled with joy and the Holy Spirit.

PSALM RESPONSE
Psalm 100:3c

We are his people, the sheep of his flock.

SECOND READING
Revelation 7:9, 14b–17

I, John, had a vision of a great multitude, which no one could count, from every nation, race, people, and tongue. They stood before the throne and before the Lamb, wearing white robes and holding palm branches in their hands.

Then one of the elders said to me, "These are the ones who have survived the time of great distress; they have washed their robes and made them white in the blood of the Lamb.

"For this reason they stand before God's throne
    and worship him day and night in his temple.
The one who sits on the throne will shelter them.
They will not hunger or thirst anymore,
    nor will the sun or any heat strike them.
For the Lamb who is in the center of the throne
    will shepherd them
    and lead them to springs of life-giving water,
    and God will wipe away every tear from their eyes."

GOSPEL
John 10:27–30

Jesus said: "My sheep hear my voice; I know them, and they follow me. I give them eternal life, and they shall never perish. No one can take them out of my hand. My Father, who has given them to me, is greater than all, and no one can take them out of the Father's hand. The Father and I are one."

❖ *Understanding the Word*

Animosity arose between the apostles and certain segments within the Jewish community. This caused Paul to discontinue ministering to the Jews and to turn to the Gentiles. The passage might suggest that all the Jews rejected the gospel and only Greek-born Jews were open to it, when in fact it was probably only the leaders of the synagogue who contradicted Paul and blasphemed against Jesus. Paul reinterprets a Servant Song of Isaiah, which declares that salvation will come to the Gentiles through the agency of the people of God. He thus claims that he, Paul, will be God's light to the Gentiles.

The multitude in John's vision is international in character. The people come from every nation, race, people, and tongue, thus fulfilling a promise made to Abraham that he would be the father of a host of nations (Genesis 17:4). The "blood of the Lamb" is a reference to Christ's redemptive sacrifice. It is also a reference to the baptism of the individuals gathered together, for it was through baptism that they were incorporated into Christ's death. It is because they have endured and have been made pure by Christ that they can stand before God and worship day and night without end.

Jesus' sheep hear his voice, recognize it, and follow him. This image implies intimate knowledge between Jesus and his followers and unquestioning trust on the part of the followers. Jesus promises that if the sheep heed his voice they will never perish. Since he wields power over death, he will certainly protect them from lesser evils. He has the right to exercise this kind of authority over the sheep because they have been given to him by God. All that Jesus says and does is the actual embodiment of God's will and not just behavior that conforms to it. Since Jesus and his Father are so closely joined, the shepherd who cares for the sheep is indeed one with God.

God spoke through the prophet Ezekiel, promising to shepherd Israel (Ezekiel 34:11ff), so it is not surprising that Jesus himself used the image of the shepherd to speak of his mission. Nor was it surprising that the first mission of his apostles was described as being sent out to gather the lost sheep of Israel (Matthew 10:6). Going further, in his own ministry, Jesus reached out to those beyond the boundaries of Judaism, bringing healing to some Gentiles by exorcising their demons (Mark 5:1ff and 7:24ff). And the vision of Revelation reveals the Lamb as one who shepherds people of every nation, race, and tongue.

The role of shepherding was given to Peter in the Gospels, while the example and letters of Paul certainly show his own acceptance of this role in the various communities of Gentiles. Today's first reading presents Paul as the one who will be God's instrument in bringing God's light, Christ, to the Gentiles outside Israel through his preaching. The Greek word for "good" (*kilos*) used to characterize the shepherd does not refer to moral character—though that is certainly a necessary attribute of all shepherds—but this particular word indicates that the shepherd is one who is "good at" shepherding. This helpful distinction challenges all who are called to participate in ministry in whatever capacity, however small, that concerns the nurturing and care of God's people. Competence and skill must accompany holiness and wisdom. When all these qualities are in play, there is greater certitude that the Church will have good shepherds.

❖ Consider/Discuss

- Have you experienced Jesus as a Good Shepherd?
- How does your calling to be a disciple involve you in the work of the Good Shepherd, caring for his lambs and sheep, being good at bringing others closer to God?

❖ *Responding to the Word*

Gentle Shepherd, continue to raise up good shepherds for your church. May all you have called to shepherd your people continue to be attentive to the guidance of your voice and follow your example in all that they do. Direct and protect our shepherds as they tend to your people.

April 28, 2013

FIFTH SUNDAY OF EASTER

Today's Focus: Work for Everyone, Guaranteed

The work of the church's first leaders continues in our day, as we discover in reading Acts. This work will eventually usher in the new age spoken of in today's second reading, but it begins even now when we live out the first and last commandment of John's Gospel.

FIRST READING
Acts 14:21–27

After Paul and Barnabas had proclaimed the good news to that city and made a considerable number of disciples, they returned to Lystra and to Iconium and to Antioch. They strengthened the spirits of the disciples and exhorted them to persevere in the faith, saying, "It is necessary for us to undergo many hardships to enter the kingdom of God." They appointed elders for them in each church and, with prayer and fasting, commended them to the Lord in whom they had put their faith. Then they traveled through Pisidia and reached Pamphylia. After proclaiming the word at Perga they went down to Attalia. From there they sailed to Antioch, where they had been commended to the grace of God for the work they had now accomplished. And when they arrived, they called the church together and reported what God had done with them and how he had opened the door of faith to the Gentiles.

PSALM RESPONSE
Psalm 145:1

I will praise your name for ever, my king and my God.

SECOND READING
Revelation 21: 1–5a

Then I, John, saw a new heaven and a new earth. The former heaven and the former earth had passed away, and the sea was no more. I also saw the holy city, a new Jerusalem, coming down out of heaven from God, prepared as a bride adorned for her husband. I heard a loud voice from the throne saying, "Behold, God's dwelling is with the human race. He will dwell with them and they will be his people and God himself will always be with them as their God. He will wipe every tear from their eyes, and there shall be no more death or mourning, wailing or pain, for the old order has passed away."

The One who sat on the throne said, "Behold, I make all things new."

GOSPEL
John 13: 31–33a, 34–35

When Judas had left them, Jesus said, "Now is the Son of Man glorified, and God is glorified in him. If God is glorified in him, God will also glorify him in himself, and God will glorify him at once. My children, I will be with you only a little while longer. I give you a new commandment: love one another. As I have loved you, so you also should love one another. This is how all will know that you are my disciples, if you have love for one another."

The suffering that Paul and Barnabas were forced to endure is referred to as the "birth pangs" of the Messiah, the inevitable suffering that occurs when one passes from "this age" to the "age of fulfillment." These men were not independent missionaries. They were sent forth by the church in Antioch, and it was to that same church that they reported what was accomplished through them. It is important to note that the success of the mission is credited to God. Still, it was through Paul that the door of faith, an opportunity to believe in salvation through Jesus Christ, was opened for the Gentiles.

The new heaven and new earth do not merely suggest transformation or renewal; they describe something entirely new. The new Jerusalem is a sacred place where God dwells in a very special way. The old order has passed away, along with death and tears. In fulfillment of the prophetic promise, God will comfort the people who mourn, wiping away their tears. The reading ends in a summary note: All things are made new. While "new" is the eschatological catchword, the present tense of the verb indicates that God's new creative action is unfolding now.

The hour of Jesus' death is the hour of his glorification. He is glorified both in his willingness to obey God even unto death, and in God's glorification of him by making his sacrifice effective for the salvation of all. Jesus tenderly admonishes his disciples to love one another. Since he will not remain with these loved ones for long, the love that they show one another will be the earthly counterpart of the mutual glorification of God and Jesus himself. They are to love one another with the same self-sacrificing love that Jesus has shown them. Such love will be the universal sign of discipleship of Jesus. The love that the followers of Jesus have for one another shows forth the glory of God.

❖ Reflecting on the Word

We go from Acts' record of the early days of the church to a vision of the final coming of God's kingdom. In Acts, those first days were a time of building up and strengthening the community. Paul and Barnabas moved from town to town: Elytra, Conium, Antioch, Epicedia, Pamphylia, Pergo, and Attala. Their work was preaching to convert, lifting the spirits of believers and encouraging their perseverance, and appointing local leaders.

Revelation offers an idealized vision of how the work begun then will turn out: a new heaven and earth, a holy city where God will dwell with the human race and will wipe away all tears caused by death and pain. Of particular interest is the phrase "the sea was no more," the sea being a symbol of chaos and destructive powers.

How will this come about? How will this activity be sustained through persecution, sin, and human weakness? The Gospel holds the key—by living the new commandment Jesus gave to his disciples: "Love one another as I have loved you." In this way, Christ continues to be glorified and God glorified in him.

The names of the cities may have changed. Now the work continues in Arlington, Baltimore, Newton, Flossmoor, Arroyo Grande, San Jose, among others. But whether cities or towns, a new creation will only result if a community of believers, under dedicated leadership, perseveres in loving as Christ loved. When this happens, the seeds of Resurrection life are certain to bear fruit.

✤ Consider/Discuss

- Have you accepted your job assignment?
- Could God be calling you to move on to "a different city," some new place to love as Christ loved?

✤ *Responding to the Word*

Your commandment to love as you loved us, Lord Jesus, with a willingness to give generously, not counting the cost, is frightening to most of us most of the time. Give us your companionship, which we surely need, and increase our hope in the fulfillment you have promised. We place our trust in you.

May 5, 2013

SIXTH SUNDAY OF EASTER

Today's Focus: Membership Qualifications

Membership in the church has been a debated topic since the beginning. Who belongs? Who doesn't? We seem to hear one set of qualifications in today's first reading and another implied in the Gospel. But there is a common denominator. Thank God— literally!—for the Holy Spirit.

FIRST READING
Acts 15:1–2, 22–29

Some who had come down from Judea were instructing the brothers, "Unless you are circumcised according to the Mosaic practice, you cannot be saved." Because there arose no little dissension and debate by Paul and Barnabas with them, it was decided that Paul, Barnabas, and some of the others should go up to Jerusalem to the apostles and elders about this question.

The apostles and elders, in agreement with the whole church, decided to choose representatives and to send them to Antioch with Paul and Barnabas. The ones chosen were Judas, who was called Barsabbas, and Silas, leaders among the brothers. This is the letter delivered by them:

"The apostles and the elders, your brothers, to the brothers in Antioch, Syria, and Cilicia of Gentile origin: greetings. Since we have heard that some of our number who went out without any mandate from us have upset you with their teachings and disturbed your peace of mind, we have with one accord decided to choose representatives and to send them to you along with our beloved Barnabas and Paul, who have dedicated their lives to the name of our Lord Jesus Christ. So we are sending Judas and Silas who will also convey this same message by word of mouth: 'It is the decision of the Holy Spirit and of us not to place on you any burden beyond these necessities, namely, to abstain from meat sacrificed to idols, from blood, from meats of strangled animals, and from unlawful marriage. If you keep free of these, you will be doing what is right. Farewell.' "

PSALM RESPONSE
Psalm 67:4

O God, let all the nations praise you!

SECOND READING
Revelation 21: 10–14, 22–23

The angel took me in spirit to a great, high mountain and showed me the holy city Jerusalem coming down out of heaven from God. It gleamed with the splendor of God. Its radiance was like that of a precious stone, like jasper, clear as crystal. It had a massive, high wall, with twelve gates where twelve angels were stationed and on which names were inscribed, the names of the twelve tribes of the Israelites. There were three gates facing east, three north, three south, and three west. The wall of the city had twelve courses of stones as its foundation, on which were inscribed the twelve names of the twelve apostles of the Lamb.

I saw no temple in the city for its temple is the Lord God almighty and the Lamb. The city had no need of sun or moon to shine on it, for the glory of God gave it light, and its lamp was the Lamb.

GOSPEL
John 14:23–29

Jesus said to his disciples: "Whoever loves me will keep my word, and my Father will love him, and we will come to him and make our dwelling with him. Whoever does not love me does not keep my words; yet the word you hear is not mine but that of the Father who sent me.

"I have told you this while I am with you. The Advocate, the Holy Spirit, whom the Father will send in my name, will teach you everything and remind you of all that I told you. Peace I leave with you; my peace I give to you. Not as the world gives do I give it to you. Do not let your hearts be troubled or afraid. You heard me tell you, 'I am going away and I will come back to you.' If you loved me, you would rejoice that I am going to the Father; for the Father is greater than I. And now I have told you this before it happens, so that when it happens you may believe."

❖ *Understanding the Word*

The question of conditions for membership was one of the most serious disputes that raged in the first years of the church. Since the Jesus movement was originally an internal Jewish renewal, the Jewish Christians continued to observe the religious practices of their former faith, and they expected the same of Gentile converts. However, Paul allowed his Gentile converts to refrain from Jewish observance. An official letter from the Jerusalem church decided the issue. Though requiring minimal observance, this decree affirmed the belief that salvation came only from Jesus and not even indirectly through the law.

The vision of the holy city Jerusalem coming down out of heaven recalls several prophecies of ancient Israel, particularly from the book of the prophet Ezekiel (see Ezekiel 40:2; 48:30–35). Coming from God, the city is radiant with the splendor of God. The new Jerusalem is founded on the apostolic teaching; the role played by the tribes of Israel is not as evident. Perhaps they reflect an element of Jewish eschatology that expected the restoration of the twelve tribes at the end-time. There is no temple in this new city, because the risen Christ is the place where God and human beings now meet.

Love is the fundamental message of Jesus' last discourse. He calls for a demanding kind of love, one that is as self-sacrificing as was his own. Jesus and his Father make an abiding dwelling with those who love like this. Like Jesus, the Holy Spirit is sent by the Father. The Spirit is not a substitute for Jesus, but is an emissary, participating in the mission of Jesus by reminding the disciples of the things that Jesus taught them. Jesus' words end on a note of reassurance. He bequeaths his peace. This is more than a wish; it is a blessing that includes all of the benefits of the Resurrection. Jesus' peace is grounded in his relationship with his Father and his self-sacrificing love of the world.

❖ Reflecting on the Word

Groucho Marx once said, "I don't want to belong to any club that would have someone like me for a member." We laugh because usually the opposite is the case. We don't want to belong to any club that would have anyone very different from me as a member. The Church, however, is true to its calling when the welcome mat is out for all.

Acts today gives us a "tweeter's" version of the early council of Jerusalem on the issue of whether Gentiles can be received into the community without circumcision and accepting the Law of Moses. Take some time to read all of Chapter 15 to hear the three important speeches that determined the conditions for the outcome of this debate. The final decision was reached under two influences: "the Holy Spirit and us"—the "us" being Peter, Barnabas and Paul, and James, leader of the church in Jerusalem.

In a more intimate manner of expression, though no less binding, Jesus speaks about the requirements for having the Father and him come to dwell with the disciples: "Whoever loves me will keep my word." That "word" we heard last week, his great commandment: Love one another as I have loved you. Jesus gives further assurance: "The Holy Spirit, whom the Father will send in my name, will teach you everything and remind you of all that I told you."

In both instances the Holy Spirit is recognized. May the Holy Spirit always continue to work on the Church's membership drive and guide the deliberations of its leaders.

❖ Consider/Discuss

- What do you see as necessary for being a member of the Catholic Church?
- Do you know what the Church declares necessary for being a member in good standing?

❖ Responding to the Word

Holy Spirit, you descended upon Christ at his baptism, guided him through his ministry, and were his first gift after the Father raised him from the dead. Continue to be with his body, the Church, to guide its work so that all its members live according to his word.

May 9 or 12, 2013

THE ASCENSION OF THE LORD

Today's Focus: A Comfort and a Challenge

The feast of the Ascension opens our eyes to the ongoing role of the risen Lord in our lives and deepens our awareness of the reason we hold on to hope. No matter what is happening in our world, the power of God is at work to transform all creation.

FIRST READING
Acts 1:1–11

In the first book, Theophilus, I dealt with all that Jesus did and taught until the day he was taken up, after giving instructions through the Holy Spirit to the apostles whom he had chosen. He presented himself alive to them by many proofs after he had suffered, appearing to them during forty days and speaking about the kingdom of God. While meeting with them, he enjoined them not to depart from Jerusalem, but to wait for "the promise of the Father about which you have heard me speak; for John baptized with water, but in a few days you will be baptized with the Holy Spirit."

When they had gathered together they asked him, "Lord, are you at this time going to restore the kingdom to Israel?" He answered them, "It is not for you to know the times or seasons that the Father has established by his own authority. But you will receive power when the Holy Spirit comes upon you, and you will be my witnesses in Jerusalem, throughout Judea and Samaria, and to the ends of the earth." When he had said this, as they were looking on, he was lifted up, and a cloud took him from their sight. While they were looking intently at the sky as he was going, suddenly two men dressed in white garments stood beside them. They said, "Men of Galilee, why are you standing there looking at the sky? This Jesus who has been taken up from you into heaven will return in the same way as you have seen him going into heaven."

PSALM RESPONSE
Psalm 47:6

God mounts his throne to shouts of joy: a blare of trumpets for the Lord.

Brothers and sisters: May the God of our Lord Jesus Christ, the Father of glory, give you a Spirit of wisdom and revelation resulting in knowledge of him. May the eyes of your hearts be enlightened, that you may know what is the hope that belongs to his call, what are the riches of glory in his inheritance among the holy ones, and what is the surpassing greatness of his power for us who believe, in accord with the exercise of his great might: which he worked in Christ, raising him from the dead and seating him at his right hand in the heavens, far above every principality, authority, power, and dominion, and every name that is named not only in this age but also in the one to come. And he put all things beneath his feet and gave him as head over all things to the church, which is his body, the fullness of the one who fills all things in every way.

– or –

Christ did not enter into a sanctuary made by hands, a copy of the true one, but heaven itself, that he might now appear before God on our behalf. Not that he might offer himself repeatedly, as the high priest enters each year into the sanctuary with blood that is not his own; if that were so, he would have had to suffer repeatedly from the foundation of the world. But now once for all he has appeared at the end of the ages to take away sin by his sacrifice. Just as it is appointed that men and women die once, and after this the judgment, so also Christ, offered once to take away the sins of many, will appear a second time, not to take away sin but to bring salvation to those who eagerly await him.

Therefore, brothers and sisters, since through the blood of Jesus we have confidence of entrance into the sanctuary by the new and living way he opened for us through the veil, that is, his flesh, and since we have "a great priest over the house of God," let us approach with a sincere heart and in absolute trust, with our hearts sprinkled clean from an evil conscience and our bodies washed in pure water. Let us hold unwaveringly to our confession that gives us hope, for he who made the promise is trustworthy.

GOSPEL
Luke 24:46–53

Jesus said to his disciples: "Thus it is written that the Christ would suffer and rise from the dead on the third day and that repentance, for the forgiveness of sins, would be preached in his name to all the nations, beginning from Jerusalem. You are witnesses of these things. And behold I am sending the promise of my Father upon you; but stay in the city until you are clothed with power from on high."

Then he led them out as far as Bethany, raised his hands, and blessed them. As he blessed them he parted from them and was taken up to heaven. They did him homage and then returned to Jerusalem with great joy, and they were continually in the temple praising God.

❖ Understanding the Word

The confusion of the apostles provided Jesus the opportunity for one final instruction. He promised them the power of the Spirit to guide them in their endeavors. The cloud that took him from their sight is a traditional symbol of the presence of God. The two men in white garments are reminiscent of the two men at the tomb who announced the Resurrection. Though these men state that Jesus will return as he left them, the symbolic nature of this description prevented the disciples and us from knowing just what that might mean. Along with these disciples, we will have to depend upon the Spirit.

The prayer from Ephesians is for a threefold spiritual enlightenment, an enlightenment of the inner eyes. The petitioner asks that believers might know 1) the hope of the calling that they have received from God, 2) the riches of the glory of God's inheritance, and 3) the surpassing greatness of God's power to those who believe. These marvels have already taken place; it is for the believers to acknowledge them in awe. The view of Christ contained in this passage is quite exalted. Having been raised from the dead, Christ now sits at God's right hand, high above all of the other heavenly creatures.

In his last instruction to his disciples, Jesus explains how his death and resurrection had been foretold. There can be no question about the veracity of these events. As witnesses to them, the disciples are now to proclaim to all the nations that he did indeed die and rise, that he did preach repentance and forgiveness of sins. This last instruction was meant not only to bring the disciples themselves to Resurrection faith but also to commission them to bring this faith to the world. The actual description of the Ascension is quite brief in this account. There is neither grief nor fear on the part of the disciples. In fact, they return rejoicing and continue worshiping publicly in the temple.

One year I missed celebrating the Ascension. I live in D.C., which celebrates it on a Sunday, but happened to be in New Jersey on that Sunday, where it had already been celebrated the previous Thursday. I really did miss celebrating it. I have come to have a deep love for this feast, finding it both comforting and challenging.

It's not a feast that brings an end to Jesus' work. Rather, it marks Jesus' transition from a limited sphere of activity—preaching, teaching, healing, living, and dying within the geographical space of Israel and its environs two thousand years ago—to the exalted position of being in glory at the Father's right hand, interceding for us all, with "all things beneath his feet," having been given "as head over all things to the church, which is his body, the fullness of the one who fills all things in every way" (Ephesians 1:23). This is a most comforting vision of Jesus and his ongoing role of praying for all creation.

The challenge comes from Luke's two versions of the Ascension, reminding us that Jesus was not signaling "mission accomplished." Note how Jesus quickly dismisses the suggestion that now was the time for Israel to be restored to a position of power as in the good old days of King David. Instead, Jesus prepares them for the next phase of God's plan for the world: working under the power of the Holy Spirit. A great deal of work remains to be done. So . . . don't stand around looking up. Get moving!

❖ Consider/Discuss

- What does it mean to say that Jesus sits at the right hand of the Father?
- Are angels whispering for you to "move on" and take up some work that invites your bearing witness to Christ?

❖ *Responding to the Word*

We thank you, Father, for the assurance that we have One who constantly intercedes for us. We thank you for making us part of your plan as co-workers. Enlighten the eyes of our hearts so we may see where you wish us to go and what you want us to do.

May 12, 2013

SEVENTH SUNDAY OF EASTER

Today's Focus: Let Us Pray

We witness three prayers today. Stephen prays in the spirit of Jesus on the cross as he is being stoned. The prayer in Revelation, imitating the Spirit and the church, fittingly concludes this book of visions. At the Last Supper Jesus prays that all be united with him and the Father.

FIRST READING
Acts 7:55–60

Stephen, filled with the Holy Spirit, looked up intently to heaven and saw the glory of God and Jesus standing at the right hand of God, and Stephen said, "Behold, I see the heavens opened and the Son of Man standing at the right hand of God." But they cried out in a loud voice, covered their ears, and rushed upon him together. They threw him out of the city, and began to stone him. The witnesses laid down their cloaks at the feet of a young man named Saul. As they were stoning Stephen, he called out, "Lord Jesus, receive my spirit." Then he fell to his knees and cried out in a loud voice, "Lord, do not hold this sin against them"; and when he said this, he fell asleep.

PSALM RESPONSE
Psalm 97:1a, 9a

The Lord is king, the most high over all the earth.

SECOND READING
Revelation 22: 12–14, 16–17, 20

I, John, heard a voice saying to me: "Behold, I am coming soon. I bring with me the recompense I will give to each according to his deeds. I am the Alpha and the Omega, the first and the last, the beginning and the end."

Blessed are they who wash their robes so as to have the right to the tree of life and enter the city through its gates.

"I, Jesus, sent my angel to give you this testimony for the churches. I am the root and offspring of David, the bright morning star."

The Spirit and the bride say, "Come." Let the hearer say, "Come." Let the one who thirsts come forward, and the one who wants it receive the gift of life-giving water.

The one who gives this testimony says, "Yes, I am coming soon." Amen! Come, Lord Jesus!

GOSPEL
John 17:20–26

Lifting up his eyes to heaven, Jesus prayed, saying: "Holy Father, I pray not only for them, but also for those who will believe in me through their word, so that they may all be one, as you, Father, are in me and I in you, that they also may be in us, that the world may believe that you sent me. And I have given them the glory you gave me, so that they may be one, as we are one, I in them and you in me, that they may be brought to perfection as one, that the world may know that you sent me, and that you loved them even as you loved me. Father, they are your gift to me. I wish that where I am they also may be with me, that they may see my glory that you gave me, because you loved me before the foundation of the world. Righteous Father, the world also does not know you, but I know you, and they know that you sent me. I made known to them your name and I will make it known, that the love with which you loved me may be in them and I in them."

❖ Understanding the Word

If the members of the Sanhedrin had believed what Stephen was alleging, they would have had to conclude that Jesus' claims about himself had been true, and that they had wrongfully put him to death. Instead, they closed their hearts, covered their ears, and sentenced Stephen to stoning. No reason is given for the presence of the young Saul (Paul). Was he a member of a local synagogue? Was he merely a spectator? Whatever the reason, here Stephen, not Paul, is the hero, the one who successfully patterns his life and death after that of his Master.

In the reading from Revelation, the risen Jesus announces that he is the Alpha and the Omega, the first and the last, the beginning and the end. These are all polar pairs, which indicate that he encompasses everything. He also identifies himself with two messianic titles: the root or branch of David, and the bright morning star, which announces the new day. Though he announces that he will judge everyone not merely according to their faith but according to their deeds, his attention is focused on those who have been faithful. This reading suggests that the Lord's coming is something to look forward to with joy.

Jesus prays for the unity of all believers, a unity that does not merely resemble the unity that exists between Jesus and his Father, but actually participates in it. Furthermore, joined to Jesus, believers share in the glory of Jesus that was manifested through his death, resurrection, and exaltation. Believers are to manifest this divine union to the world so that the world will see not only that God sent Jesus, but also that God loves believers with the same love with which Jesus is loved. Having made God's name known to believers, Jesus asks that these believers might be with him. If the love with which God loves Jesus resides in those who believe in him, Jesus himself will abide in them.

118

We witness three intense moments of prayer in today's scriptures. The first is Stephen's prayer as he is about to be stoned. Filled with the Holy Spirit, he sees a vision of Jesus at the Father's throne. As a crowd is beginning to stone him, he prays, "Lord Jesus, receive my spirit." As Jesus entrusted himself to the Father, Stephen entrusts himself to Jesus. Then Stephen also makes a prayer asking forgiveness for his killers.

In the Gospel we witness the final words of Jesus' great prayer at the Last Supper, a prayer for those future generations who will come to believe because of those who preach the gospel. This profound prayer asks that all believers participate in the communion Jesus has with the Father, entering into the mystical indwelling of the Father in the Son and the Son in the Father. The communion in the very life of the Father and the Son will come about as the work of the Spirit.

In the final vision in the book of Revelation, John the seer invites us to join him in the simplest prayer of all, initiated by the Spirit and the bride, the church of the future, calling out to the One who is the Alpha and the Omega, the beginning and the end, the bright morning star: "Come, Lord Jesus, come!"

The Easter season's final gifts before the feast of Pentecost are prayers naming the Spirit's work: our surrender to the Lord, forgiveness of others, communion in the Trinity, the final coming of the Lord.

✤ *Consider/Discuss*

- Do these prayers reflect your needs?
- What would you want your final prayer to be?

✤ *Responding to the Word*

Come, Lord Jesus, come this day into my life. Send your Spirit to draw me more fully into the intimate communion you share with your Father and with all believers. Help me to pray with attentiveness and commitment the prayer you gave us: Our Father . . .

May 19, 2013

PENTECOST SUNDAY

Today's Focus: Holy Spirit, Mega-Gift

The Easter season concludes with the great feast of Pentecost, celebrating the giving of the Holy Spirit and the birth of the church. The Spirit comes as the final stage of God's love affair with the world. Through the Spirit God continues to touch our lives.

FIRST READING
Acts 2:1–11

When the time for Pentecost was fulfilled, they were all in one place together. And suddenly there came from the sky a noise like a strong driving wind, and it filled the entire house in which they were. Then there appeared to them tongues as of fire, which parted and came to rest on each one of them. And they were all filled with the Holy Spirit and began to speak in different tongues, as the Spirit enabled them to proclaim.

Now there were devout Jews from every nation under heaven staying in Jerusalem. At this sound, they gathered in a large crowd, but they were confused because each one heard them speaking in his own language. They were astounded, and in amazement they asked, "Are not all these people who are speaking Galileans? Then how does each of us hear them in his native language? We are Parthians, Medes, and Elamites, inhabitants of Mesopotamia, Judea and Cappadocia, Pontus and Asia, Phrygia and Pamphylia, Egypt and the districts of Libya near Cyrene, as well as travelers from Rome, both Jews and converts to Judaism, Cretans and Arabs, yet we hear them speaking in our own tongues of the mighty acts of God."

PSALM RESPONSE
Psalm 104:30

Lord, send out your Spirit, and renew the face of the earth.

SECOND READING
1 Corinthians 12:3b–7, 12–13

Brothers and sisters: No one can say, "Jesus is Lord," except by the Holy Spirit. There are different kinds of spiritual gifts but the same Spirit; there are different forms of service but the same Lord; there are different workings but the same God who produces all of them in everyone. To each individual the manifestation of the Spirit is given for some benefit.

As a body is one though it has many parts, and all the parts of the body, though many, are one body, so also Christ. For in one Spirit we were all baptized into one body, whether Jews or Greeks, slaves or free persons, and we were all given to drink of one Spirit.

120

– or –

Romans 8:8–17 Brothers and sisters: Those who are in the flesh cannot please God. But you are not in the flesh; on the contrary, you are in the spirit, if only the Spirit of God dwells in you. Whoever does not have the Spirit of Christ does not belong to him. But if Christ is in you, although the body is dead because of sin, the spirit is alive because of righteousness. If the Spirit of the one who raised Jesus from the dead dwells in you, the one who raised Christ from the dead will give life to your mortal bodies also, through his Spirit that dwells in you. Consequently, brothers and sisters, we are not debtors to the flesh, to live according to the flesh. For if you live according to the flesh, you will die, but if by the Spirit you put to death the deeds of the body, you will live.

For those who are led by the Spirit of God are sons of God. For you did not receive a spirit of slavery to fall back into fear, but you received a Spirit of adoption, through whom we cry, "Abba, Father!" The Spirit himself bears witness with our spirit that we are children of God, and if children, then heirs, heirs of God and joint heirs with Christ, if only we suffer with him so that we may also be glorified with him.

GOSPEL On the evening of that first day of the week, when the doors were
John 20:19–23 locked, where the disciples were, for fear of the Jews, Jesus came and stood in their midst and said to them, "Peace be with you." When he had said this, he showed them his hands and his side. The disciples rejoiced when they saw the Lord. Jesus said to them again, "Peace be with you. As the Father has sent me, so I send you." And when he had said this, he breathed on them and said to them, "Receive the Holy Spirit. Whose sins you forgive are forgiven them, and whose sins you retain are retained."

– or –

John 14:15–16, Jesus said to his disciples: "If you love me, you will keep my com-
23b–26 mandments. And I will ask the Father, and he will give you another Advocate to be with you always.

"Whoever loves me will keep my word, and my Father will love him, and we will come to him and make our dwelling with him. Those who do not love me do not keep my words; yet the word you hear is not mine but that of the Father who sent me.

"I have told you this while I am with you. The Advocate, the Holy Spirit whom the Father will send in my name, will teach you everything and remind you of all that I told you."

The Jewish feast of Pentecost was one of the three major pilgrim festivals of Israel, hence the presence in Jerusalem of devout Jews from every nation. Since the people who experienced the unusual occurrence understood the bold proclamations of the Spirit–filled disciples, the miracle seems to have been speech in foreign tongues, not ecstatic speech (glossolalia). In other words, there was a miracle in hearing as well as in speaking. This outpouring of the Spirit and the preaching of the gospel to all nations point to the gathering of all peoples into the reign of God.

To claim that Jesus was Lord was to set up a rivalry between his followers and the political authorities who were called "Lord." This claim placed Christians at great risk for their lives. The word was also used in Greek as a substitute for God's personal name. Therefore, its use implied that Jesus was divine. Paul insists that the spiritual gifts were not given for the self-aggrandizement but for the benefit of the entire community. He then compares the diversity found within the community to the human body. Each part has its own unique function, but all parts work for the good of the whole.

In John's account, the Resurrection and bestowal of the Spirit occurred on the same day. Previously, religious meaning was given to the Sabbath. The Resurrection ushered in a new age, and so importance is now given to the first day of the week. The wish for peace, a common Jewish greeting, was also a prayer for the blessings of the end-times. Jesus uses it here as a declaration of the arrival of that time of fulfillment. The closed doors underscore the mysterious character of Jesus' risen body. The wounds in his hands and side show that he is not a figment of their imaginations, or a ghost, but the person they knew. With the bestowal of the Spirit, the disciples are authorized to continue the mission of Jesus.

✦ Reflecting on the Word

I heard a noted theologian quip that we might possibly think of the Holy Spirit as the Cinderella of the Trinity because the Holy Spirit does the work while the Father and the Son get the attention. Everyone laughed—but our readings today highlight the many ways the Holy Spirit enters our lives and gets to work.

Begin with the images of the Spirit found in today's scripture: a strong, driving wind; hovering tongues of fire; the lavisher of languages; the giver of spiritual gifts; the breath of the risen Lord; the power of forgiveness—and these are only a few of the names given to the Holy Spirit. Turn to the Gospel of John, in which Jesus refers to the Spirit as the Paraclete or Advocate, the Teacher, the Witness.

Find the Sequence for the feast of Pentecost in a worship aid and you will discover even more insights into the role of the Spirit cast in a poetic form: father of the poor, the comforter, sweet refreshment, grateful coolness, healer of wounds, renewer of our strength. And my two favorite lines: "Bend the stubborn heart and will;/Melt the frozen, warm the chill."

The work of the Holy Spirit is to bring us to life and then to make us life-givers for others. Paul reminds us that all the gifts of the Spirit are given for the common good.

The church was born after this mega-gift was given to a small group of disciples who were disciples of a crucified Galilean. The Spirit is truly the Gift That Keeps On Giving.

❖ Consider/Discuss

- Which name for the Holy Spirit best describes the role the Spirit has played in your life?
- What gift of the Spirit would you ask for, not only for yourself, but for the good of those you love?

❖ Responding to the Word

Come, Holy Spirit; bring peace, mercy, forgiveness, justice, and wisdom to our world and its leaders. Come, Holy Spirit; fill the hearts of your faithful and enkindle in them the fire of your love. Come, Holy Spirit; make your home in me that I might bring your light into the world.

Notes

We may think that the themes associated with Ordinary Time are not particularly engaging, because they are often basic instructions. However, it is in this teaching that we discover what it means to be a follower of Jesus, and such instruction is always challenging. The readings move easily from one area of life to another. Sometimes they open us to new challenges, but most of the time they are like reruns, lessons that we may already have learned but must always learn anew. These readings do not contain trivial themes. On the contrary, they address many of the realities of everyday life, realities that are frequently overlooked because of their ordinariness. Ordinary does not mean banal. It is the warp and woof of life; it is the normal place where we encounter God and so, even if we take a vacation from the responsibilities that we carry throughout the year, the readings of this period of the year remind us that there is no vacation from our responsibilities of discipleship.

The first readings insist that those chosen by God have a serious responsibility to be faithful to the law; no one is exempt from its observance. These readings from the wisdom tradition and from the prophets offer a kind of kaleidoscope of images and themes that call to mind aspects of our religious tradition and challenge us to shape our own lives in accord with the theology found there. These readings also lay bare our human weakness and our propensity for sin. Finally, the greatness of God is evident in the teachings on Creation, on the Resurrection, and on the coming of God at the end-time. Many of the second readings from various Letters consist of instructions that ground the believers in faith. Other passages provide examples of how disciples might live out the faith that they profess.

As the Gospel readings recount the public ministry of Jesus, they also uncover the contours of discipleship. One's discipleship is shaped by the way one perceives Jesus. Those who accept the challenge that he offers will participate in his ministry. Like him, they will know both success and failure. Actually, the fundamental charge of the disciple is to proclaim by word and by example that the only good in life that endures is commitment to God in Christ.

The readings for this time in the liturgical year create a mosaic of both brilliant colors and muted hues. The boldest colors draw us to the divine nature of Christ. This is reflected in the picture of the historical Jesus that is sketched. In the shadow of the figure of the Lord we see the disciples, called to participate in the life of Christ and to further the establishment of the reign of God. As the disciples become more and more like their Lord, their ministry and life become more and more brilliant in color.

May 26, 2013

THE MOST HOLY TRINITY

Today's Focus: A God Who Delights

The image of Divine Wisdom playing at creation captures the joy God takes in this great work. This joy leads to the outpouring of grace called God's plan of salvation which continues to unfold in our own day. The life of the Trinity flows ever outward, embracing us and all creation in communion.

FIRST READING
Proverbs 8: 22–31

Thus says the wisdom of God:
"The LORD possessed me, the beginning of his ways,
  the forerunner of his prodigies of long ago;
from of old I was poured forth,
  at the first, before the earth.
When there were no depths I was brought forth,
  when there were no fountains or springs of water;
before the mountains were settled into place,
  before the hills, I was brought forth;
while as yet the earth and fields were not made,
  nor the first clods of the world.
"When the Lord established the heavens I was there,
  when he marked out the vault over the face of the deep;
when he made firm the skies above,
  when he fixed fast the foundations of the earth;
when he set for the sea its limit,
  so that the waters should not transgress his command;
then was I beside him as his craftsman,
  and I was his delight day by day,
playing before him all the while,
  playing on the surface of his earth;
  and I found delight in the human race."

PSALM RESPONSE
Psalm 8:2a

O Lord, our God, how wonderful your name in all the earth!

SECOND READING
Romans 5:1–5

Brothers and sisters: Therefore, since we have been justified by faith, we have peace with God through our Lord Jesus Christ, through whom we have gained access by faith to this grace in which we stand, and we boast in hope of the glory of God. Not only that, but we even boast of our afflictions, knowing that affliction produces endurance, and endurance, proven character, and proven character, hope, and hope does not disappoint, because the love of God has been poured out into our hearts through the Holy Spirit that has been given to us.

GOSPEL
John 16:12–15 Jesus said to his disciples: "I have much more to tell you, but you cannot bear it now. But when he comes, the Spirit of truth, he will guide you to all truth. He will not speak on his own, but he will speak what he hears, and will declare to you the things that are coming. He will glorify me, because he will take from what is mine and declare it to you. Everything that the Father has is mine; for this reason I told you that he will take from what is mine and declare it to you."

❖ Understanding the Word

The created world is beautifully portrayed in today's reading. There is no cosmic battle here, as is found in some of the other ancient creation myths. There is only one God who effortlessly establishes the entire universe in tranquility and order. There is rejoicing in this created world. God delights in Woman Wisdom; Woman Wisdom rejoices before God. Wisdom also takes delight in the inhabited part of the earth and in the human race. The last verse leaves us on an open threshold, gazing at the universe that unfolds before us, aware that this mysterious primordial figure of Wisdom has a special interest in us.

According to Paul, the justification of the Roman Christians is an accomplished fact. They have already been reconciled with God; their guilt has already been forgiven. Though God is really the author of their justification, it has been accomplished through their faith in Jesus Christ, who through his death and resurrection has reconciled all people with God. Believers still wait in hope for God's ultimate glory. Here is an example of Paul's already-but-not-yet thinking about the endtimes. The Trinitarian nature of Paul's faith and teaching is clear: Christ brings us to God, and the Spirit comes to us from that same God.

The Gospel explains the relationship between the Father, Jesus, and the Spirit by relating all three to the teaching of Jesus. The Spirit will fill the void caused by Jesus' absence, not so much with a presence as with a form of teaching. It will be through the unfolding of this teaching that the Spirit will glorify Jesus, and reveal him to be the chosen one of God. It was from the Father that the Spirit heard the teachings of Jesus, and then it was also from the Father that the Spirit was sent to bring these teachings to fruition. The Spirit glorifies Jesus by bringing to light the deeper truth of his teaching, teaching that also belongs to God.

We begin and conclude most of our efforts to pray with the simple words "In the name of the Father and of the Son and of the Holy Spirit." Many times a hurried gesture accompanies these words, touching forehead, chest, and each shoulder. But think for a moment about that gesture that makes a cross on our bodies, as it moves from mind to heart to the width of our bodies. Reflect on those words. How often our familiarity with this action can become a rote gesture and a hurriedly mumbled phrase.

The mystery of the Trinity is central to our faith. Our God is one yet three, three yet one. No matter which way you say it, the mystery doesn't become any more comprehensible or less baffling. At the heart of this mystery is the reality of our loving God who created our world and all the worlds beyond ours, who has given us generous access by the gift of faith in Jesus Christ, and who has poured divine love into our hearts through the Holy Spirit, the first gift to us at Baptism.

What can possibly make sense of this? I would hold up one phrase from today's readings for meditation. Divine Wisdom speaks of herself as being the Lord's delight while creation was taking place, playing before the Lord day by day. Then there is that beautiful conclusion when Wisdom says, "And I found delight in the human race." God's Wisdom delights in us! Can we return the favor?

✤ Consider/Discuss

- Do you think of God as taking delight in the works of creation, salvation, and sanctification?
- How does having "God's love poured into your heart" lead you to take delight in God?

✤ Responding to the Word

God of creation, you sent your Son, Jesus, to bring us fullness of life, leading us into communion with you through the Holy Spirit. May we be a source of delight for you, and be worthy of the creation you have entrusted to our care. We thank you for all that has been, is, and will be.

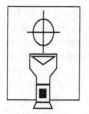

June 2, 2013

THE MOST HOLY BODY AND BLOOD OF CHRIST

Today's Focus: A Meal Rich in Blessing

We move from a meal in which the king-priest Melchizedek offers Abram bread, wine, and a blessing, to one in which Jesus offers his disciples bread and wine blessed into his body and blood, to a meal in which Jesus offers a multitude bread and fish blessed into abundance—each sheds light on the Eucharistic meal we share.

FIRST READING
Genesis 14: 18–20

In those days, Melchizedek, king of Salem, brought out bread and wine, and being a priest of God Most High, he blessed Abram with these words:
"Blessed be Abram by God Most High,
    the creator of heaven and earth;
and blessed be God Most High,
    who delivered your foes into your hand."
Then Abram gave him a tenth of everything.

PSALM RESPONSE
Psalm 110:4b

You are a priest for ever, in the line of Melchizedek.

SECOND READING
1 Corinthians 11: 23–26

Brothers and sisters: I received from the Lord what I also handed on to you, that the Lord Jesus, on the night he was handed over, took bread, and, after he had given thanks, broke it and said, "This is my body that is for you. Do this in remembrance of me." In the same way also the cup, after supper, saying, "This cup is the new covenant in my blood. Do this, as often as you drink it, in remembrance of me." For as often as you eat this bread and drink the cup, you proclaim the death of the Lord until he comes.

GOSPEL
Luke 9:11b–17

Jesus spoke to the crowds about the kingdom of God, and he healed those who needed to be cured. As the day was drawing to a close, the Twelve approached him and said, "Dismiss the crowd so that they can go to the surrounding villages and farms and find lodging and provisions; for we are in a deserted place here." He said to them, "Give them some food yourselves." They replied, "Five loaves and two fish are all we have, unless we ourselves go and buy food for all these people." Now the men there numbered about five thousand. Then he said to his disciples, "Have them sit down in groups of about fifty." They did so and made them all sit down. Then taking the five loaves and the two fish, and looking up to heaven, he said the blessing over them, broke them, and gave them to the disciples to set before the crowd. They all ate and were satisfied. And when the leftover fragments were picked up, they filled twelve wicker baskets.

❖ Understanding the Word

Names play a very important role in the first story. The name Melchizedek comes from the Hebrew words for "my king" and "righteous." Salem is probably a shortened form of the name Jerusalem, the Jebusite city that was ultimately captured by David and made the capital of his kingdom. The words pronounced by Melchizedek are both a blessing for Abram and an exclamation of praise of God Most High. Abram then offers a tenth of his goods to Melchizedek. Thus, the story introduces us to the importance of the city of Jerusalem with its king and its cultic life.

In describing his version of the Last Supper, Paul used technical and formulaic language: what he received, he now hands down. He did not receive the tradition in direct revelation from the Lord, but by word of mouth, the usual way a religious heritage is transmitted. Jesus' sharing of the blessed bread and cup was a prophetic symbolic action that anticipated his death. In the memorial celebration, the past, the present, and the future are brought together: the past in the commemoration of his death; the present in the ritual of remembrance itself; the future in his *parousía*, his coming again.

The eucharistic overtones in the feeding of the multitude are obvious: he blessed . . . he broke . . . he gave to eat. It is difficult to know whether the historical Jesus actually spoke these words, and if so, whether it was done with an eye to his last supper, which was itself a foreshadowing of the final messianic banquet. However, we can be certain that the Gospel writer wanted these connections to be made. This feeding account might also allude to the final meal in the reign of God. The apostles are actually the ones through whom the crowds experience the munificence of Jesus. The author of the Gospel shows that Jesus provides for his people through the agency of the church. The many-leveled meaning of the story rests on the miraculous abundance that God provides through Jesus.

While the first reading sounds like an ancient forerunner of the Mass, even including a collection, what it really presents is a post-battle victory dinner, hosted by Melchizedek, with Abram giving the king and priest some of the spoils won in battle. Even so, the heart of this reading is Melchizedek blessing God over bread and wine and asking a blessing for Abram.

We then hear Paul speak about his handing on the tradition he received, recounting the meal Jesus shared at the Last Supper before he was handed over to suffer and die. Bread was broken and named his body; the cup of wine was shared as a sign of the new covenant to be enacted through the shedding of his blood. In doing this throughout future generations, the community would proclaim Christ's saving death until his return.

The multitude Jesus once fed with a few blessed loaves and fish now has become the people of God, a people of faith, also having suffered through the centuries, ever hungry for the living bread and thirsty for the saving cup, anticipating the banquet we shall share in the kingdom.

This meal continues to make Christ present as priest, as sacrificial offering, and as food that nourishes his body, the Church. Whenever we participate, we join with Christ, our head, and with all who have preceded us, giving praise and thanks for all blessings to the Father in the power of the Holy Spirit.

✦ Consider/Discuss

- What does the presence of Christ in the Eucharist mean for community life?
- How does this meal that nourishes us relate to the hungers in today's world?

✦ Responding to the Word

We give you thanks, loving God, for the nourishment and strength we continue to receive in this sacrament of the Eucharist. Keep us aware that we live in a world hungry for food that strengthens the body and food that nourishes the spirit. Impel us to respond to the needs of your hungry children.

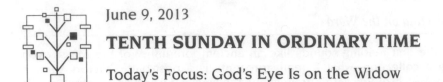

TENTH SUNDAY IN ORDINARY TIME

Today's Focus: God's Eye Is on the Widow

God's care reaches out to two heartbroken widows, restoring to them a future that had suddenly disappeared with the deaths of their sons. God's power is at work through the word of the prophet Elijah; the Father visits his people in the flesh in his son Jesus.

FIRST READING
1 Kings 17:17–24

Elijah went to Zarephath of Sidon to the house of a widow. The son of the mistress of the house fell sick, and his sickness grew more severe until he stopped breathing. So she said to Elijah, "Why have you done this to me, O man of God? Have you come to me to call attention to my guilt and to kill my son?" Elijah said to her, "Give me your son." Taking him from her lap, he carried the son to the upper room where he was staying, and put him on his bed. Elijah called out to the LORD: "O LORD, my God, will you afflict even the widow with whom I am staying by killing her son?" Then he stretched himself out upon the child three times and called out to the LORD: "O LORD, my God, let the life breath return to the body of this child." The LORD heard the prayer of Elijah; the life breath returned to the child's body and he revived. Taking the child, Elijah brought him down into the house from the upper room and gave him to his mother. Elijah said to her, "See! Your son is alive." The woman replied to Elijah, "Now indeed I know that you are a man of God. The word of the LORD comes truly from your mouth."

PSALM RESPONSE
Psalm 30:2a

I will praise you, Lord, for you have rescued me.

SECOND READING
Galatians 1:11–19

I want you to know, brothers and sisters, that the gospel preached by me is not of human origin. For I did not receive it from a human being, nor was I taught it, but it came through a revelation of Jesus Christ.

For you heard of my former way of life in Judaism, how I persecuted the church of God beyond measure and tried to destroy it, and progressed in Judaism beyond many of my contemporaries among my race, since I was even more a zealot for my ancestral traditions. But when God, who from my mother's womb had set me apart and called me through his grace, was pleased to reveal his Son to me, so that I might proclaim him to the Gentiles, I did not immediately consult flesh and blood, nor did I go up to Jerusalem to those who were apostles before me; rather, I went into Arabia and then returned to Damascus.

Then after three years I went up to Jerusalem to confer with Cephas and remained with him for fifteen days. But I did not see any other of the apostles, only James the brother of the Lord.

GOSPEL
Luke 7:11–17

Jesus journeyed to a city called Nain, and his disciples and a large crowd accompanied him. As he drew near to the gate of the city, a man who had died was being carried out, the only son of his mother, and she was a widow. A large crowd from the city was with her. When the Lord saw her, he was moved with pity for her and said to her, "Do not weep." He stepped forward and touched the coffin; at this the bearers halted, and he said, "Young man, I tell you, arise!" The dead man sat up and began to speak, and Jesus gave him to his mother. Fear seized them all, and they glorified God, exclaiming, "A great prophet has arisen in our midst," and "God has visited his people." This report about him spread through the whole of Judea and in all the surrounding region.

❖ Understanding the Word

As was the custom of the day, the woman in the first account offers hospitality to one in need, but then she suffers misfortune. She links the illness of her son with the entrance of the prophet into their lives. It is not the power from the body of the prophet that restores the boy, but the power of God working through the prophet. When her son is restored to her alive, the woman responds with an act of faith. Her living son is proof that God's power works through this man of God, in a foreign land, for the benefit of a widow.

Paul admits that he was originally a zealous adherent to the traditions of the ancestors, probably a reference to the oral traditions that the Pharisees developed as they interpreted the scriptures to meet the needs of their time. He certainly knew about Jesus, for he persecuted some of his followers. Paul asserts his independence from other apostles, insisting that he is now a disciple of no one but Jesus Christ. While such insistence reveals a man of strong conviction, it may have been seen by some as arrogant self-confidence. Paul must have realized this, for he credited the grace of God for his change of heart.

Jesus and his disciples encounter a funeral procession leaving the city that they are about to enter. The deceased is the only son of a widowed woman. This is an unusual miracle, for Jesus seems to have performed it out of his own deep emotion rather than in response to someone else's request or demonstration of faith. The vulnerable position in society of this widow is the same as that of the widow of Zarephath of Sidon in the first reading. Not only is she suffering the grief of loss, she now is also bereft of a legal advocate. The miracle demonstrates the presence of the reign of God in the lives of people who believe.

Widows were not merry in the Bible. They were not high on Israel's scale of social importance, nor on that of other countries in biblical times. A widow was in trouble if she did not have a son or another male in the family to care for her. God's compassion for widows shines through here.

There is no faith in evidence on the part of either widow. Neither asks Elijah or Jesus to do anything. If anything, the widow of Zarephath blames the prophet for the death of her son: "Why have you done this to me, O man of God?" This could be the grief speaking or an assumption that a foreign prophet's presence attracted divine attention in some punishing way. But the prophet's prayer has God restore the child's life.

Compassion for the widow moves Jesus: "When the Lord saw her, he was moved with pity for her and said to her, 'Do not weep.' " Jesus does nothing more than speak to the young man, "Young man, I tell you, arise!" And the dead man sits up, speaking—a nice touch by Luke. The young man returns to life speaking. What were his first words?

One wonders what God makes of our age, when the precarious condition of widows in the past has become the ongoing plight of so many women, young and old, across all cultures in the world. How many see their children die before them, the cost of diseases that could be averted, even cured, or needless wars between genocidal factions?

❖ Consider/Discuss

- How would you describe the condition of women in today's world?
- Where and how is Jesus calling us to act today to relieve the plight of women?

❖ Responding to the Word

Jesus, Son of Mary, you befriended the Samaritan woman as well as Martha and Mary. You heard the plea of the Syro-Phoenician woman and raised the widow's son. You liberated Mary Magdalene from her demons and spoke out for the woman at the house of Simon the Pharisee. Bless our efforts to serve women in our world.

June 16, 2013

ELEVENTH SUNDAY IN ORDINARY TIME

Today's Focus: Grant to Us, O Lord, a Heart Renewed

Today's readings balance last week's. Then we saw God's care for women, sending prophets to restore deceased sons to their heart-broken widowed mothers. Today we witness God's care for men, sending prophets to penetrate the hardened hearts of a king and a Pharisee.

FIRST READING
2 Samuel 12: 7–10, 13

Nathan said to David: "Thus says the LORD God of Israel: 'I anointed you king of Israel. I rescued you from the hand of Saul. I gave you your lord's house and your lord's wives for your own. I gave you the house of Israel and of Judah. And if this were not enough, I could count up for you still more. Why have you spurned the Lord and done evil in his sight? You have cut down Uriah the Hittite with the sword; you took his wife as your own, and him you killed with the sword of the Ammonites. Now, therefore, the sword shall never depart from your house, because you have despised me and have taken the wife of Uriah to be your wife.' " Then David said to Nathan, "I have sinned against the LORD." Nathan answered David: "The LORD on his part has forgiven your sin: you shall not die."

PSALM RESPONSE
Psalm 32:5c

Lord, forgive the wrong I have done.

SECOND READING
Galatians 2:16, 19–21

Brothers and sisters: We who know that a person is not justified by works of the law but through faith in Jesus Christ, even we have believed in Christ Jesus that we may be justified by faith in Christ and not by works of the law, because by works of the law no one will be justified. For through the law I died to the law, that I might live for God. I have been crucified with Christ; yet I live, no longer I, but Christ lives in me; insofar as I now live in the flesh, I live by faith in the Son of God who has loved me and given himself up for me. I do not nullify the grace of God; for if justification comes through the law, then Christ died for nothing.

GOSPEL
Luke 7:36 — 8:3
or 7:36–50

A Pharisee invited Jesus to dine with him, and he entered the Pharisee's house and reclined at table. Now there was a sinful woman in the city who learned that he was at table in the house of the Pharisee. Bringing an alabaster flask of ointment, she stood behind him at his feet weeping and began to bathe his feet with her tears. Then she wiped them with her hair, kissed them, and anointed them with the ointment. When the Pharisee who had invited him saw this he said to himself, "If this man were a prophet, he would know who and what sort of woman this is who is touching him, that she is a sinner." Jesus said to him in reply, "Simon, I have something to say to you." "Tell me, teacher," he said. "Two people were in debt to a certain creditor; one owed five hundred days' wages and the other owed fifty. Since they were unable to repay the debt, he forgave it for both. Which of them will love him more?" Simon said in reply, "The one, I suppose, whose larger debt was forgiven." He said to him, "You have judged rightly."

Then he turned to the woman and said to Simon, "Do you see this woman? When I entered your house, you did not give me water for my feet, but she has bathed them with her tears and wiped them with her hair. You did not give me a kiss, but she has not ceased kissing my feet since the time I entered. You did not anoint my head with oil, but she anointed my feet with ointment. So I tell you, her many sins have been forgiven because she has shown great love. But the one to whom little is forgiven, loves little." He said to her, "Your sins are forgiven." The others at table said to themselves, "Who is this who even forgives sins?" But he said to the woman, "Your faith has saved you; go in peace."

[Afterward he journeyed from one town and village to another, preaching and proclaiming the good news of the kingdom of God. Accompanying him were the Twelve and some women who had been cured of evil spirits and infirmities, Mary, called Magdalene, from whom seven demons had gone out, Joanna, the wife of Herod's steward Chuza, Susanna, and many others who provided for them out of their resources.]

✛ Understanding the Word

Nathan chastises David for his adultery. The king is reminded of the blessings that God bestowed upon him. When David took the wife of Uriah, he not only committed adultery with her, but he also cut off Uriah's line of descent. Uriah's murder merely brought this fact to completion. The episode also reveals the precarious position that women held in this society. Their procreative potential made them both cherished and vulnerable. The punishment shows clearly that the king may have been chosen by God and lavished with blessings, but he was still accountable to the law like every other Israelite.

Paul contrasts observance of the law with the power of the death and resurrection of Christ. Though faithful to the law during his lifetime, in death Jesus moved out of the realm of the law, and by his resurrection he moved beyond it. Joined to Jesus, believers die to the law through the death of Jesus and live for God through his resurrection. According to Paul, either justification comes through the law, and then Christ died in vain; or justification comes through faith in Jesus Christ, and then life according to the law has been transcended.

The dinner to which Jesus was invited must have been either a banquet or a Sabbath meal, because those eating were reclining. The woman had not been invited, yet she seems to have had free access to the dinner, suggesting that it was not a strictly private affair. Because Jesus does not rebuff her, Simon concludes that he does not know that she is a sinner, and consequently, he could not be a prophet. Jesus' parable shows that he does indeed know about the woman, and he is aware of Simon's thoughts as well. Jesus' last words to the woman reveal the progression of her transformation: her faith was the basis of her love; her love was demonstrated in her contrition. Jesus recognized this, and rewarded her.

✥ Reflecting on the Word

Nathan's message to King David could not have been any more pointed: God says, "I have given you all that you have, and you have taken away all that your devoted soldier Uriah had: his wife and his life.'" David acknowledges his sin, confessing his guilt, and God shows mercy, forgiving him.

After hearing Jesus preach, a woman responds with repentance to his message announcing the coming of God's reign. She comes to the house of Simon the Pharisee to express her grateful heart for all to see. Simon, however, is a harder nut to crack. As Nathan did with David, Jesus tells a story, hoping to penetrate Simon's judgmental heart. Simon gets the point, but we don't know whether it stays in his head without reaching his heart.

God sent Jesus to liberate people, to bring them to a fuller life. We see Jesus trying to free both men and women from what imprisons them, and to bring them out of the darkness and into the light of communion with God and with each other. We see how quickly God responds to David's confession and how appreciatively Jesus speaks of the woman to Simon.

One hopes that Simon came to himself at some point and was able to receive the good news of God's kingdom so near to his grasp. One hopes he came to know God's generous forgiveness for his sins, whether many or few, great or small. One hopes he came to recognize Jesus as truly God's prophet and Son.

✤ *Consider/Discuss*

- Do our "little" sins lead us to be judgmental of others?
- Do we know that no sin is beyond God's forgiveness?

✤ *Responding to the Word*

You are our forgiving Father who desires to lift any burden caused by sin. Give us the courage to confess honestly what we have done and what we have failed to do. When we sin, save us from despair and keep our eyes on your merciful love, revealed to us by your Son, Jesus.

June 23, 2013

TWELFTH SUNDAY IN ORDINARY TIME

Today's Focus: The Unexpected Messiah

The first three Gospels each contain the scene in which Jesus turns to the disciples and asks them, "Who do you say that I am?" In Luke, Peter replies "The Christ of God." Jesus then explains who he thinks he is, and what that means for him, for them, and for us today.

FIRST READING
Zechariah 12: 10–11; 13:1

Thus says the LORD: I will pour out on the house of David and on the inhabitants of Jerusalem a spirit of grace and petition; and they shall look on him whom they have pierced, and they shall mourn for him as one mourns for an only son, and they shall grieve over him as one grieves over a firstborn.

On that day the mourning in Jerusalem shall be as great as the mourning of Hadadrimmon in the plain of Megiddo.

On that day there shall be open to the house of David and to the inhabitants of Jerusalem, a fountain to purify from sin and uncleanness.

PSALM RESPONSE
Psalm 63:2b

My soul is thirsting for you, O Lord my God.

SECOND READING
Galatians 3: 26–29

Brothers and sisters: Through faith you are all children of God in Christ Jesus. For all of you who were baptized into Christ have clothed yourselves with Christ. There is neither Jew nor Greek, there is neither slave nor free person, there is not male and female; for you are all one in Christ Jesus. And if you belong to Christ, then you are Abraham's descendant, heirs according to the promise.

GOSPEL
Luke 9:18–24

Once when Jesus was praying in solitude, and the disciples were with him, he asked them, "Who do the crowds say that I am?" They said in reply, "John the Baptist; others, Elijah; still others, 'One of the ancient prophets has arisen.' " Then he said to them, "But who do you say that I am?" Peter said in reply, "The Christ of God." He rebuked them and directed them not to tell this to anyone.

He said, "The Son of Man must suffer greatly and be rejected by the elders, the chief priests, and the scribes, and be killed and on the third day be raised."

Then he said to all, "If anyone wishes to come after me, he must deny himself and take up his cross daily and follow me. For whoever wishes to save his life will lose it, but whoever loses his life for my sake will save it."

In today's Gospel, Jesus is praying in a certain place and uses the opportunity for reflection to inform the disciples about his identity and theirs. Jesus clarifies what it means to be God's messiah (Christ). It means to "suffer greatly," to endure rejection, then to be killed. The disciples must be willing to take up a cross if they wish to follow Jesus.

The position of these events is instructive. Right before them we read that Jesus had sent the disciples out on a mission during which they had preached and healed (Luke 9:1–6). Upon their return, they witnessed Jesus' multiplication of the five loaves and two fishes so that five thousand were fed. Moreover, Jesus had told them that they were to do the same: "Give them some food yourselves" (9:13). Thus, the disciples are filled with examples of the power of the ministry that they are to undertake. Lest they think that ministry is a move from power to power, Jesus takes the opportunity to tell them that the way of ministry is the path that he will take from suffering to glory.

The section that follows today's Gospel reading is about the transfiguration of Jesus, and it is also helpful for determining the significance of today's readings. Only in Luke's account of the Transfiguration do we hear that Moses and Elijah were speaking with Jesus about "his exodus that he was going to accomplish in Jerusalem" (9:31). These words of theirs pick up Jesus' exhortation to the disciples that they must come after him by denying themselves and following him (9:23).

Luke would have the disciples realize that they are to exercise a powerful ministry for others while participating in their own exodus by following Jesus. The images of the Exodus and of taking up the cross to follow Jesus imply the rigors of a difficult time filled with suffering. They also imply, however, that the end of the journey is the Promised Land and resurrection.

❖ *Reflecting on the Word*

The apostles were probably not all that different from the other members of their families or their friends. They were not very different from the other Jews of their day. Indeed, given the expectations and hopes we have for our own leaders today, we would not have answered Jesus much differently. They were waiting for the Messiah to come, and once he came, life would be good again.

They expected the Messiah (which means "Anointed One") to come in power and might; a liberator like Moses, who led God's people out of slavery; a great king like David, who brought the people of the divided northern and southern kingdoms into one nation. How wonderful would this new era be, ushered in by such a Messiah!

Imagine their surprise when Jesus rebukes Peter for saying that he is "The Christ [Messiah] of God" (9:20). Greater their surprise when Jesus goes on to say that he must suffer greatly, be rejected by their religious leaders, and be killed—but also be raised from death on the third day (9:22). It is fair to wonder if, in their shock, they even heard the part about being raised. The ultimate stunning news, however, would have been that to follow their Messiah, they must be willing to deny themselves, taking up their crosses every day.

A person like this Messiah would not get a lot of votes, even today. But it is through faith in Christ Jesus, Anointed One of God, that we have become children of God. And so we are called, as Paul tells us, to clothe ourselves with Christ (Galatians 3:27), another way of saying "Take up your cross, every day."

✤ Consider/Discuss

- If Jesus asked you "Who do you say that I am?" what would your answer be?
- In what ways does daily life call upon you to take up your cross? What form does this command take in the life of the whole Church?

✤ Responding to the Word

Jesus Christ, our Messiah, let us be clothed with your risen glory, as each day we walk with you, carrying the cross that life calls on us to bear. Increase our faith in you; help us to know your gracious loving presence with us always.

June 30, 2013

THIRTEENTH SUNDAY IN ORDINARY TIME

Today's Focus: Kingdom Fitness

Different circumstances call for different forms of fitness. Television offers viewers a variety of competitive programs demanding particular skills: singing, dancing, cooking, traveling quickly to a particular destination, or simply being the last survivor. Being a disciple of Jesus Christ also calls for a certain kind of fitness.

FIRST READING
1 Kings 19:16b, 19–21

The LORD said to Elijah: "You shall anoint Elisha, son of Shaphat of Abel-meholah, as prophet to succeed you."

Elijah set out and came upon Elisha, son of Shaphat, as he was plowing with twelve yoke of oxen; he was following the twelfth. Elijah went over to him and threw his cloak over him. Elisha left the oxen, ran after Elijah, and said, "Please, let me kiss my father and mother goodbye, and I will follow you." Elijah answered, "Go back! Have I done anything to you?" Elisha left him, and taking the yoke of oxen, slaughtered them; he used the plowing equipment for fuel to boil their flesh, and gave it to his people to eat. Then Elisha left and followed Elijah as his attendant.

PSALM RESPONSE
Psalm 16:5a

You are my inheritance, O Lord.

SECOND READING
Galatians 5:1, 13–18

Brothers and sisters: For freedom Christ set us free; so stand firm and do not submit again to the yoke of slavery.

For you were called for freedom, brothers and sisters. But do not use this freedom as an opportunity for the flesh; rather, serve one another through love. For the whole law is fulfilled in one statement, namely, *You shall love your neighbor as yourself.* But if you go on biting and devouring one another, beware that you are not consumed by one another.

I say, then: live by the Spirit and you will certainly not gratify the desire of the flesh. For the flesh has desires against the Spirit, and the Spirit against the flesh; these are opposed to each other, so that you may not do what you want. But if you are guided by the Spirit, you are not under the law.

GOSPEL
Luke 9:51–62

When the days for Jesus' being taken up were fulfilled, he resolutely determined to journey to Jerusalem, and he sent messengers ahead of him. On the way they entered a Samaritan village to prepare for his reception there, but they would not welcome him because the destination of his journey was Jerusalem. When the disciples James and John saw this they asked, "Lord, do you want us to call down fire from heaven to consume them?" Jesus turned and rebuked them, and they journeyed to another village.

As they were proceeding on their journey someone said to him, "I will follow you wherever you go." Jesus answered him, "Foxes have dens and birds of the sky have nests, but the Son of Man has nowhere to rest his head."

And to another he said, "Follow me." But he replied, "Lord, let me go first and bury my father." But he answered him, "Let the dead bury their dead. But you, go and proclaim the kingdom of God." And another said, "I will follow you, Lord, but first let me say farewell to my family at home." To him Jesus said, "No one who sets a hand to the plow and looks to what was left behind is fit for the kingdom of God."

❖ Understanding the Word

Elijah's symbolic act of throwing his cloak over Elisha indicates that Elisha has been invested with the power and authority of Elijah. It also suggests that a new generation of prophets is on the horizon. This account describes the conflict that exists between two fundamental responsibilities: fidelity to the call from God and fidelity to one's primary family obligations. Elisha has been commissioned by God to be a prophet, and it is up to him to decide whether or not he can make the radical break from the past that this commission requires.

Paul states that Christ did not free the Galatians from one form of bondage only to have them submit to another. Habits of mind and heart, addictions of all kinds, retain their hold even after they are renounced. Freedom itself is a frightening thing, but it requires the willing renunciation of whatever might enslave them. Paul also insists that the freedom to which the Galatians have been called is not an invitation to license. Though no longer under the bondage of the law, the Galatians are not free to live lawless lives. They are expected to "love your neighbor as yourself" (cf. Leviticus 19:18).

Some people of Samaria remained in Israel during the Exile and intermarried with neighboring foreigners. Because of this, the returning Jews considered them ritually unclean and kept them from helping with rebuilding the temple. The Samaritans then built their own temple on Mt. Gerizim, and they refused hospitality to Jews who traveled through Samaria on the way to worship in Jerusalem. Jesus encountered three prospective followers along the way. The first one enthusiastically offers commitment; the other two wish to postpone joining Jesus until they have put their immediate affairs in order. Jesus emphasizes the demands that discipleship will exact. His followers must be willing to relinquish all. While followers should be enthusiastic in their dedication, they should also be prepared to pay the price of wholehearted commitment.

One quality is essential for being a disciple—commitment. When Elisha asks the prophet's permission to kiss his parents good-bye, Elijah answers somewhat ambiguously, but Elisha realizes this is the hour of decision. He not only kills and cooks his oxen but burns the plow they came with, wiping out all connection to his past trade. There is no report on how his parents felt about this, but it signals Elisha's commitment. Eventually, it won him a double portion of Elijah's spirit.

Jesus outlines the fitness program his disciples must measure up to: an ability to live without the comforts of home, a freedom from any ties to family that might prevent preaching the kingdom of God, and the ability to live such a life with total commitment and without any regret. All this is the work of the Spirit within us, liberating us from what can hold us in place, unable to move and help bring God's kingdom into the world.

When Paul talks about Christ setting us free for freedom, he too refers to casting off any yoke that could bind or enslave us. Like Jesus, Paul voices a call to live by the Spirit, that breath of God that blows us where it wills. The Spirit can free us from any inclination either to "bite and devour" another, as in calling down fire from heaven on them, or to be consumed by others who wish us harm. By surrendering to the Spirit, we will become fit.

✤ Consider/Discuss

- What kind of commitment have you made to be a disciple of the Lord?
- How do you understand what it means to be free? Do some kinds of freedom end up enslaving you?

✤ *Responding to the Word*

Lord, we ask you for the freedom that truly frees us to love as you love, to have the mind that was in Christ Jesus, and to allow us to empty ourselves so you can fill us. Make us fit for the work of the kingdom through the gift of your Spirit.

July 7, 2013

FOURTEENTH SUNDAY IN ORDINARY TIME

Today's Focus: The Joy of Evangelizing

Joy rings through all three readings today from three preachers. The prophet proclaims that God will spread prosperity over Jerusalem, giving comfort and delight. Paul announces that God will give peace and mercy to all who accept the new creation realized through Christ's saving death. And Jesus sends out preachers who return rejoicing.

FIRST READING
Isaiah 66: 10–14c

Thus says the LORD:
Rejoice with Jerusalem and be glad because of her,
    all you who love her;
exult, exult with her,
    all you who were mourning over her!
Oh, that you may suck fully
    of the milk of her comfort,
that you may nurse with delight
    at her abundant breasts!
For thus says the LORD:
Lo, I will spread prosperity over Jerusalem like a river,
    and the wealth of the nations like an overflowing torrent.
As nurslings, you shall be carried in her arms,
    and fondled in her lap;
as a mother comforts her child,
    so will I comfort you;
    in Jerusalem you shall find your comfort.

When you see this, your heart shall rejoice
    and your bodies flourish like the grass;
the LORD's power shall be known to his servants.

PSALM RESPONSE
Psalm 66:1

Let all the earth cry out to God with joy.

SECOND READING
Galatians 6: 14–18

Brothers and sisters: May I never boast except in the cross of our Lord Jesus Christ, through which the world has been crucified to me, and I to the world. For neither does circumcision mean anything, nor does uncircumcision, but only a new creation. Peace and mercy be to all who follow this rule and to the Israel of God.

From now on, let no one make troubles for me; for I bear the marks of Jesus on my body.

The grace of our Lord Jesus Christ be with your spirit, brothers and sisters. Amen.

GOSPEL
Luke 10:1–12,
17–20 or 10:1–9

At that time the Lord appointed seventy-two others whom he sent ahead of him in pairs to every town and place he intended to visit. He said to them, "The harvest is abundant but the laborers are few; so ask the master of the harvest to send out laborers for his harvest. Go on your way; behold, I am sending you like lambs among wolves. Carry no money bag, no sack, no sandals; and greet no one along the way. Into whatever house you enter, first say, 'Peace to this household.' If a peaceful person lives there, your peace will rest on him; but if not, it will return to you. Stay in the same house and eat and drink what is offered to you, for the laborer deserves his payment. Do not move about from one house to another. Whatever town you enter and they welcome you, eat what is set before you, cure the sick in it and say to them, 'The kingdom of God is at hand for you.' [Whatever town you enter and they do not receive you, go out into the streets and say, 'The dust of your town that clings to our feet, even that we shake off against you.' Yet know this: the kingdom of God is at hand. I tell you, it will be more tolerable for Sodom on that day than for that town."

The seventy-two returned rejoicing, and said, "Lord, even the demons are subject to us because of your name." Jesus said, "I have observed Satan fall like lightning from the sky. Behold, I have given you the power to 'tread upon serpents' and scorpions and upon the full force of the enemy and nothing will harm you. Nevertheless, do not rejoice because the spirits are subject to you, but rejoice because your names are written in heaven."]

❖ Understanding the Word

Isaiah characterizes Jerusalem as a nursing mother, ready to give of herself, feeding her inhabitants from the fullness of her own body. She carries the people, fondles and comforts them. This same maternal metaphor then characterizes God. The metaphor of water is also employed to describe Jerusalem's life-giving properties. This is a powerful image, since Israel was bounded on several sides by deserts or barren wilderness. On the day Jerusalem is transformed, the people will rejoice with their hearts and their bones. The power of God will shine forth from the restored city, and the people of God will rejoice.

Paul speaks of the death of Jesus and of his own suffering. Jesus died as a convicted felon, and Paul boasts in the sign of this death. The centrality of the cross has turned the world upside down. Joined to the death and resurrection of Jesus, Paul has struck a death blow to the world and its system of values, and that world is now dead to him. Faith in the power of the cross of Jesus, not circumcision, effects membership in the people of God. Thus women and men from every race and ethnic origin are welcome in this community.

Jesus uses two metaphors to represent the mission of his disciples: harvest, and lambs among wolves. Harvest suggests that the seventy-two have only to gather up the fruits of the work of others. Still, the field of ministry is threatening and the missionaries themselves are vulnerable as lambs. They are to trust in God and depend upon the hospitality of those to whom they go. The urgency of the time precludes usual social niceties. Peace! will suffice as an adequate greeting. The people will witness the power of God triumphant over the powers of evil. As important as are the wondrous deeds that they will be able to perform, more wondrous still will be the fact that their names will be inscribed in the heavenly book.

❖ Reflecting on the Word

From the beginning, spreading the word about the kingdom of God was at the top of Jesus' priority list. He began his own ministry preaching that the kingdom of God was near, indeed, "at hand." The good news of God's presence in the world was the primary work given to his apostles when he sent them out. Later, as Luke records, Jesus sent out seventy-two others. And after he had risen, he commanded all disciples to do this until the end of time.

Jesus' directives to the seventy-two are still practical: travel in twos, travel light, don't dawdle, bring peace with you, don't fuss over accommodations, eat and drink what is offered. Their work was to heal and preach. If there was no interest, move on. One might wonder whether more could have been accomplished if they had not been paired up, but anyone who goes out armed only with the gospel realizes how good it is to have companionship in this important work.

Pope Benedict XVI is calling for all Catholics to participate in a "new evangelization," one marked by a new ardor, new methods, and new expressions. Consider ardor; it means having zeal, fire, passion. Ardor flows from joy. The Church's joy as the new Jerusalem comes from knowing we are saved by Christ's death and resurrection. By our baptism we are part of a new creation. Now is our time to witness to Christ, sharing our faith in Jesus, and knowing he is with us, as the head of his Body, the Church.

❖ Consider/Discuss

- Do you accept the calling to be one who witnesses to the gospel and participates in this mission of the Church?
- Does your love for Jesus Christ enable you to talk about him and what he means to you, when the opportunity presents itself?

❖ Responding to the Word

Loving Lord Jesus, you continue to ask us to go forth and bring word about the living God you taught us to call Father, the God who loves us as a mother who wishes to comfort us. Fill us with your Spirit, who gives us courage and commitment to the message of the gospel.

July 14, 2013

FIFTEENTH SUNDAY IN ORDINARY TIME

Today's Focus: Our Good Neighbor God

God sent Jesus to re-form our hearts, to re-create them, to transform them into more loving and open hearts. The Gospel challenges the old saying the poet Robert Frost once quoted, "Good fences make good neighbors." Jesus educates us into another vision of what makes a good neighbor.

FIRST READING
Deuteronomy 30:10–14

Moses said to the people: "If only you would heed the voice of the LORD, your God, and keep his commandments and statutes that are written in this book of the law, when you return to the LORD, your God, with all your heart and all your soul.

"For this command that I enjoin on you today is not too mysterious and remote for you. It is not up in the sky, that you should say, 'Who will go up in the sky to get it for us and tell us of it, that we may carry it out?' Nor is it across the sea, that you should say, 'Who will cross the sea to get it for us and tell us of it, that we may carry it out?' No, it is something very near to you, already in your mouths and in your hearts; you have only to carry it out."

PSALM RESPONSE
Psalm 69:33

Turn to the Lord in your need, and you will live.

SECOND READING
Colossians 1: 15–20

Christ Jesus is the image of the invisible God,
    the firstborn of all creation.
For in him were created all things in heaven and on earth,
    the visible and the invisible,
        whether thrones or dominions or principalities or powers;
    all things were created through him and for him.
He is before all things,
    and in him all things hold together.
He is the head of the body, the church.
He is the beginning, the firstborn from the dead,
    that in all things he himself might be preeminent.
For in him all the fullness was pleased to dwell,
    and through him to reconcile all things for him,
        making peace by the blood of his cross
        through him, whether those on earth or those in heaven.

GOSPEL
Luke 10:25–37

There was a scholar of the law who stood up to test Jesus and said, "Teacher, what must I do to inherit eternal life?" Jesus said to him, "What is written in the law? How do you read it?" He said in reply,

You shall love the Lord, your God,
with all your heart,
with all your being,
with all your strength,
and with all your mind,
and your neighbor as yourself.

He replied to him, "You have answered correctly; do this and you will live."

But because he wished to justify himself, he said to Jesus, "And who is my neighbor?" Jesus replied, "A man fell victim to robbers as he went down from Jerusalem to Jericho. They stripped and beat him and went off leaving him half-dead. A priest happened to be going down that road, but when he saw him, he passed by on the opposite side. Likewise a Levite came to the place, and when he saw him, he passed by on the opposite side. But a Samaritan traveler who came upon him was moved with compassion at the sight. He approached the victim, poured oil and wine over his wounds and bandaged them. Then he lifted him up on his own animal, took him to an inn, and cared for him. The next day he took out two silver coins and gave them to the innkeeper with the instruction, 'Take care of him. If you spend more than what I have given you, I shall repay you on my way back.' Which of these three, in your opinion, was neighbor to the robbers' victim?" He answered, "The one who treated him with mercy." Jesus said to him, "Go and do likewise."

❖ Understanding the Word

Moses instructs the people about the law's importance and its accessibility. To those who may say that the law is too difficult to understand or too lofty to observe, Moses replies: No! It is neither mysterious nor remote. Even a cursory examination will show that while it is indeed the word of God, it comes to us through human experience. In other words, the law of God is as close to us as is our own human life. This is a bold claim because it identifies human experience as the place where the word of God is to be found.

The exalted description of Christ in the second reading extols the divine character and activity of Christ rather than his human nature and earthly existence. Paul characterizes Christ as the image of God, firstborn, the beginning, the head of the church. Each image adds a significant dimension to our understanding of Christ. Christ occupies the place of preeminence over the rest of creation, a preeminence that makes creation dependent upon him. Using the metaphor of body, Paul depicts both the union that exists between Christ and the church and the preeminence that is Christ's as head of that body. Finally, Christ is seen as the agent of reconciliation.

A lawyer challenges Jesus' knowledge of the law. Jesus shows that he knows and conforms to that law, and then he turns the lawyer's challenge back on him by asking him to answer his own questions. The lawyer quotes the two passages from scripture that encompass all of one's responsibilities. Jesus responds with a parable in which he changes the question from "Who is my neighbor?" to "What does it mean to be a neighbor?" The lawyer had asked about required works and is instructed about heartfelt love. The admonition is striking: Go and do likewise! Put aside racial or religious prejudices in order to meet the needs of others! Put aside all other responsibilities in order to love the other!

❖ Reflecting on the Word

The word "neighbor" is rooted in the Old English words "near" (*neah*) and "a dweller" (*gebur*). A neighbor, then, is one who dwells near. As a boy, I lived in what was called a row home; all the houses on our street were attached. Our neighbors were those who literally lived next door.

Today's readings take the definition of a neighbor beyond physical nearness. When the lawyer asks Jesus, "Who is my neighbor?" he was asking about the requirement of the law that commanded that one love one's neighbor as oneself. Jesus' answer went to the heart of the issue. To be a neighbor was to reach out to help anyone in need, setting aside any barriers that either society or selfishness might set up. To be a neighbor was to open one's heart to another, recognizing in the other the image of the God who created them. To be a neighbor was to treat another with mercy.

When Moses said God's law was "something very near, already in your mouths and in your hearts," he was presenting God as a true neighbor, as near as our heartbeat. When Paul said Jesus was both the image of the invisible God and the head of his body, the church, could any image better capture the nearness of Christ and his church? St. Teresa of Ávila echoed this when she said, "Christ has no body now but yours, no hands or feet on earth but yours. Yours are the eyes through which Christ's compassion looks upon the world."

❖ Consider/Discuss

- Is the basic choice to be either a neighbor whose love touches other lives, or a parasite that lives off other lives?
- Can being a member of Christ's body move you to drawing nearer to someone today?

❖ Responding to the Word

God, who placed your law in our hearts, help us to remember your nearness to us in the depths of our being, and to allow your Son's law of love to guide what we see, say, and do. Increase our openness to your Spirit and how your Spirit guides us.

July 21, 2013

SIXTEENTH SUNDAY IN ORDINARY TIME

Today's Focus: Crossing Boundaries

Two tales of boundary crossings are offered today. God crosses over into the everyday lives of Abraham and Sarah, and Jesus approves Mary's crossing over into territory that traditionally belonged to the men of her world: sitting as a disciple at the feet of the Master. God won't be restricted to staying within our lines.

FIRST READING
Genesis 18: 1–10a

The LORD appeared to Abraham by the terebinth of Mamre, as he sat in the entrance of his tent, while the day was growing hot. Looking up, Abraham saw three men standing nearby. When he saw them, he ran from the entrance of the tent to greet them; and bowing to the ground, he said: "Sir, if I may ask you this favor, please do not go on past your servant. Let some water be brought, that you may bathe your feet, and then rest yourselves under the tree. Now that you have come this close to your servant, let me bring you a little food, that you may refresh yourselves; and afterward you may go on your way." The men replied, "Very well, do as you have said."

Abraham hastened into the tent and told Sarah, "Quick, three measures of fine flour! Knead it and make rolls." He ran to the herd, picked out a tender, choice steer, and gave it to a servant, who quickly prepared it. Then Abraham got some curds and milk, as well as the steer that had been prepared, and set these before the three men; and he waited on them under the tree while they ate.

They asked Abraham, "Where is your wife Sarah?" He replied, "There in the tent." One of them said, "I will surely return to you about this time next year, and Sarah will then have a son."

PSALM RESPONSE
Psalm 15:1a

He who does justice will live in the presence of the Lord.

SECOND READING
Colossians 1: 24–28

Brothers and sisters: Now I rejoice in my sufferings for your sake, and in my flesh I am filling up what is lacking in the afflictions of Christ on behalf of his body, which is the church, of which I am a minister in accordance with God's stewardship given to me to bring to completion for you the word of God, the mystery hidden from ages and from generations past. But now it has been manifested to his holy ones, to whom God chose to make known the riches of the glory of this mystery among the Gentiles; it is Christ in you, the hope for glory. It is he whom we proclaim, admonishing everyone and teaching everyone with all wisdom, that we may present everyone perfect in Christ.

Jesus entered a village where a woman whose name was Martha welcomed him. She had a sister named Mary who sat beside the Lord at his feet listening to him speak. Martha, burdened with much serving, came to him and said, "Lord, do you not care that my sister has left me by myself to do the serving? Tell her to help me." The Lord said to her in reply, "Martha, Martha, you are anxious and worried about many things. There is need of only one thing. Mary has chosen the better part and it will not be taken from her."

❖ Understanding the Word

The reading from Genesis follows a classic story form well known in the ancient Near East: heavenly beings come in disguise to a humble home, are shown hospitality, and announce a future birth.

Abraham is portrayed here as the perfect host. One of the visitors foretells the birth of Sarah's son. Sarah's significance is clear. She is named rather than merely identified as Abraham's wife. The child is identified as her son rather than Abraham's. Obviously this woman will play an important role in the life of this child. All of this points to the extraordinary nature of the yet unborn child.

Paul rejoices in his sufferings, for he believes that they will benefit the Colossian Christians. He would never say that the sufferings of Jesus were in any way lacking in their atoning efficacy. Rather, he believed that, joined to Jesus, his own sufferings had merit and could be seen as part of the sufferings that would inaugurate the messianic age. Ultimately, the real message that Paul proclaims is Christ the risen Lord. To borrow from the great Jewish rabbi Hillel, everything else is commentary! However, commentary is necessary for us to understand the specific impact of the message in every time and place.

Martha welcomes Jesus into her house. She is not merely overwhelmed with the traditional household duties; she is fulfilling the customary responsibilities of hospitality. The word "service" has specific ministerial connotations. Mary sits at Jesus' feet, the customary place of a disciple. In their own ways, both sisters are faithful disciples of Jesus, one listening to his word and the other performing service. Jesus is not being asked to intervene in a domestic squabble. He is being asked to set priorities. Last Sunday we saw that attention to the person in need is to be preferred over the fulfillment of one's everyday responsibilities. The story of Martha and Mary seems to be another example of this principle.

❖ Reflecting on the Word

It is instructive to look at the maps found in most Bibles. You get a sense of how "man-made" (here meaning "made by males") boundaries are. The boundary lines of the biblical world at the time of the Exodus yield to those at the time of King David and then again to those of the world at the time of Babylonian ascendency, and on to the time of Jesus and the early church. The shifting boundaries are a constant over the centuries.

The two stories today reveal a seismic shift in boundaries between God and us. Up until this time in the story of Abraham, God had spoken with Abraham, but now God comes for a home visit. A boundary of intimacy is crossed. Abraham provides a meal and waits on the Lord. In response, God tells Sarah that, after a quarter of a century of hearing the promise, she will have a son by next year.

When Jesus said to Martha that Mary had chosen the better part, he was also approving a shift in boundaries. There were physical boundaries in the Jewish home, "male space" and "female space." By sitting at the feet of Jesus, Mary had crossed the line. Only a disciple of a teacher would do this and only a man could be a disciple. When Martha notes that Mary is not where she belongs, helping in the kitchen, Jesus makes clear where he stands—and where Mary can sit. All part of a new creation, and not yet a finished one either.

✦ Consider/Discuss

- What boundaries have changed in your lifetime?
- What boundaries still need to be changed, opening up more shared space?

✦ Responding to the Word

Loving God, you set the boundaries of earth, sky, and sea. In doing this, you provide a place for us to live responsibly and work happily in your creation. Direct our efforts to be as hospitable as Abraham was to passing strangers and as innovative as Jesus was with his friends Martha and Mary.

July 28, 2013

SEVENTEENTH SUNDAY IN ORDINARY TIME

Today's Focus: Persisting in Prayer

Both Genesis and Luke call us to be persistent when praying to God. They also reveal something important about the God we are praying to, the God of Abraham and the God of Jesus. And Colossians reminds us that we pray as those who have been buried and raised with Christ in baptism.

FIRST READING
Genesis 18: 20–32

In those days, the LORD said: "The outcry against Sodom and Gomorrah is so great, and their sin so grave, that I must go down and see whether or not their actions fully correspond to the cry against them that comes to me. I mean to find out."

While Abraham's visitors walked on farther toward Sodom, the LORD remained standing before Abraham. Then Abraham drew nearer and said: "Will you sweep away the innocent with the guilty? Suppose there were fifty innocent people in the city; would you wipe out the place, rather than spare it for the sake of the fifty innocent people within it? Far be it from you to do such a thing, to make the innocent die with the guilty so that the innocent and the guilty would be treated alike! Should not the judge of all the world act with justice?" The LORD replied, "If I find fifty innocent people in the city of Sodom, I will spare the whole place for their sake." Abraham spoke up again: "See how I am presuming to speak to my Lord, though I am but dust and ashes! What if there are five less than fifty innocent people? Will you destroy the whole city because of those five?" He answered, "I will not destroy it, if I find forty-five there." But Abraham persisted, saying, "What if only forty are found there?" He replied, "I will forbear doing it for the sake of the forty." Then Abraham said, "Let not my Lord grow impatient if I go on. What if only thirty are found there?" He replied, "I will forbear doing it if I can find but thirty there." Still Abraham went on, "Since I have thus dared to speak to my Lord, what if there are no more than twenty?" The LORD answered, "I will not destroy it, for the sake of the twenty." But he still persisted: "Please, let not my Lord grow angry if I speak up this last time. What if there are at least ten there?" He replied, "For the sake of those ten, I will not destroy it."

PSALM RESPONSE
Psalm 138:3a

Lord, on the day I called for help, you answered me.

Brothers and sisters: You were buried with him in baptism, in which you were also raised with him through faith in the power of God, who raised him from the dead. And even when you were dead in transgressions and the uncircumcision of your flesh, he brought you to life along with him, having forgiven us all our transgressions; obliterating the bond against us, with its legal claims, which was opposed to us, he also removed it from our midst, nailing it to the cross.

Jesus was praying in a certain place, and when he had finished, one of his disciples said to him, "Lord, teach us to pray just as John taught his disciples." He said to them, "When you pray, say:
Father, hallowed be your name,
your kingdom come.
Give us each day our daily bread
and forgive us our sins
for we ourselves forgive everyone in debt to us,
and do not subject us to the final test."

And he said to them, "Suppose one of you has a friend to whom he goes at midnight and says, 'Friend, lend me three loaves of bread, for a friend of mine has arrived at my house from a journey and I have nothing to offer him,' and he says in reply from within, 'Do not bother me; the door has already been locked and my children and I are already in bed. I cannot get up to give you anything.' I tell you, if he does not get up to give the visitor the loaves because of their friendship, he will get up to give him whatever he needs because of his persistence.

"And I tell you, ask and you will receive; seek and you will find; knock and the door will be opened to you. For everyone who asks, receives; and the one who seeks, finds; and to the one who knocks, the door will be opened. What father among you would hand his son a snake when he asks for a fish? Or hand him a scorpion when he asks for an egg? If you then, who are wicked, know how to give good gifts to your children, how much more will the Father in heaven give the Holy Spirit to those who ask him?"

❖ Understanding the Word

The account of the dialogue between Abraham and God over the fate of Sodom and Gomorrah is actually a discussion about the nature of divine justice. In traditional societies there is a tension between communal guilt and innocence and individual guilt and innocence. More emphasis is given to the group than to the individual member. At issue in this passage is the extent to which the righteousness of a few people can balance the sinfulness of most. The story demonstrates the power of the righteous. God is willing to allow a few righteous people to save many.

Paul describes the effects of the triumph of the power of God in the lives of believers as it is manifested in the resurrection of Christ. He does this by relating Christ's burial in the grave of the earth with the burial of Christians in the waters of baptism. Paul's argument moves from consideration of actual physical death to spiritual death, the condition of those who, because of sin, are separated from God, who is the source of life. It is important to note that it was precisely while they were sinners that they were saved. The debt owed because of transgressions of the past has been canceled.

Jesus' own practice of prayer prompted his disciples to ask for direction in their prayer, just as the disciples of other religious leaders asked to be taught to pray. Jesus' discourse on prayer can be divided into three separate but related segments: the Lord's Prayer itself (vv. 1–4), an example of persistence in prayer (vv. 5–8), and the assurance of that prayer will be heard (vv. 19–13). There is question about whether this passage should be seen as an actual prayer or as a pattern to follow when praying. The persistence with which one should pray is characterized by the story of the man who woke his sleeping friend. This entire discourse encourages the disciples to persevere in prayer.

❖ Reflecting on the Word

In this delightful story from the book of Genesis, Abraham is presented as being on such intimate terms with God that God not only talks things over with Abraham, but responds to Abraham's gentle nudging. Notice how Abraham first "draws nearer" to God, asking if God will really sweep away the innocent with the guilty. Then he increases the pressure: "Should not the judge of all the world act with justice?" Quite of bit of chutzpah there! In the end, God momentarily yields to Abraham's persuasive—and persistent—intercession.

Jesus urges his disciples to persist in prayer to God, after teaching his prayer to them. This great prayer is the basis for our approaching God with persistence. We are told to call God Father, and then to make two prayers of praise and three petitions to God. Those praying move from blessing and praising God's name and sovereignty to asking for our most basic needs: bread, forgiveness, and deliverance from evil. Jesus follows the gift of his prayer with advice and encouragement.

His advice is to persist; his encouragement is to remember that God is a father who loves his children. God will not refuse the gift of the Spirit to those who have been buried with Christ and have already been raised with him in baptism. As the author of the Letter to the Colossians reminds us, God brought you to life along with Christ even when you were dead in sin. How could God refuse us anything that was truly good for us?

❖❖ Consider/Discuss

- Do you have confidence that God will hear your prayer?
- Do you ask for the Holy Spirit to help you in your prayer?

❖❖ Responding to the Word

Lord, may I come to know the truth of the words of today's response: "Lord, on the day I called for help, you answered me." May we rest peacefully in that assurance that we have received a Spirit of adoption that allows us to cry, "Abba, Father."

August 4, 2013

EIGHTEENTH SUNDAY IN ORDINARY TIME

Today's Focus: Lasting Riches

Today's readings begin by speaking to anxiety and worry. Qoheleth ("Teacher") announces that everything in life is futile, transitory, empty. The psalmist then reminds us that we all go back to dust. But wait, the Gospel offers hope. Within Jesus' words is a call to discover where our real treasure is, reinforced by the reading from Colossians.

FIRST READING
Ecclesiastes 1:2; 2:21–23

Vanity of vanities, says Qoheleth,
    vanity of vanities! All things are vanity!

Here is one who has labored with wisdom and knowledge and skill, and yet to another who has not labored over it, he must leave property. This also is vanity and a great misfortune. For what profit comes to man from all the toil and anxiety of heart with which he has labored under the sun? All his days sorrow and grief are his occupation; even at night his mind is not at rest. This also is vanity.

PSALM RESPONSE
Psalm 90:1

If today you hear his voice, harden not your hearts.

SECOND READING
Colossians 3: 1–5, 9–11

Brothers and sisters: If you were raised with Christ, seek what is above, where Christ is seated at the right hand of God. Think of what is above, not of what is on earth. For you have died, and your life is hidden with Christ in God. When Christ your life appears, then you too will appear with him in glory.

Put to death, then, the parts of you that are earthly: immorality, impurity, passion, evil desire, and the greed that is idolatry. Stop lying to one another, since you have taken off the old self with its practices and have put on the new self, which is being renewed, for knowledge, in the image of its creator. Here there is not Greek and Jew, circumcision and uncircumcision, barbarian, Scythian, slave, free; but Christ is all and in all.

GOSPEL
Luke 12:13–21

Someone in the crowd said to Jesus, "Teacher, tell my brother to share the inheritance with me." He replied to him, "Friend, who appointed me as your judge and arbitrator?" Then he said to the crowd, "Take care to guard against all greed, for though one may be rich, one's life does not consist of possessions."

Then he told them a parable. "There was a rich man whose land produced a bountiful harvest. He asked himself, 'What shall I do, for I do not have space to store my harvest?' And he said, 'This is what I shall do: I shall tear down my barns and build larger ones.

There I shall store all my grain and other goods and I shall say to myself, "Now as for you, you have so many good things stored up for many years, rest, eat, drink, be merry!" ' But God said to him, 'You fool, this night your life will be demanded of you; and the things you have prepared, to whom will they belong?' Thus will it be for all who store up treasure for themselves but are not rich in what matters to God."

❖ Understanding the Word

The word "vanity" means breath or vapor. It denotes a transitory nature or the lack of substance. "Vanity of vanities" is a way of expressing the superlative. Qoheleth is saying that everything is transitory. He is not passing judgment on living itself, but on the anticipation of future satisfaction. Our own transitory nature places the future in jeopardy, and so it is vain to place our hope of satisfaction there. This does not mean that we should refrain from commitment and hard work. It does suggest that the real fruits of our actions are found in the actions themselves rather than in what we might be able to enjoy of them in the future.

The Colossians are told to set their minds on the things of heaven because they are now joined to the risen Christ. Christ's life is the new source for their own lives, and they will share in his ultimate manifestation in glory. Their transformation is characterized as putting off the old self and putting on the new, as one would change clothing. Finally, Paul insists that in this new way of living distinctions such as race, religious origin, gender, culture, or social status no longer feed bias or discrimination. Such distinctions need not be separations. Christ is the exclusive and determining force in all.

Jesus is approached by a man who wants him to act as arbiter between himself and his brother. Jesus uses this encounter as an occasion to teach a lesson about the futility of a life spent in amassing material possessions. The rich man is not censured because of his wealth, but because of the greed that underlies his actions. The man's death is not a punishment for his greed. It is simply the end of his life of excess. It points out the futility of that life. Jesus draws out the moral of his story. It is foolish to devote one's life to the amassing of goods and to be bereft in what matters to God.

What are your three major worries? What gets you tossing and turning at night? Money? Family? The future? Work? Then the book of Ecclesiastes is for you. There is some comfort in its world-weary wisdom. All is passing—life, love, property, worries. What good does it do to worry yourself to death? Death will come soon enough when God turns us all back to dust (that's a little of the psalmist thrown in, for further emphasis). Now, into the week!

Thank God for Jesus. He certainly is a wise teacher in today's Gospel, side-stepping a request to get involved in family bickering over an inheritance. His work was about getting people into the kingdom, not getting people to share the family gold. Even so, Jesus draws a lesson from this situation for the crowd: Avoid greed. Don't reduce your life to what you accumulate.

To bring it home, he tells about a rich man so sure he is going to be around tomorrow that he plans on stockpiling all his goods for himself so he can "rest, eat, drink, and be merry" for the rest of his days. But God has other plans for him.

Jesus' wisdom: Be rich in what matters to God. Colossians agrees: Think of what is above, of Christ at God's right hand, of the glory that awaits you. Make Christ your all and God your treasure. Remember that the goal is transformation, not accumulation. So, put on that new self; put on Christ.

✢ Consider/Discuss

- What have you changed by worrying?
- Do you accept Jesus as your teacher? What is he trying to teach you today?

✢ Responding to the Word

Jesus, teach me to place my life and the lives of those I love in your hands. Help me to be rich in what matters to God, and to put on the new person who is the fulfillment of the Father's plan for me. Give us all wisdom of heart.

August 11, 2013

NINETEENTH SUNDAY IN ORDINARY TIME

Today's Focus: Trustworthy Servants of a Trustworthy God

From Abraham and his descendants to Moses and the Israelites to Jesus and his disciples, God was revealed as being trustworthy for keeping any promises made. Therefore, God deserves having men and women who are trustworthy in return. To serve such a God is to find a Father who will be pleased to give us the kingdom.

**FIRST
READING**
Wisdom 18:6–9

The night of the passover was known beforehand to our fathers,
    that, with sure knowledge of the oaths in which they put
    their faith,
they might have courage.
Your people awaited the salvation of the just
    and the destruction of their foes.
For when you punished our adversaries,
    in this you glorified us whom you had summoned.
For in secret the holy children of the good were offering sacrifice
    and putting into effect with one accord the divine institution.

**PSALM
RESPONSE**
Psalm 33:12b

Blessed the people the Lord has chosen to be his own.

In the shorter form of the reading, the passage in brackets is omitted.

**SECOND
READING**
*Hebrews 11:
1–2, 8–19 or
11:1–2, 8–12*

Brothers and sisters: Faith is the realization of what is hoped for and evidence of things not seen. Because of it the ancients were well attested.

By faith Abraham obeyed when he was called to go out to a place that he was to receive as an inheritance; he went out, not knowing where he was to go. By faith he sojourned in the promised land as in a foreign country, dwelling in tents with Isaac and Jacob, heirs of the same promise; for he was looking forward to the city with foundations, whose architect and maker is God. By faith he received power to generate, even though he was past the normal age—and Sarah herself was sterile—for he thought that the one who had made the promise was trustworthy. So it was that there came forth from one man, himself as good as dead, descendants as numerous as the stars in the sky and as countless as the sands on the seashore.

[All these died in faith. They did not receive what had been promised but saw it and greeted it from afar and acknowledged themselves to be strangers and aliens on earth, for those who speak thus show that they are seeking a homeland. If they had been thinking of the land from which they had come, they would have had opportunity to return. But now they desire a better homeland, a heavenly one. Therefore, God is not ashamed to be called their God, for he has prepared a city for them.

By faith Abraham, when put to the test, offered up Isaac, and he who had received the promises was ready to offer his only son, of whom it was said, "Through Isaac descendants shall bear your name." He reasoned that God was able to raise even from the dead, and he received Isaac back as a symbol.]

In the shorter form of the reading, the passages in brackets are omitted.

GOSPEL
Luke 12:32–48
or 12:35–40

Jesus said to his disciples: ["Do not be afraid any longer, little flock, for your Father is pleased to give you the kingdom. Sell your belongings and give alms. Provide money bags for yourselves that do not wear out, an inexhaustible treasure in heaven that no thief can reach nor moth destroy. For where your treasure is, there also will your heart be.]

"Gird your loins and light your lamps and be like servants who await their master's return from a wedding, ready to open immediately when he comes and knocks. Blessed are those servants whom the master finds vigilant on his arrival. Amen, I say to you, he will gird himself, have them recline at table, and proceed to wait on them. And should he come in the second or third watch and find them prepared in this way, blessed are those servants. Be sure of this: if the master of the house had known the hour when the thief was coming, he would not have let his house be broken into. You also must be prepared, for at an hour you do not expect, the Son of Man will come."

[Then Peter said, "Lord, is this parable meant for us or for everyone?" And the Lord replied, "Who, then, is the faithful and prudent steward whom the master will put in charge of his servants to distribute the food allowance at the proper time? Blessed is that servant whom his master on arrival finds doing so. Truly, I say to you, the master will put the servant in charge of all his property. But if that servant says to himself, 'My master is delayed in coming,' and begins to beat the menservants and the maidservants, to eat and drink and get drunk, then that servant's master will come on an unexpected day and at an unknown hour and will punish the servant severely and assign him a place with the unfaithful. That servant who knew his master's will but did not make preparations nor act in accord with his will shall be beaten severely; and the servant who was ignorant of his master's will but acted in a way deserving of a severe beating shall be beaten only lightly. Much will be required of the person entrusted with much, and still more will be demanded of the person entrusted with more."]

The reading from Wisdom reinterprets the account of the plagues experienced in Egypt. It contrasts the plight of the Israelites and that of the Egyptians, showing how God reversed the very means employed by the Egyptians to afflict the Israelites. The Egyptians themselves were smitten, while the Israelites escaped unscathed. The focus in this account is on the providence of God in sparing the Israelites. For Israel there was always a point of pride in these wondrous feats. However, they were ultimately accomplished for the glory of God's name, never for the glory of Israel itself.

The author of Hebrews states that faith is an openness of mind and heart, not merely a set of propositions. He turns to Abraham's faith to illustrate this. Abraham was willing to leave his home for a land he did not know. His faith became apparent again at the conception of Isaac. Finally, Abraham's faith was manifested in his willingness to respond to God's command to sacrifice that son of promise. The prospect of Isaac's death demonstrates his trust that the God who brought life from a man who was "as good as dead" could bring about the life of this son.

Jesus' address to his disciples reveals the tender nature of their relationship. The metaphor of a flock suggests both intimate knowledge and wholehearted commitment on the part of the shepherd. He assures them that, regardless of how demanding his teaching might seem, it has their best interests at heart. He announces that the reign of God is theirs, and he then exhorts them to live lives that demonstrate their citizenship in that realm. He directs them to be watchful, instructing them to be prepared like servants awaiting the return of the householder. He links the return of the householder with the coming of the Son of Man. Since there is no telling when he will arrive, loyal servants must be prepared at all times.

❖❖ *Reflecting on the Word*

The author of Hebrews calls our attention to the faith of Abraham. Abraham's faith showed itself in his willingness to depart from his home and leave his kin, to trust a promise that his descendants would outnumber the stars, and to be willing to trust God to provide even when God asked him to sacrifice the son who guaranteed the promised future. Through all this a covenant was initiated.

Moses and his people trusted God to take them from the slavery of Egypt to freedom. God's trustworthiness was shown over the coming centuries, not only by leading them into a promised land, but into a covenantal relationship that found itself renewed again and again, despite Israel's infidelities.

With Jesus came a new covenant in his blood, and a call to his followers to replace any fear they might have with an abiding trust in the Father to give them the promised kingdom. He spoke about having a fidelity that would characterize them as good servants in the household of faith. The hallmarks of this fidelity would be watchfulness for the master's return, a commitment to guarding the treasures of the household and caring for its members, and an abiding bond among those who serve.

The stakes of being a good servant are great: either to earn the respect of the master on his return or to lose it, to receive the gratitude of a master who would serve them or to see only sadness and disappointment in his eyes.

✛ Consider/Discuss

- How do you respond to the call to be a trustworthy servant?
- What form does service to the Lord and the divine household take in your life?

✛ Responding to the Word

Jesus, you have promised that if we are faithful in serving you, as you have been in serving the Father's will by your life and death, then you will invite us to recline at table on your return and you will wait on us. Help us to find in this promise good reason to serve you.

August 15, 2013

THE ASSUMPTION OF THE BLESSED VIRGIN MARY

Today's Focus: Mary, Mother of Hope

The Assumption can be thought of as Mary being taken away from us, removed from the earth and its concerns. We can imagine her dwelling with her Son in inaccessible light, far from the cares of our lives. That is not its meaning; it is a feast calling us to hope.

FIRST READING
Revelation 11: 19a; 12:1–6a, 10ab

God's temple in heaven was opened, and the ark of his covenant could be seen in the temple.

A great sign appeared in the sky, a woman clothed with the sun, with the moon beneath her feet, and on her head a crown of twelve stars. She was with child and wailed aloud in pain as she labored to give birth. Then another sign appeared in the sky; it was a huge red dragon, with seven heads and ten horns, and on its heads were seven diadems. Its tail swept away a third of the stars in the sky and hurled them down to the earth. Then the dragon stood before the woman about to give birth, to devour her child when she gave birth. She gave birth to a son, a male child, destined to rule all the nations with an iron rod. Her child was caught up to God and his throne. The woman herself fled into the desert where she had a place prepared by God.

Then I heard a loud voice in heaven say:
"Now have salvation and power come,
    and the kingdom of our God
    and the authority of his Anointed One."

PSALM RESPONSE
Psalm 45:10bc

The queen stands at your right hand, arrayed in gold.

SECOND READING
1 Corinthians 15:20–27

Brothers and sisters: Christ has been raised from the dead, the firstfruits of those who have fallen asleep. For since death came through man, the resurrection of the dead came also through man. For just as in Adam all die, so too in Christ shall all be brought to life, but each one in proper order: Christ the firstfruits; then, at his coming, those who belong to Christ; then comes the end, when he hands over the kingdom to his God and Father, when he has destroyed every sovereignty and every authority and power. For he must reign until he has put all his enemies under his feet. The last enemy to be destroyed is death, for "he subjected everything under his feet."

GOSPEL
Luke 1:39–56

Mary set out and traveled to the hill country in haste to a town of Judah, where she entered the house of Zechariah and greeted Elizabeth. When Elizabeth heard Mary's greeting, the infant leaped in her womb, and Elizabeth, filled with the Holy Spirit, cried out in a loud voice and said, "Blessed are you among women, and blessed is the fruit of your womb. And how does this happen to me, that the mother of my Lord should come to me? For at the moment the sound of your greeting reached my ears, the infant in my womb leaped for joy. Blessed are you who believed that what was spoken to you by the Lord would be fulfilled."

And Mary said:

"My soul proclaims the greatness of the Lord;
my spirit rejoices in God my Savior
for he has looked upon his lowly servant.
From this day all generations will call me blessed:
the Almighty has done great things for me,
and holy is his Name.
He has mercy on those who fear him
in every generation.
He has shown the strength of his arm,
and has scattered the proud in their conceit.
He has cast down the mighty from their thrones,
and has lifted up the lowly.
He has filled the hungry with good things,
and the rich he has sent away empty.
He has come to the help of his servant Israel
for he has remembered his promise of mercy,
the promise he made to our fathers,
to Abraham and his children for ever."

Mary remained with her about three months and then returned to her home.

❖ Understanding the Word

Two signs appear in the heavens, a pregnant woman and the cosmic dragon. She is no ordinary woman. Rather she is depicted as an astral being, superior even to the moon. The twelve stars symbolize the signs of the zodiac, the seven-headed dragon a cosmic monster. Her child is described in royal terms. He is destined to shepherd all of the nations and to rule with a rod of iron, an image of harsh punishment. He is rescued from the threat of the dragon and caught up to the throne of God. His mother is also protected by God, but she flees into the wilderness.

The reading from Paul brings together several of his most treasured themes. Christ is identified as the first fruits of those who have fallen asleep. His resurrection contains the promise of resurrection for all who are joined to him. Paul argues that through sin Adam brought death into the world. In a similar manner, joined in faith to Christ, we are all brought to life. Paul seems to suggest that there is an interval between the end of the world and the final end when Christ will hand the fruits of his victory over to God.

Mary greets Elizabeth with a customary salutation, but it causes the child in Elizabeth's womb to leap with joy. It is as if Mary is the ark and the child within her is the glory of God. In response to this wondrous experience, Elizabeth exalts first Mary and then her child. Mary's hymn of praise has strong parallels in the victory hymns of Miriam (Exodus 15:1–18), Hannah (1 Samuel 2:1–10), and Judith (Judith 16:1–17). While the first section of the prayer describes the great things that God did for Mary, the last verses list some of the past blessings enjoyed by Israel. Mary's hymn of praise suggests that the marvels accomplished in her are a final example of God's mercy. The salvation of God's people has finally come.

❖ Reflecting on the Word

The feast of the Assumption offers hope. What has been done for Mary will be done for us. Our God, the Creator of all that is, has intended from the beginning that creation would share in the fullness of light and life. God's purpose is to bring all creation into the life of the Trinity.

Today's readings are rich in images of being lifted up. In Revelation, we find the image of the child being *caught up* to God and God's throne, safe from the threat of the dragon intent on devouring the child. Paul writes to the Corinthians that just as Christ has been *raised up*, the first fruits, the beginning of the harvest, so too in him all shall be restored to life. And the Gospel gives us Mary's great prayer, her only extended speech in scripture, when she sings her song of praise to God: "My soul proclaims the greatness of the Lord . . . (who) has *lifted up* the lowly."

The Assumption of Mary also lifts us up in hope. What has been done for her will be done for all of us who have been redeemed by Christ, if we commit ourselves to dying and rising with him. She is the mother of and model for all disciples. Her words at the Annunciation, "Be it done to me according to your word," began a life of surrender to God's will. This yielding led to her being taken into the presence of God, where she prays for us in union with her Son.

❖ Consider/Discuss

- Can you see in this feast a promise of hope for all who are faithful to the Lord?
- Can you see a challenge to surrender to God, who will lift you into fullness of life?

❖ Responding to the Word

Mary, help us to find Christ, knowing that when we "do whatever he tells you" (John 2:5), we follow your example of surrendering our will to the Father. Give us the hope that springs from a trusting faith in the Father and shows itself in love for one another.

August 18, 2013

TWENTIETH SUNDAY IN ORDINARY TIME

Today's Focus: Focus, Focus, Focus

Today's focus is focus. Jeremiah was a model of keeping his message in focus, while all the leaders, political and religious, had lost it. Jesus' words put the focus on himself first, then on his followers. And Hebrews is a clear call to focus in order to win the race.

FIRST READING
Jeremiah 38:4–6, 8–10

In those days, the princes said to the king: "Jeremiah ought to be put to death; he is demoralizing the soldiers who are left in this city, and all the people, by speaking such things to them; he is not interested in the welfare of our people, but in their ruin." King Zedekiah answered: "He is in your power"; for the king could do nothing with them. And so they took Jeremiah and threw him into the cistern of Prince Malchiah, which was in the quarters of the guard, letting him down with ropes. There was no water in the cistern, only mud, and Jeremiah sank into the mud.

Ebed-melech, a court official, went there from the palace and said to him: "My lord king, these men have been at fault in all they have done to the prophet Jeremiah, casting him into the cistern. He will die of famine on the spot, for there is no more food in the city." Then the king ordered Ebed-melech the Cushite to take three men along with him, and draw the prophet Jeremiah out of the cistern before he should die.

PSALM RESPONSE
Psalm 40:14b

Lord, come to my aid!

SECOND READING
Hebrews 12:1–4

Brothers and sisters: Since we are surrounded by so great a cloud of witnesses, let us rid ourselves of every burden and sin that clings to us and persevere in running the race that lies before us while keeping our eyes fixed on Jesus, the leader and perfecter of faith. For the sake of the joy that lay before him he endured the cross, despising its shame, and has taken his seat at the right of the throne of God. Consider how he endured such opposition from sinners, in order that you may not grow weary and lose heart. In your struggle against sin you have not yet resisted to the point of shedding blood.

GOSPEL
Luke 12:49–53

Jesus said to his disciples: "I have come to set the earth on fire, and how I wish it were already blazing! There is a baptism with which I must be baptized, and how great is my anguish until it is accomplished! Do you think that I have come to establish peace on the earth? No, I tell you, but rather division. From now on a household of five will be divided, three against two and two against three; a father will be divided against his son and a son against his father, a mother against her daughter and a daughter against her mother, a mother-in-law against her daughter-in-law and a daughter-in-law against her mother-in-law."

❖ *Understanding the Word*

The reading from Jeremiah is a drama of national crisis, prophetic involvement, and political power plays. Jerusalem is under siege and seems to be losing the battle. The prophet's message has demoralized the soldiers. Such behavior is considered an act of treason punishable by death. Placed in a cistern, Jeremiah is saved by a foreigner. The unrest in the kingdom is almost tangible. Not only do the people have to contend with a nation that is mightier than they are, but there is no stability in their own government and they are divided over the matter of prophetic proclamation. Jeremiah appears to be the center of contention.

The author of Hebrews argues that just as athletic games were often held in large amphitheaters, which could accommodate throngs of spectators, so Christians are surrounded by a great cloud of witnesses. Just as athletes are spurred on by the cheers of the people in the stands, so Christians are encouraged by those who have preceded them. Success in athletics requires that one have a goal that is kept uppermost in one's mind. Jesus should be the goal continually held before the eyes of the Christian. Like athletes on the field, the Christians are urged to strain further and further.

Jesus says that he has come to cast fire on the earth and to cause division at the very heart of human society. While Jesus himself is a man of peace, the message that he proclaims is clearly divisive. Many of the claims he makes cut to the core of our dominant social and religious customs and understanding. He makes demands on people that challenge them to the very heart of their being. He insists that commitment to him and his message must take precedence over any political and even kinship loyalties. This is the cause of the division described in the passage. The animosity that Jesus generates is the cause of his own rejection and ultimate suffering and death.

Losing focus can be dangerous to your health. A man recalled in an interview how he had taken his eyes off the road for only three seconds to check his cell phone, when he smashed into the car in front of him. An expert on the addictive nature of digital technology suggested that when driving, cell phone owners should throw it out of reach in the back seat of the car. Cell phones are a danger to our focus on the road.

Jesus shifts how we usually focus on him today—not as preaching or teaching or healing or shepherding, but as casting fire on the earth; not as peacemaker but as divider. This might not make us too happy. Who wants an incendiary Jesus torching the land, or Jesus the homebreaker causing trouble in our family relationships? But Luke's focus on Jesus cannot be tossed aside

Like Jeremiah, Jesus had to tell people what they didn't want to hear: that Jerusalem was going to be destroyed, that it wasn't enough to think God would protect the citizens simply because they laid claim to the temple, the law, or the Sabbath. Laying claims didn't matter if you didn't live them. Laying claim to Jesus means living as a disciple of Jesus, keeping your eyes on Jesus as our "leader and perfecter of faith." Faith ties, not blood ties, are what matter. Jesus came to bring into being a new family through his saving death and resurrection. That's the faith focus.

✢ Consider/Discuss

- Have you ever had an experience of losing focus when navigating, or being called to, the digital world (cell phone, Internet, texting)?
- What is Jesus calling our attention to, when he says he has come to set the earth on fire, or to bring division, not peace?

✢ Responding to the Word

Jesus, you came to enlighten the eyes of our hearts so that we might see you as our leader, hear you as the very Word of God, and follow you along the way you have led. Do not let us grow weary and lose heart, but set our spirits afire with your life-giving Spirit.

August 25, 2013

TWENTY-FIRST SUNDAY IN ORDINARY TIME

Today's Focus: Discipline, Not Entitlement

We have all run into it on occasion—that sense of entitlement some (maybe even we!) have presumed, a claim to be treated differently, as "special." It can be due to a relationship, a skill, a reward, or simply a gift. God's word cuts through any such claims today with two strong images.

FIRST READING
Isaiah 66:18-21

Thus says the LORD: I know their works and their thoughts, and I come to gather nations of every language; they shall come and see my glory. I will set a sign among them; from them I will send fugitives to the nations: to Tarshish, Put and Lud, Mosoch, Tubal and Javan, to the distant coastlands that have never heard of my fame, or seen my glory; and they shall proclaim my glory among the nations. They shall bring all your brothers and sisters from all the nations as an offering to the LORD, on horses and in chariots, in carts, upon mules and dromedaries, to Jerusalem, my holy mountain, says the LORD, just as the Israelites bring their offering to the house of the LORD in clean vessels. Some of these I will take as priests and Levites, says the LORD.

PSALM RESPONSE
Mark 16:15

Go out to all the world and tell the Good News.

SECOND READING
Hebrews 12: 5-7, 11–13

Brothers and sisters, You have forgotten the exhortation addressed to you as children:
"My son, do not disdain the discipline of the Lord
    or lose heart when reproved by him;
for whom the Lord loves, he disciplines;
    he scourges every son he acknowledges."
Endure your trials as "discipline"; God treats you as sons. For what "son" is there whom his father does not discipline? At the time, all discipline seems a cause not for joy but for pain, yet later it brings the peaceful fruit of righteousness to those who are trained by it.

So strengthen your drooping hands and your weak knees. Make straight paths for your feet, that what is lame may not be disjointed but healed.

171

GOSPEL
Luke 13:22–30

Jesus passed through towns and villages, teaching as he went and making his way to Jerusalem. Someone asked him, "Lord, will only a few people be saved?" He answered them, "Strive to enter through the narrow gate, for many, I tell you, will attempt to enter but will not be strong enough. After the master of the house has arisen and locked the door, then will you stand outside knocking and saying, 'Lord, open the door for us.' He will say to you in reply, 'I do not know where you are from.' And you will say, 'We ate and drank in your company and you taught in our streets.' Then he will say to you, 'I do not know where you are from. Depart from me, all you evildoers!' And there will be wailing and grinding of teeth when you see Abraham, Isaac, and Jacob and all the prophets in the kingdom of God and you yourselves cast out. And people will come from the east and the west and from the north and the south and will recline at table in the kingdom of God. For behold, some are last who will be first, and some are first who will be last."

❖ Understanding the Word

Isaiah announces that even foreign people are called together by God, and will become a sign to other foreigners of the glory that they themselves have seen. This vision is quite surprising, for Israel was not a nation that engaged in much missionary activity. Both the universal nature and the cultic character of the vision become clear. People stream to Jerusalem from all four directions. They all come to worship on God's holy mountain. What is most amazing is that from these foreign people God will call forth priests and Levites. Both ethnic privilege and cultic regulations are set aside.

The author of Hebrews softens the view that suffering is discipline from God by appealing to the relationship of parent to child. If it is out of love and concern that parents discipline their children, then suffering can be seen as rigorous training from God that can strengthen us. According to the wisdom tradition, an individual must choose one of two paths, the way of the wise or the way of the foolish. The path referred to here is the way of the wise athlete, and the advice given admonishes the runner to make sure that the path is straight so that there will be no mishap.

Jesus is questioned about the number of people saved. He gives no direct answer, but turns the focus from curiosity about the salvation of others to concern about one's own future. His words illustrate the surprising reversals that the reign of God will bring forth. Salvation is not promised exclusively to one group rather than another. It will be surprising to see who is saved and who is not. Insiders will be kept outside and outsiders will be brought in; Jews will be barred from the messianic banquet while Gentiles will feast at it; outcasts will be welcome, but religious elites will not. While this is true only of some members of each group, the reversals are startling.

The first image is found in Hebrews. No talk of being father's "little darling" or mother's "favorite pet" here. We get a comparison of God as a father who disciplines his child, even "scourges" every son he acknowledges. Now that certainly is a tough image to take, especially in a culture so attuned to the horrors of child abuse. But the time of the Letter to the Hebrews was a different culture, subscribing to the old adage "Spare the rod and spoil the child." What is important is the notion of discipline. So let's set the scourge aside and take up the issue of discipline—the discipline necessary to run a race, to "strengthen your drooping hands and your weak knees, (to) make straight paths for your feet, that what is lame may not be disjointed but healed." Healing what is weak is the goal of this discipline.

The second image is Jesus as the gatekeeper who is telling us that the gate into the kingdom is a narrow one, so strive (there's that note of discipline, again) to enter it. Jesus isn't into numbers and doesn't answer the question asked. He simply urges us to be strong enough to get through the gate. And any claims of "You knew me years ago, Jesus" or "You knew my mother and grandmother" won't matter. Furthermore, prepare to be surprised when you see at who is getting through the gate into the kingdom.

The bottom line today: Strive, discipline yourself—feeling entitled won't get you in.

❖ Consider/Discuss

- Is discipline necessary in your life? What kind?
- What is the key to getting through the "narrow gate"?

❖ *Responding to the Word*

Lord, teach us what we need to know to run the race, to gain entry through the narrow gate, to reach your kingdom. May we realize that you have called us to work with you to bring about the kingdom in our world. Give us the dedication to persevere in this goal.

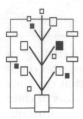

September 1, 2013

TWENTY-SECOND SUNDAY IN ORDINARY TIME

Today's Focus: Good Advice or Good News?

We can hear a call to be humble in today's readings: "Conduct your affairs with humility and you will be loved . . . " (Sirach 3:17). Jesus' words at a dinner party apply this advice to table etiquette: "Don't rush to take the place of honor." But there is more here than first meets the ear.

FIRST READING
Sirach 3:17–18, 20, 28–29

My child, conduct your affairs with humility,
and you will be loved more than a giver of gifts.
Humble yourself the more, the greater you are,
and you will find favor with God.
What is too sublime for you, seek not,
into things beyond your strength search not.
The mind of a sage appreciates proverbs,
and an attentive ear is the joy of the wise.
Water quenches a flaming fire,
and alms atone for sins.

PSALM RESPONSE
Psalm 68:11b

God, in your goodness, you have made a home for the poor.

SECOND READING
Hebrews 12: 18–19, 22–24a

Brothers and sisters: You have not approached that which could be touched and a blazing fire and gloomy darkness and storm and a trumpet blast and a voice speaking words such that those who heard begged that no message be further addressed to them. No, you have approached Mount Zion and the city of the living God, the heavenly Jerusalem, and countless angels in festal gathering, and the assembly of the firstborn enrolled in heaven, and God the judge of all, and the spirits of the just made perfect, and Jesus, the mediator of a new covenant, and the sprinkled blood that speaks more eloquently than that of Abel.

GOSPEL
Luke 14:1, 7–14

On a sabbath Jesus went to dine at the home of one of the leading Pharisees, and the people there were observing him carefully.

He told a parable to those who had been invited, noticing how they were choosing the places of honor at the table. "When you are invited by someone to a wedding banquet, do not recline at table in the place of honor. A more distinguished guest than you may have been invited by him, and the host who invited both of you may approach you and say, 'Give your place to this man,' and then you would proceed with embarrassment to take the lowest place. Rather, when you are invited, go and take the lowest place so that when the host comes to you he may say, 'My friend, move up to a higher position.' Then you will enjoy the esteem of your companions at the table. For everyone who exalts himself will be humbled, but the one who humbles himself will be exalted." Then he said to the host who invited him, "When you hold a lunch or a dinner, do not invite your friends or your brothers or your relatives or your wealthy neighbors, in case they may invite you back and you have repayment. Rather, when you hold a banquet, invite the poor, the crippled, the lame, the blind; blessed indeed will you be because of their inability to repay you. For you will be repaid at the resurrection of the righteous."

❖ Understanding the Word

The author of Sirach admonishes the student to be content with things that are within the realm of possibility. Since this is a discourse on humility, it implies that one might attempt the impossible in order to promote one's reputation in the eyes of others. Still, the only way we discover whether or not we are attempting the impossible is to try. Failure to achieve our goals will help us to recognize our limitations. It is precisely in situations of ambiguity such as this that we both exercise our wisdom and gain more.

The second reading contains a comparison between ancient Israel's experience of God on Mount Sinai and the experience of God on the transformed Mount Zion at the end of time. The fire and thunder of the first experience discouraged access to the divine; not so the second experience. Furthermore, the efficacy of the blood of the innocent Christ is compared to the blood of the innocent Abel and not to that of the Passover sacrifice. Hence, the second experience is not so much a repudiation of the first covenant as it is a description of the final fulfillment accomplished by means of the second.

Jesus tells a parable that addresses proper seating at banquets. This was a very important issue, for one's place at table was indicative of the degree of honor with which the host regarded the guest. The story shows the folly in presuming importance at a public banquet, and it challenges the arrogance of those who think that they are more important than they really are. Jesus turns priorities upside down, criticizing the practice of inviting only those able to reciprocate in kind.

His disciples should give to those who are in need, the very people who cannot advance one's sense of honor, but who might in fact undermine one's reputation. At this Sabbath dinner, Jesus first redefines what honorable behavior is, and then he redefines who are honored guests.

✤ Reflecting on the Word

Sirach's call to act with humility in our affairs connects nicely with Jesus' words to take the last place rather than the place of honor in the dining room. Humility scores more points with others than presumption or pride, even with God. But Jesus is offering more than good advice.

Keep in mind that Jesus was at dinner with Pharisees and lawyers, and that he has just finished healing a man with dropsy who was right in front of him, and it was the Sabbath. Jesus could never seem to stop working on the Sabbath, even in front of people "observing him carefully."

Jesus then tells them a parable, that is, a story with a punch, one that upends the expectations of the listeners. Jesus is proclaiming how things are to be in the kingdom of God—and for those who work to bring about God's kingdom come about even now. In the Kingdom, the last will be first; in the Kingdom, the least will be honored and feted; in the Kingdom, generosity will replace entitlement.

God's plan is not to duplicate Mt. Sinai with its gloomy darkness and fearful words, but God's dinner parties will take place on Mt. Zion, the heavenly Jerusalem, with angels in festal gathering, and the chosen all shining and joyful. Those in attendance will know they are there because of the blood of the Lamb that won them mercy before the throne of God. We prepare for this by showing generosity now.

✤ Consider/Discuss

- Can you hear good news in today's Gospel, how living in the kingdom can start even now?
- How does today's Gospel shed light on what Sunday Mass is about?

✤ Responding to the Word

Generous God, you have invited us to the table of the Word and the table of the Eucharist, where we are nourished and where we learn what it means to live as children of the Kingdom. Thank you for this generous gift. May it continue to shape our lives.

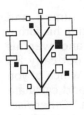

September 8, 2013

TWENTY-THIRD SUNDAY IN ORDINARY TIME

Today's Focus: The Cost of a Re-Newed World

Jesus lays out what it costs to be his disciple and calls his listeners to consider this carefully before signing on. Using the metaphors of building a tower and going to battle, he sketches what a renewed world demands: commitment to him, the One who embodies the wisdom of God.

FIRST READING
Wisdom 9: 13–18b

Who can know God's counsel,
　　or who can conceive what the LORD intends?
For the deliberations of mortals are timid,
　　and unsure are our plans.
For the corruptible body burdens the soul
　　and the earthen shelter weighs down the mind
　　　　that has many concerns.
And scarce do we guess the things on earth,
　　and what is within our grasp we find with difficulty;
　　but when things are in heaven, who can search them out?
Or who ever knew your counsel, except you had given wisdom
　　and sent your holy spirit from on high?
And thus were the paths of those on earth made straight.

PSALM RESPONSE
Psalm 90:1

In every age, O Lord, you have been our refuge.

SECOND READING
Philemon 9–10, 12–17

I, Paul, an old man, and now also a prisoner for Christ Jesus, urge you on behalf of my child Onesimus, whose father I have become in my imprisonment; I am sending him, that is, my own heart, back to you. I should have liked to retain him for myself, so that he might serve me on your behalf in my imprisonment for the gospel, but I did not want to do anything without your consent, so that the good you do might not be forced but voluntary. Perhaps this is why he was away from you for a while, that you might have him back forever, no longer as a slave but more than a slave, a brother, beloved especially to me, but even more so to you, as a man and in the Lord. So if you regard me as a partner, welcome him as you would me.

GOSPEL
Luke 14:25–33

Great crowds were traveling with Jesus, and he turned and addressed them, "If anyone comes to me without hating his father and mother, wife and children, brothers and sisters, and even his own life, he cannot be my disciple. Whoever does not carry his own cross and come after me cannot be my disciple. Which of you wishing to construct a tower does not first sit down and calculate the cost to see if there is enough for its completion? Otherwise, after laying the foundation and finding himself unable to finish the work the onlookers should laugh at him and say, 'This one began to build but did not have the resources to finish.' Or what king marching into battle would not first sit down and decide whether with ten thousand troops he can successfully oppose another king advancing upon him with twenty thousand troops? But if not, while he is still far away, he will send a delegation to ask for peace terms. In the same way, anyone of you who does not renounce all his possessions cannot be my disciple."

❖ *Understanding the Word*

Wisdom insists that no one can fathom the mind of God; no one can know God's will. Yet, we are required to live in accord with that will. The wisdom tradition states that frequently we discover new things about our world and our lives even before we have an understanding of our discoveries. It also acknowledges that there is a dimension to human beings that seeks a wisdom beyond that achieved by reflection on experience alone. The realization of human limitation prompted the author to exclaim that we will attain the wisdom we so sorely seek only if God bestows it upon us.

Paul's Letter to Philemon is a personal appeal to Philemon to accept back with no recriminations a slave who had escaped his household and his control. Though Paul does not criticize slavery itself, he does suggest a way of relating with the slave that will eventually undermine the philosophy that undergirds slavery. Since he taught that in Christ there are no longer slaves or free persons, but that all are children of God, he relies on Philemon's own understanding of mutual brotherhood and sisterhood in Christ to transform his attitude toward Onesimus. Now he challenges Philemon to witness to his own belief in this teaching.

Jesus explains the cost of discipleship. He insists on three conditions for true discipleship. His followers must subordinate everything to commitment to him, even the closest family ties. They must also be willing to bear the suffering that following him will entail. The burden will differ from person to person, but the requirement is the same—wholehearted commitment. Finally, they will be called on to relinquish all their possessions. Total commitment to Jesus requires the willingness to give up the comfort and security of a stable family life, as well as the willingness to spend all one has on that venture. Whoever cannot make such a wholehearted commitment cannot be his disciple.

Does Jesus really mean this? Hate my parents? My siblings? My spouse and children? Hate myself and spend my life carrying "my cross"? "Give up all possessions"? Is this another example of Jesus' hyperbole, like when he said, "If your hand offends you cut it off. If your eye leads you to sin, pluck it out"? What are we getting ourselves into, if we follow Jesus?

We are getting into the most radical commitment of our lives—to accept Christ as our Lord and Savior. We are committing to him and his mission to bring new life to the world, and to bring all our relationships into our life in him. We commit to work at having that mind in us that was in Christ Jesus.

We are getting ourselves into bringing about a re-newed world, where a new sense of family moves us beyond blood ties, a new sense of self takes us beyond personal fulfillment, a new sense of relationship to possessions carries us beyond "shop, shop, shop."

Paul was inviting Philemon to enter into this new world. Philemon's slave, Onesimus, his "property," had run away, a capital offense, punishable even by death. Paul asks the slave owner to take back the slave as a brother in Christ. One wonders what a different world we might have if this short letter (only twenty-five verses) had been read, preached, and heard yearly over the centuries.

So count the cost, know what's at stake, and commit this day to Christ the Lord.

✤ *Consider/Discuss*

- What tower are you building? What battle are you willing to engage in for the sake of the kingdom of God?
- Do you love and trust Jesus enough to follow him daily?

✤ *Responding to the Word*

All-wise and all-knowing God, give us a share in your wisdom and the courage to commit to building up your kingdom in our world. Give us the strength to fight against all that is evil and destructive of your creation. Send your Spirit that we might live more fully in Christ.

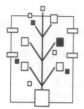

September 15, 2013

TWENTY-FOURTH SUNDAY IN ORDINARY TIME

Today's Focus: God Is Always ISO (In Search Of)

"This saying is trustworthy and deserves full acceptance: Christ came into the world to save sinners" (1 Timothy 1:15). These words take us into the heart of the mystery of our salvation. Three parables in today's Gospel reinforce them, inviting us to think of our God as a shepherd, a woman searching for a coin, and a merciful father.

FIRST READING
Exodus 32: 7–11, 13–14

The Lord said to Moses, "Go down at once to your people, whom you brought out of the land of Egypt, for they have become depraved. They have soon turned aside from the way I pointed out to them, making for themselves a molten calf and worshiping it, sacrificing to it and crying out, 'This is your God, O Israel, who brought you out of the land of Egypt!' I see how stiff-necked this people is," continued the Lord to Moses. "Let me alone, then, that my wrath may blaze up against them to consume them. Then I will make of you a great nation."

But Moses implored the Lord, his God, saying, "Why, O Lord, should your wrath blaze up against your own people, whom you brought out of the land of Egypt with such great power and with so strong a hand? Remember your servants Abraham, Isaac, and Israel, and how you swore to them by your own self, saying, 'I will make your descendants as numerous as the stars in the sky; and all this land that I promised, I will give your descendants as their perpetual heritage.' " So the Lord relented in the punishment he had threatened to inflict on his people.

PSALM RESPONSE
Luke 15:18

I will rise and go to my father.

SECOND READING
1 Timothy 1: 12–17

Beloved: I am grateful to him who has strengthened me, Christ Jesus our Lord, because he considered me trustworthy in appointing me to the ministry. I was once a blasphemer and a persecutor and arrogant, but I have been mercifully treated because I acted out of ignorance in my unbelief. Indeed, the grace of our Lord has been abundant, along with the faith and love that are in Christ Jesus. This saying is trustworthy and deserves full acceptance: Christ Jesus came into the world to save sinners. Of these I am the foremost. But for that reason I was mercifully treated, so that in me, as the foremost, Christ Jesus might display all his patience as an example for those who would come to believe in him for everlasting life. To the king of ages, incorruptible, invisible, the only God, honor and glory forever and ever. Amen.

In the shorter form of the reading, the passage in brackets is omitted.

GOSPEL
Luke 15:1–32 or
15:1–10

Tax collectors and sinners were all drawing near to listen to Jesus, but the Pharisees and scribes began to complain, saying, "This man welcomes sinners and eats with them." So to them he addressed this parable. "What man among you having a hundred sheep and losing one of them would not leave the ninety-nine in the desert and go after the lost one until he finds it? And when he does find it, he sets it on his shoulders with great joy and, upon his arrival home, he calls together his friends and neighbors and says to them, 'Rejoice with me because I have found my lost sheep.' I tell you, in just the same way there will be more joy in heaven over one sinner who repents than over ninety-nine righteous people who have no need of repentance.

"Or what woman having ten coins and losing one would not light a lamp and sweep the house, searching carefully until she finds it? And when she does find it, she calls together her friends and neighbors and says to them, 'Rejoice with me because I have found the coin that I lost.' In just the same way, I tell you, there will be rejoicing among the angels of God over one sinner who repents."

[Then he said, "A man had two sons, and the younger son said to his father, 'Father give me the share of your estate that should come to me.' So the father divided the property between them. After a few days, the younger son collected all his belongings and set off to a distant country where he squandered his inheritance on a life of dissipation. When he had freely spent everything, a severe famine struck that country, and he found himself in dire need. So he hired himself out to one of the local citizens who sent him to his farm to tend the swine. And he longed to eat his fill of the pods on which the swine fed, but nobody gave him any. Coming to his senses he thought, 'How many of my father's hired workers have more than enough food to eat, but here am I, dying from hunger. I shall get up and go to my father and I shall say to him, "Father, I have sinned against heaven and against you. I no longer deserve to be called your son; treat me as you would treat one of your hired workers." ' So he got up and went back to his father. While he was still a long way off, his father caught sight of him, and was filled with compassion. He ran to his son, embraced him and kissed him. His son said to him, 'Father, I have sinned against heaven and against you; I no longer deserve to be called your son.' But his father ordered his servants, 'Quickly bring the finest robe and put it on him; put a ring on his finger and sandals on his feet. Take the fattened calf and slaughter it. Then let us celebrate with a feast, because this son of mine was dead, and has come to life again; he was lost, and has been found.' Then the celebration began. Now the older son had been out in the field and, on his way back, as he neared the house, he heard the sound of music and dancing.

He called one of the servants and asked what this might mean. The servant said to him, 'Your brother has returned and your father has slaughtered the fattened calf because he has him back safe and sound.' He became angry, and when he refused to enter the house, his father came out and pleaded with him. He said to his father in reply, 'Look, all these years I served you and not once did I disobey your orders; yet you never gave me even a young goat to feast on with my friends. But when your son returns, who swallowed up your property with prostitutes, for him you slaughter the fattened calf.' He said to him, 'My son, you are here with me always; everything I have is yours. But now we must celebrate and rejoice, because your brother was dead and has come to life again; he was lost and has been found.' "]

❖ Understanding the Word

After the people make themselves a molten calf and worship it, God accuses them of being stiff-necked. It is probably here more than anywhere else that the greatness of Moses is seen. He pleads for the preservation of the people of whom he is a member. He first insists that the Israelites are God's very own special people, delivered from Egypt. It would be a shame to destroy them now. He then appeals to the promises that God made to the ancestors. How could God possibly renege on them? God listens to the entreaty of Moses; God does relent; God does give the people another chance.

Paul's words open with an expression of gratitude for God's goodness toward him. He admits that previously he had hunted down and stood in judgment over the followers of Jesus. For this reason, he is a perfect example of one who deserves punishment at the hands of God. He stresses his sinfulness so that he can emphasize God's mercy. He insists that the greater his own failure, the more remarkable is God's success in him. In fact, according to Paul, that is the very reason that God took the passionate persecutor and transformed him into an apostle. Paul's own change of heart reveals the breadth of Christ's patience.

The Pharisees and scribes had criticized Jesus for keeping company with tax collectors and sinners, people who were considered social outcasts. They maintained that Jesus' association with them contaminated him as well. In contrast, Jesus saw this association as an opportunity for opening the reign of God to all. Using parables, Jesus drew lines of contrast between the religious leaders and those the leaders have marginalized. The stories depict the extravagant solicitude of the shepherd and the woman to demonstrate the extent to which God will go to rescue even one lost individual. The parable of the prodigal son contrasts God's openness to repentant sinners and the closed-mindedness of those who consider themselves faithful.

The interaction today between Moses and God serves more as a contrast than a parallel with today's Gospel. When God informs Moses of plans to start over again with Moses alone, and to let his wrath "blaze up against" the people for worshiping a golden calf, Moses has to remind God of the covenant's promises. God does relent. In contrast, Jesus embodies the mercy of God, who sent Jesus for our salvation.

Jesus was sent to search out the one sheep who wandered off, to turn the house upside down to recover the misplaced coin, and to welcome back that deliberately lost son, allowing him the time to "come to his senses" and the freedom to choose to return home. Jesus is not the placating voice, tamping down God's fiery anger, but the Father's obedient Son, doing the Father's will by reaching out with mercy and compassion. As Paul writes, Christ came into the world to save sinners. We put our trust in this.

We can see ourselves in any of these roles: one who wanders off, or becomes accidentally lost, or deliberately goes away—all of which leads to our being in a place we don't belong, sometimes in a condition we are ashamed of. We can even be the one who doesn't go off physically but whose heart is far from the Father, living our lives in bitterness, anger, resentment, or a refusal to forgive. Christ tells us his Father can't wait for us to end up back where we belong—in our Father's embrace.

✢ Consider/Discuss

- Do you need to be reminded of the Father's great love for us all?
- Does God need you to seek out someone who has wandered off, or even gotten deliberately lost?

✢ *Responding to the Word*

Forgiving God, we join St. Paul in saying thank you for giving us Christ as a source of strength. May the words of Christ continue to move our hearts into knowing and trusting your love more deeply. Thank you for giving us a place at your table. To you be honor and glory.

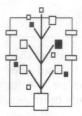

September 22, 2013

TWENTY-FIFTH SUNDAY IN ORDINARY TIME

Today's Focus: The Bottom Line

The bottom line of today's Gospel is the bottom line disciples are to consider when examining their use of money and possessions: "You cannot serve both God and mammon." Created in God's image, called to fidelity in a new covenant in Christ, and empowered by the Holy Spirit, we are to avoid "mammon sickness."

FIRST READING
Amos 8:4–7

Hear this, you who trample upon the needy
    and destroy the poor of the land!
"When will the new moon be over," you ask,
    "that we may sell our grain,
    and the sabbath, that we may display the wheat?
We will diminish the ephah,
    add to the shekel,
    and fix our scales for cheating!
We will buy the lowly for silver,
    and the poor for a pair of sandals;
    even the refuse of the wheat we will sell!"
The Lord has sworn by the pride of Jacob:
    Never will I forget a thing they have done!

PSALM RESPONSE
Psalm 113: 1a, 7b

Praise the Lord who lifts up the poor.

SECOND READING
1 Timothy 2: 1–8

Beloved: First of all, I ask that supplications, prayers, petitions, and thanksgivings be offered for everyone, for kings and for all in authority, that we may lead a quiet and tranquil life in all devotion and dignity. This is good and pleasing to God our savior, who wills everyone to be saved and to come to knowledge of the truth.
    For there is one God.
    There is also one mediator between God and men,
    the man Christ Jesus,
    who gave himself as ransom for all.
This was the testimony at the proper time. For this I was appointed preacher and apostle—I am speaking the truth, I am not lying—, teacher of the Gentiles in faith and truth.
    It is my wish, then, that in every place the men should pray, lifting up holy hands, without anger or argument.

GOSPEL
Luke 16:1–13 or
16:10–13

Jesus said to his disciples, ["A rich man had a steward who was reported to him for squandering his property. He summoned him and said, 'What is this I hear about you? Prepare a full account of your stewardship, because you can no longer be my steward.' The steward said to himself, 'What shall I do, now that my master is taking the position of steward away from me? I am not strong enough to dig and I am ashamed to beg. I know what I shall do so that, when I am removed from the stewardship, they may welcome me into their homes.' He called in his master's debtors one by one. To the first he said, 'How much do you owe my master?' He replied, 'One hundred measures of olive oil.' He said to him, 'Here is your promissory note. Sit down and quickly write one for fifty.' Then to another the steward said, 'And you, how much do you owe?' He replied, 'One hundred kors of wheat.' The steward said to him, 'Here is your promissory note; write one for eighty.' And the master commended that dishonest steward for acting prudently.

"For the children of this world are more prudent in dealing with their own generation than are the children of light. I tell you, make friends for yourselves with dishonest wealth, so that when it fails, you will be welcomed into eternal dwellings.] The person who is trustworthy in very small matters is also trustworthy in great ones; and the person who is dishonest in very small matters is also dishonest in great ones. If, therefore, you are not trustworthy with dishonest wealth, who will trust you with true wealth? If you are not trustworthy with what belongs to another, who will give you what is yours? No servant can serve two masters. He will either hate one and love the other, or be devoted to one and despise the other. You cannot serve both God and mammon."

❖ Understanding the Word

Amos denounces the unscrupulous merchants for their false piety, their avarice, their dishonest business practices, and their exploitation of the poor and defenseless. The judgment of God is passed on these unrighteous individuals in the form of an irrevocable oath. Amos prophesied to the northern kingdom, referred to here as Jacob. As this oracle shows, the people of privilege frequently took advantage of the vulnerable poor. God swears an oath against such pride, showing that the evil perpetrated by it will not be forgotten; it will be avenged. This is truly an oracle of judgment.

The major point of Paul's instruction to Timothy seems to be the all-inclusive scope of Christian prayer. Twice Paul states that prayers should be offered for all people. Special attention is given to civic leaders. Thus, Christianity was not fundamentally inimical toward those who wielded worldly power. Besides, if all power comes from God, as Christians believed, then rightful leaders govern by God's authority, and this authority should be respected. Paul is urging prayer for the conversion of these leaders. If they are converted, they will recognize and accept the teachings of the gospel, and all will be able to live tranquil lives.

Jesus tells a story of a manager who rewrote the debts of his employer in order to ensure a financial future for himself as he faced dismissal. The story has raised many questions, because Jesus seems to commend unscrupulous behavior. Actually, Jesus uses this particular incident to make a religious point. He states that the children of this age (children of the world) have more practical wisdom than do children of light. The real point of the story is found in the last verse. Though shrewd in the ways of the world, the steward chose to serve his own financial needs rather than the economic interests of his employer. Rather than choose to serve the master of the household (God), he chose his own personal interests (mammon).

✛ Reflecting on the Word

The word "mammon" is Aramaic and means property, not only money, but also any possession. More than twenty-five years ago, Fr. John Haughey, S.J. wrote a thoughtful book entitled *The Holy Use of Money: Personal Finances in the Light of the Christian Faith*. He described the condition of "mammon sickness" as having three interrelated aspects: running after things, a numbness in our relationships, and a divided consciousness regarding God.

Today's readings invite us to take our spiritual temperatures to see if we are suffering from a low-grade, or even a more severe, case of "mammon sickness." The prophet Amos rails not simply against dishonest business practices in buying and selling, but more importantly how pursuing wealth can diminish honoring God on the Sabbath and lead to "trampling upon the needy and destroying the poor of the land." The prophetic voice shouts out to proclaim God's love and care for the poor; wealth can exclude such love and care from our daily lives.

The parable Jesus tells and the sayings that follow call for more consideration than space allows, but note that the master's seeming admiration is for his steward's "prudence" or "shrewdness" in using money to make friends. Jesus then contrasts how the children of this world deal with their own kind more astutely than the children of the light. Succinctly put, use mammon to help others. There can be a holy use of money, to care for those most in need, thereby giving glory to God.

✛ Consider/Discuss

- Do you see mammon/money as seducer or sacrament?
- God or mammon—whom do you serve? How do you know?

✛ Responding to the Word

God of justice, you are our true wealth and you have entrusted us with the goods of all creation. May we use them wisely and work to see that all have a just share in them. Form us into just and generous stewards, modeled after the image of your Son.

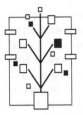

September 29, 2013

TWENTY-SIXTH SUNDAY IN ORDINARY TIME

Today's Focus: Open the Gate

As the gap between rich and the poor widens, God's Word could not be more "in your face." Look around; look at your life. "Woe to the complacent," wails Amos. "Pursue righteousness . . . Lay hold of eternal life," urges Paul. "Listen to 'Resurrection Man' before it is too late," counsels Luke.

FIRST READING
Amos 6:1a, 4–7

Thus says the LORD the God of hosts:
Woe to the complacent in Zion!
Lying upon beds of ivory,
    stretched comfortably on their couches,
they eat lambs taken from the flock,
    and calves from the stall!
Improvising to the music of the harp,
    like David, they devise their own accompaniment.
They drink wine from bowls
    and anoint themselves with the best oils;
    yet they are not made ill by the collapse of Joseph!
Therefore, now they shall be the first to go into exile,
    and their wanton revelry shall be done away with.

PSALM RESPONSE
Psalm 146:1b

Praise the Lord, my soul!

SECOND READING
1 Timothy 6: 11–16

But you, man of God, pursue righteousness, devotion, faith, love, patience, and gentleness. Compete well for the faith. Lay hold of eternal life, to which you were called when you made the noble confession in the presence of many witnesses. I charge you before God, who gives life to all things, and before Christ Jesus, who gave testimony under Pontius Pilate for the noble confession, to keep the commandment without stain or reproach until the appearance of our Lord Jesus Christ that the blessed and only ruler will make manifest at the proper time, the King of kings and Lord of lords, who alone has immortality, who dwells in unapproachable light, and whom no human being has seen or can see. To him be honor and eternal power. Amen.

Jesus said to the Pharisees: "There was a rich man who dressed in purple garments and fine linen and dined sumptuously each day. And lying at his door was a poor man named Lazarus, covered with sores, who would gladly have eaten his fill of the scraps that fell from the rich man's table. Dogs even used to come and lick his sores. When the poor man died, he was carried away by angels to the bosom of Abraham. The rich man also died and was buried, and from the netherworld, where he was in torment, he raised his eyes and saw Abraham far off and Lazarus at his side. And he cried out, 'Father Abraham, have pity on me. Send Lazarus to dip the tip of his finger in water and cool my tongue, for I am suffering torment in these flames.' Abraham replied, 'My child, remember that you received what was good during your lifetime while Lazarus likewise received what was bad; but now he is comforted here, whereas you are tormented. Moreover, between us and you a great chasm is established to prevent anyone from crossing who might wish to go from our side to yours or from your side to ours.' He said, 'Then I beg you, father, send him to my father's house, for I have five brothers, so that he may warn them, lest they too come to this place of torment.' But Abraham replied, 'They have Moses and the prophets. Let them listen to them.' He said, 'Oh no, father Abraham, but if someone from the dead goes to them, they will repent.' Then Abraham said, 'If they will not listen to Moses and the prophets, neither will they be persuaded if someone should rise from the dead.' "

❖ Understanding the Word

The prophet Amos does not denounce wealth itself, but the complacency that often accompanies it. He is distressed because the affluent entertain themselves with wantonness while the social structure of the northern kingdom of Israel disintegrates. He censures the habit of self-indulgence at feasts. The wealthy dine on the meat of lambs and calves, the very animals that were used for sacrifice. Their fastidious tastes expose their arrogance. Perhaps the most excessive example of dissolute dining is their manner of drinking wine. Not content to sip from goblets, they guzzle from wide-mouthed bowls. One can only imagine the result of such drinking.

Paul's address to Timothy contains a fourfold message. He exhorts him to pursue virtue, to fight for the faith, to grasp eternal life, and to keep the commandments. While these are responsibilities of all Christians, Paul expects that Timothy will fulfill them in ways that reflect his pastoral office. He employs an image from athletic competition in order to illustrate the struggle that being faithful often entails. The prize that Paul has in mind is eternal life. Underscoring the seriousness of his admonitions, he charges Timothy, before God and before Christ, to obey the commandments in anticipation of Christ's glorious manifestation.

The Gospel paints a picture of radical reversals. The man who was treated as a castoff enjoys the bliss of heaven, while the one who savored life's pleasures ends up in great torment in the netherworld. The reversal of the rich man's fortune was not the consequence of the lack of moral rectitude; it resulted from his indifference to the needs of the covenant brother who lay at the gate of his home. When he asked that Lazarus be sent to warn his brothers to change their way of life (*metánoia*), he was told that if they did not heed the religious tradition that charged the wealthy to meet the needs of the poor, they would not listen to a resurrected Lazarus.

❖ Reflecting on the Word

Being complacent means to be pleased with yourself. The prophet Amos paints a vivid picture of a pampered people, lying on couches, snacking and sipping to soothing music, massaged into a state of lethargy. Then he lowers the boom: "Party's over. Get ready for exile."

Jesus also paints a portrait of ongoing indolence. Rich Man lies on his couch, dressed in luxuriant purple and soft linen, eating rich foods and drinking choice wines "each day." The problem is that he has become so anesthetized that he can't move, not even to go out to the gate where poor Lazarus lies, smelly, starving, and sickly. Then, suddenly, death pulls down the curtain.

Next scene: a reversal. The gate has become a gap, an abyss. Rich Man is on one side, Lazarus on the other. What is the point? If you enjoy this life, you will pay for it in the next? More that gates have an expiration date and we need to go through the gates life gives us now. The Latin word for gate is *porta*. The word opportunity comes from it. Every opportunity is a gate for entering into a world where we can make a difference. Who is on the other side can vary: a sick person, a sore person, a helpless person, a poor person.

And someone has come back from the dead to tell us this is our calling—Jesus, Resurrection Man. There is always some gate nearby. Open it and look at what's in front of you.

❖ Consider/Discuss

- Who is "outside the gate" in your life?
- When have you heard the voice of the Risen One call you to care for the poor?

❖ Responding to the Word

Lord Jesus, the age to come should start now. Now is the time to hear your word calling us to make this world a place of hospitality and gracious care for all. If we are complacent in any way, break through our indifference and move us to act.

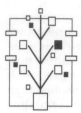

October 6, 2013

TWENTY-SEVENTH SUNDAY IN ORDINARY TIME

Today's Focus: Ask, Then Act

All three readings direct our attention to the vision that faith in God provides. Faith is a gift to be asked for and then acted on. The Gospel connects the power of even a little faith with Jesus' call to willing and obedient service to God.

FIRST READING
Habakkuk 1: 2–3; 2:2–4

How long, O LORD? I cry for help
　　but you do not listen!
I cry out to you, "Violence!"
　　but you do not intervene.
Why do you let me see ruin;
　　why must I look at misery?
Destruction and violence are before me;
　　there is strife, and clamorous discord.
Then the LORD answered me and said:
　　Write down the vision clearly upon the tablets,
　　so that one can read it readily.
For the vision still has its time,
　　presses on to fulfillment, and will not disappoint;
if it delays, wait for it,
　　it will surely come, it will not be late.
The rash one has no integrity;
　　but the just one, because of his faith, shall live.

PSALM RESPONSE
Psalm 95:8

If today you hear his voice, harden not your hearts.

SECOND READING
2 Timothy 1: 6–8, 13–14

Beloved: I remind you to stir into flame the gift of God that you have through the imposition of my hands. For God did not give us a spirit of cowardice but rather of power and love and self-control. So do not be ashamed of your testimony to our Lord, nor of me, a prisoner for his sake; but bear your share of hardship for the gospel with the strength that comes from God.

Take as your norm the sound words that you heard from me, in the faith and love that are in Christ Jesus. Guard this rich trust with the help of the Holy Spirit that dwells within us.

GOSPEL
Luke 17:5–10

The apostles said to the Lord, "Increase our faith." The Lord replied, "If you have faith the size of a mustard seed, you would say to this mulberry tree, 'Be uprooted and planted in the sea,' and it would obey you.

"Who among you would say to your servant who has just come in from plowing or tending sheep in the field, 'Come here immediately and take your place at table'? Would he not rather say to him, 'Prepare something for me to eat. Put on your apron and wait on me while I eat and drink. You may eat and drink when I am finished'? Is he grateful to that servant because he did what was commanded? So should it be with you. When you have done all you have been commanded, say, 'We are unprofitable servants; we have done what we were obliged to do.' "

❖ Understanding the Word

The circumstances within which Habakkuk finds himself are overwhelming: violence, ruin, misery, and destruction. He faces strife and discord. It seems to be more than he can handle, and so he cries out to God: Why? Why do I have to be a witness to all of this desolation, especially since you do not seem to be open to my call for help? Finally, God responds with a vision, not an answer. Without telling the prophet why he has had to carry the burden of suffering or how long he will have to wait, God instructs him that the righteous wait in faith.

Paul appeals to Timothy to be courageous in the face of hardship. He admonishes Timothy to renew his zeal, to be unashamed of the gospel that he preaches, to bear his share of suffering, to adhere to Paul's teaching, and to safeguard it. Paul is aware of the risk that one takes in publicly professing faith in Jesus Christ. There is a stigma attached to such bold testimony. Despite this, Timothy should be willing to accept and to embrace the suffering that will inevitably befall him as a minister of the gospel. Nothing should undermine Timothy's confidence, for he can be strong with the strength that comes from God.

Two independent sayings constitute the Gospel reading: the power of faith and the responsibilities of discipleship. Jesus' attitude is so different from that of the apostles. They ask for an increase of faith; Jesus speaks about its nature. They are interested in quantity; Jesus is concerned about quality. Using the image of a household staff, he insists that though it is relatively small, it is still expected to perform several tasks—plowing, tending sheep, preparing food, and serving at table. The householder might appear unreasonable, but the story is not about being considerate. This is a teaching about the obligations of the one serving, not of the one being served.

The prophet Habakkuk asks God how long he (the prophet) will have to see violence, ruin, and misery. God answers with a vision to be written down and a call to wait patiently in faith. "The just one, because of his faith, shall live."

Paul sounds a call to interior action, urging Timothy to stir into flame the gift of God: a spirit of courage, energy, and action. Though separated by over six centuries, the prophet Habakkuk and the apostles Paul and Timothy faced suffering and destruction; all three responded by witnessing to their faith in the God of Israel. For Paul, this faith finds expression in fidelity to the gospel of Jesus Christ.

The Gospel answers two questions: how do we get this faith and what do we do with it in the face of trials? We get it by asking. Jesus tells the apostles it is not a matter of quantity but quality. A little faith can go a long way in producing results. While Luke's version of this saying of Jesus is less dramatic than Matthew's—with Luke faith can uproot a mulberry tree, while Matthew has it moving a mountain—the basic point is the same.

After his response, Jesus calls them to action. Faith flowers into service. Serving Christ, especially in the least and the needy, flows from faith. The vision faith provides carries us into making this world a better place, embodying the faith, hope, and love that can transform the world.

❖❖ Consider/Discuss

- How have you experienced the power of faith?
- Has it helped you to get through difficult times, giving you strength to uproot any obstacle and toss it in the sea of God's mercy?

❖❖ Responding to the Word

Give us faith, generous God, to carry us through whatever trials and suffering might come in the future. We believe you are with us in all life's circumstances and events, but darkness can sometimes cloud our vision. At those times, help our unbelief. Send your Spirit to strengthen us.

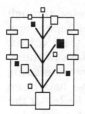

October 13, 2013

TWENTY-EIGHTH SUNDAY IN ORDINARY TIME

Today's Focus: Surprising Messengers

The word of God brings healing on many levels. Sometimes it comes through the scriptures and preaching, at other times it comes through people we would never expect. This word will not be chained, but will achieve God's purpose: our salvation. All people are forever drawn into God's life and love.

FIRST READING
2 Kings 5: 14–17

Naaman went down and plunged into the Jordan seven times at the word of Elisha, the man of God. His flesh became again like the flesh of a little child, and he was clean of his leprosy.

Naaman returned with his whole retinue to the man of God. On his arrival he stood before Elisha and said, "Now I know that there is no God in all the earth, except in Israel. Please accept a gift from your servant."

Elisha replied, "As the Lord lives whom I serve, I will not take it"; and despite Naaman's urging, he still refused. Naaman said: "If you will not accept, please let me, your servant, have two mule-loads of earth, for I will no longer offer holocaust or sacrifice to any other god except to the Lord."

PSALM RESPONSE
Psalm 98:2b

The Lord has revealed to the nations his saving power.

SECOND READING
2 Timothy 2: 8–13

Beloved: Remember Jesus Christ, raised from the dead, a descendant of David: such is my gospel, for which I am suffering, even to the point of chains, like a criminal. But the word of God is not chained. Therefore, I bear with everything for the sake of those who are chosen, so that they too may obtain the salvation that is in Christ Jesus, together with eternal glory. This saying is trustworthy:

> If we have died with him
> we shall also live with him;
> if we persevere
> we shall also reign with him.
> But if we deny him
> he will deny us.
> If we are unfaithful
> he remains faithful,
> for he cannot deny himself.

GOSPEL
Luke 17:11–19
As Jesus continued his journey to Jerusalem, he traveled through Samaria and Galilee. As he was entering a village, ten lepers met him. They stood at a distance from him and raised their voices, saying, "Jesus, Master! Have pity on us!" And when he saw them, he said, "Go show yourselves to the priests." As they were going they were cleansed. And one of them, realizing he had been healed, returned, glorifying God in a loud voice; and he fell at the feet of Jesus and thanked him. He was a Samaritan. Jesus said in reply, "Ten were cleansed, were they not? Where are the other nine? Has none but this foreigner returned to give thanks to God?" Then he said to him, "Stand up and go; your faith has saved you."

❖ Understanding the Word

The story about Naaman focuses on healing, gratitude, conversion, and worship. His cure was clearly miraculous; all he had to do was submit himself to the ritual that Elisha prescribed. This cure champions monotheism and universalism. Naaman may have needed a miracle to recognize the universal power of the God of Israel, but recognize it he did! Something else makes this story exceptional. Though there were many people suffering from leprosy in Israel, God chose to heal a foreigner. This divine act demonstrates God's love and concern for all, Israelite and non-Israelite alike.

Paul writes from prison, making his appeal to Timothy even more poignant. He exhorts his disciple to remember what is at the heart of the gospel that Paul has preached. The kind of remembering of which he speaks is a way of witnessing to the authenticity of what is remembered. In this case it points to a twofold truth: Jesus Christ is raised from the dead and he is a descendant of David. The agony and indignity that Paul bears in his imprisonment are seen by him as a share in the "birth pangs of the messiah," that necessary suffering that will precede the birth of the reign of God.

The Gospel narrative echoes the story recounted in the first reading. It is the story of a foreigner who suffered the pain and indignities of leprosy, was cured by the power of God, and returned to give thanks. He, along with his companions, had recognized Jesus earlier and had hoped for a cure. They all believed that Jesus had the power to heal them and they all went off to show themselves to the priests. What made this man unique was his gratitude. Furthermore, it was a Samaritan, one who was despised by the Jews, who showed gratitude to the Jewish wonder worker. Jesus made this point quite clearly. Once again the last (a Samaritan) will be first (held up as an example).

First, go to your Bible and read the entire fifth chapter in Second Kings for this most enjoyable story of the prophet and the Gentile general with leprosy, highlighting the power of God's word to heal. With today's familiar Gospel story of Jesus and the ten lepers, the focus is on God's salvation coming to "outsiders" like Naaman and the Samaritan as both healing and conversion. We see God's compassionate outreach for those whose leprosy placed them outside the community, for leprosy was a social stigma as well as a physical condition.

What I love in the story of Naaman is the role of the servants, the "little ones." A servant girl captured in a raid first tells Naaman's wife about "the prophet in Samaria." After Naaman arrives at Elisha's door, a servant brings the prophet's message to wash seven times in the Jordan. And finally, it is the general's own servants who convince him to follow this command when he gets all huffy about washing in the Jordan instead of the beautiful rivers back home. But down he goes and cured he is.

Leprosy is a stand-in for the condition of sin that alienates us from God and each other. God's greatest desire is that we know divine, saving grace, a desire often brought home to us by the surprising messengers God sends us—including the prophet from Nazareth who continues to surprise us after two thousand years. So be on the lookout for how God is working to draw you closer and deepen your faith.

✤ Consider/Discuss

- How has God's word brought healing into your life? How has it deepened your ongoing conversion?
- Can you think of any surprising messengers God has used to "get through" to you?

✤ Responding to the Word

Open our ears, Lord, to hear your word. Open our eyes to see the many ways you reach out to us through those you bring into our lives who help us to know you. Help us to see that all people are your beloved children, and that all earth is holy and bears your presence.

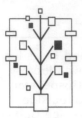

October 20, 2013

TWENTY-NINTH SUNDAY IN ORDINARY TIME

Today's Focus: Praying for Justice

One of the dominant themes in Luke's Gospel is prayer. At least seven times Jesus is presented as going off to pray and twice we find his teaching on prayer. This Sunday and next we hear parables that offer guidance on how to pray and what to pray for.

FIRST READING
Exodus 17: 8–13

In those days, Amalek came and waged war against Israel. Moses, therefore, said to Joshua, "Pick out certain men, and tomorrow go out and engage Amalek in battle. I will be standing on top of the hill with the staff of God in my hand." So Joshua did as Moses told him: he engaged Amalek in battle after Moses had climbed to the top of the hill with Aaron and Hur. As long as Moses kept his hands raised up, Israel had the better of the fight, but when he let his hands rest, Amalek had the better of the fight. Moses' hands, however, grew tired; so they put a rock in place for him to sit on. Meanwhile Aaron and Hur supported his hands, one on one side and one on the other, so that his hands remained steady till sunset. And Joshua mowed down Amalek and his people with the edge of the sword.

PSALM RESPONSE
Psalm 121:2

Our help is from the Lord, who made heaven and earth.

SECOND READING
2 Timothy 3:14 — 4:2

Beloved: Remain faithful to what you have learned and believed, because you know from whom you learned it, and that from infancy you have known the sacred Scriptures, which are capable of giving you wisdom for salvation through faith in Christ Jesus. All Scripture is inspired by God and is useful for teaching, for refutation, for correction, and for training in righteousness, so that one who belongs to God may be competent, equipped for every good work.

I charge you in the presence of God and of Christ Jesus, who will judge the living and the dead, and by his appearing and his kingly power: proclaim the word; be persistent whether it is convenient or inconvenient; convince, reprimand, encourage through all patience and teaching.

GOSPEL
Luke 18:1–8

Jesus told his disciples a parable about the necessity for them to pray always without becoming weary. He said, "There was a judge in a certain town who neither feared God nor respected any human being. And a widow in that town used to come to him and say, 'Render a just decision for me against my adversary.' For a long time the judge was unwilling, but eventually he thought, 'While it is true that I neither fear God nor respect any human being, because this widow keeps bothering me I shall deliver a just decision for her lest she finally come and strike me.' " The Lord said, "Pay attention to what the dishonest judge says. Will not God then secure the rights of his chosen ones who call out to him day and night? Will he be slow to answer them? I tell you, he will see to it that justice is done for them speedily. But when the Son of Man comes, will he find faith on earth?"

❖❖ *Understanding the Word*

Many people have been troubled by the thought that God actually directed aggressive military behavior. However, since the Israelites believed that they were God's special people, they also looked upon their enemies as God's enemies. In fighting their own battles they would be fighting God's battles. The support that Moses gets from Aaron and Hur is probably symbolic. Though Joshua and his selected companions ultimately put the Amalekites to the sword, it was really the prayer of Moses that wins the battle. However, Joshua's involvement in this victory established him as a trustworthy leader for the future.

Paul expounds on the excellence of the sacred scriptures (holy writings) and their usefulness in the lives of Christians. Timothy is reminded of those teachers from whom he learned the message of the scriptures, namely his mother, Eunice; his grandmother Lois; and more recently, Paul himself. Loyalty to his teachers is one reason for Timothy's own faithfulness to the teaching of the scriptures. Paul believed that all scripture was inspired by God and that it played a very important role in the lives of believers. Having expounded on the glories of the sacred scriptures, he solemnly charges Timothy to remain faithful to his ministerial responsibilities.

Jesus draws a very sharp contrast between a judge and a widow who comes to that judge for justice. The judge is described as fearing neither God nor human beings. By his own admission, he is devoid of such devotion. On the other hand, the woman is a widow, a member of one of the most oppressed classes in Israelite society. Though vulnerable, she is bold, a real match for the judge. He will not give in; she will not give up. The persistence of the woman becomes the model Jesus uses to describe the resoluteness required of God's chosen ones. Like the woman, they do not know when God will respond to their pleas, and so they must persist.

Possibly this parable about the widow and the unjust judge was based on a real incident. Since Luke presents Jesus as having loyal women friends who traveled with him, this story might have come from one of them. It has a nice touch of humor when the judge admits he finally gave her justice out of fear she would bop him on the head.

Earlier in this Gospel, Jesus told another parable about being persistent in prayer (11:5–8), but here persistence is connected with a particular end: to persist in praying for justice. If a powerless widow's persistence moves even an unjust judge to justice, how much more will the Father of justice listen to the prayers of his children? Jesus' words were held up to Luke's community who lived in a hostile environment, encouraging them not to lose faith that God keeps all promises. Their fulfillment had already begun in Jesus' resurrection and the gift of the Holy Spirit.

Presumably our first reading was chosen to present a weary Moses as one persisting in prayer with the help of Aaron and Hur. That this prayer results in Joshua's successfully "mowing down" the Amalekites may not particularly inspire. More helpful is Paul's advice to turn to scripture "for training in righteousness (justice)," especially keeping the psalms in mind. Today's responsorial psalm reminds us that "our help is from the Lord, who made heaven and earth." So persist in praying for justice; let not your hearts grow weary.

✛ Consider/Discuss

- What areas of injustice do you see in our world?
- Do you pray that God's justice—understood as the grace to be in right relationship with God, others, oneself, and our world—come more fully into our lives and our world?

✛ Responding to the Word

O God of justice, we ask that you send the Spirit to give us a greater dedication to bringing your justice into the world. Let our hearts not grow weary asking for this gift of the Holy Spirit. Strengthen our faith in the power of your grace to transform our lives.

October 27, 2013

THIRTIETH SUNDAY IN ORDINARY TIME

Today's Focus: Praying for Mercy

Today's parable contrasts the prayers of a Pharisee and a tax collector. Of interest is how the posture of each reflects his attitude and self-perception. Of importance is how the prayer of each weighs in with God. "The prayer of the lowly pierces the clouds," Sirach tells us. Indeed, it touches God's heart.

FIRST READING
Sirach 35: 12–14, 16–18

The LORD is a God of justice,
  who knows no favorites.
Though not unduly partial toward the weak,
  yet he hears the cry of the oppressed.
The Lord is not deaf to the wail of the orphan,
  nor to the widow when she pours out her complaint.
The one who serves God willingly is heard;
  his petition reaches the heavens.
The prayer of the lowly pierces the clouds;
  it does not rest till it reaches its goal,
nor will it withdraw till the Most High responds,
  judges justly and affirms the right,
and the Lord will not delay.

PSALM RESPONSE
Psalm 34:7a

The Lord hears the cry of the poor.

SECOND READING
2 Timothy 4: 6–8, 16–18

Beloved: I am already being poured out like a libation, and the time of my departure is at hand. I have competed well; I have finished the race; I have kept the faith. From now on the crown of righteousness awaits me, which the Lord, the just judge, will award to me on that day, and not only to me, but to all who have longed for his appearance.

At my first defense no one appeared on my behalf, but everyone deserted me. May it not be held against them! But the Lord stood by me and gave me strength, so that through me the proclamation might be completed and all the Gentiles might hear it. And I was rescued from the lion's mouth. The Lord will rescue me from every evil threat and will bring me safe to his heavenly kingdom. To him be glory forever and ever. Amen.

199

GOSPEL
Luke 18:9–14

Jesus addressed this parable to those who were convinced of their own righteousness and despised everyone else. "Two people went up to the temple area to pray; one was a Pharisee and the other was a tax collector. The Pharisee took up his position and spoke this prayer to himself, 'O God, I thank you that I am not like the rest of humanity—greedy, dishonest, adulterous—or even like this tax collector. I fast twice a week, and I pay tithes on my whole income.' But the tax collector stood off at a distance and would not even raise his eyes to heaven but beat his breast and prayed, 'O God, be merciful to me a sinner.' I tell you, the latter went home justified, not the former; for whoever exalts himself will be humbled, and the one who humbles himself will be exalted."

❖ Understanding the Word

Sirach insists that the justice of God is an established fact. He also states that God knows no favorites, neither the privileged nor the dispossessed. By making this statement he indirectly shows that, if there is any partiality, it is ours and not God's. According to covenant theology, we are all responsible for each other. The well-off are obliged to address the needs of those who suffer misfortune. This is a matter of justice, not charity. As a covenant partner, God will intervene on behalf of the poor when other covenant partners disregard their responsibilities. Sirach assures these forlorn people that their entreaties will not go unheeded.

Paul is aware that his days are numbered. His death is imminent. He faces it with the calm resignation that springs from deep faith. He states that he is being poured out like sacrificial blood. He also views his death as a departure like that of sailors weighing anchor or soldiers breaking camp. Like them, Paul has completed a demanding tour of service and is now preparing to return home. Finally, employing imagery from athletic competition, he claims that he has competed well; he has finished the race. He is confident that just as God previously rescued him from peril, so God will rescue him again.

The story of the Pharisee and the tax collector is an example of divine reversal. The Pharisee is a model of religious observance. His practices of piety exceed the requirements of the law. The tax collector, despised because he is part of the economic system put in place by the occupying Romans, asks God for mercy. He stands at a distance, not raising his eyes to heaven. The tax collector prays that his sins be expiated, and his prayer is answered. The Pharisee asks for nothing, and he receives nothing. The men's lives may have been the reverse of each other, but the judgment of Jesus exposes the real reversal.

There is a funny song in the highly irreverent musical *The Book of Mormon*. One of the two young Mormons being sent as a missionary to Uganda is a real "golden boy" with genuine expectations of doing great things. When he is paired up with a less prepossessing fellow named Callahan, he sings a song predicting the great things they will do. The song's title is "It's You and Me—But Mostly Me."

The prayer of the Pharisee falls into this category. It is not a bad prayer, we are told. The Pharisee stands before God in gratitude for many blessings. But the focus quickly shifts to "I . . . I . . . I . . . I . . . " It is the simple prayer of the tax collector that wins God's heart. Note how Jesus expresses it: "the latter went home justified." To be justified is to be in right relationship with God; it is a gift of God. Asking that God be merciful puts us in right relationship with God.

We can make our own several prayers found in Luke's first two chapters. Consider the prayer of Mary upon hearing Elizabeth's words of greeting (1:46–55), the prayer of Zechariah at the birth of John the Baptist (1:68–79), and the prayer of Simeon in the temple when he takes in his arms the Christ Child (2:29–32). Each keeps our focus on God as a God of justice and mercy. Each calls us to bow our heads humbly in recognition of who we are and who God is.

✢ Consider/Discuss

- Does God really want us bowing our heads and beating our breasts?
- Where is the line between self-acceptance, self-esteem, and self-absorption?

✢ *Responding to the Word*

When I am tempted to be boastful in my prayer, O God, help me to recall that I always stand before you as a sinner.

November 1, 2013

ALL SAINTS

Today's Focus: The Power of One

Saints are baptized into the one Body of Christ. They have given the world a taste of the reign of God over all the centuries. They are our kin, and today we give thanks for them.

FIRST READING
Revelation 7: 2–4, 9–14

I, John, saw another angel come up from the East, holding the seal of the living God. He cried out in a loud voice to the four angels who were given power to damage the land and the sea, "Do not damage the land or the sea or the trees until we put the seal on the foreheads of the servants of our God." I heard the number of those who had been marked with the seal, one hundred and forty-four thousand marked from every tribe of the Israelites.

After this I had a vision of a great multitude, which no one could count, from every nation, race, people, and tongue. They stood before the throne and before the Lamb, wearing white robes and holding palm branches in their hands. They cried out in a loud voice:
"Salvation comes from our God, who is seated on the throne,
and from the Lamb."
All the angels stood around the throne and around the elders and the four living creatures. They prostrated themselves before the throne, worshiped God, and exclaimed:
"Amen. Blessing and glory, wisdom and thanksgiving,
honor, power, and might
be to our God forever and ever. Amen."
Then one of the elders spoke up and said to me, "Who are these wearing white robes, and where did they come from?" I said to him, "My lord, you are the one who knows." He said to me, "These are the ones who have survived the time of great distress; they have washed their robes and made them white in the blood of the Lamb."

PSALM RESPONSE
Psalm 24:6

Lord, this is the people that longs to see your face.

SECOND READING
1 John 3:1–3

Beloved: See what love the Father has bestowed on us that we may be called the children of God. Yet so we are. The reason the world does not know us is that it did not know him. Beloved, we are God's children now; what we shall be has not yet been revealed. We do know that when it is revealed we shall be like him, for we shall see him as he is. Everyone who has this hope based on him makes himself pure, as he is pure.

GOSPEL When Jesus saw the crowds, he went up the mountain, and after
Matthew he had sat down, his disciples came to him. He began to teach
5:1–12a them, saying:

"Blessed are the poor in spirit,
for theirs is the kingdom of heaven.
Blessed are they who mourn,
for they will be comforted.
Blessed are the meek,
for they will inherit the land.
Blessed are they who hunger and thirst for righteousness,
for they will be satisfied.
Blessed are the merciful,
for they will be shown mercy.
Blessed are the clean of heart,
for they will see God.
Blessed are the peacemakers,
for they will be called children of God.
Blessed are they who are persecuted for the sake of righteousness,
for theirs is the kingdom of heaven.
Blessed are you when they insult you and persecute you
and utter every kind of evil against you falsely because of me.
Rejoice and be glad,
for your reward will be great in heaven."

❖ Understanding the Word

The events of the first apocalyptic vision unfold on earth; those of the second take place in heaven. Both visions depict vast assemblies of the righteous. One hundred forty-four thousand is clearly a symbolic number. Twelve is squared and then multiplied by a thousand, resulting in a number that indicates completeness. The multitude gathered around the throne comes from every nation, every race, every people, and every tongue. The universality is complete. The multitude represents those who survived the distress of the end-times because they were purified through the blood of the sacrificial Lamb. This distinction entitles them to participate in the celestial celebrations.

According to the Letter of John, love is generative, transforming. It makes believers children of God. Everything that happens in their lives is a consequence of their having been recreated as God's children. They are a new reality and consequently they are not accepted by the world, the old reality. The type of behavior they choose is frequently in opposition to society at large. The "now but not yet" of Christian eschatology (teachings about the end-time) is clearly stated. Though believers have already been reborn as children of God, their transformation has not yet been completed, nor has it been fully made known to them.

In form and content, the Beatitudes are wisdom teaching, not Christian law, as is sometimes claimed. Like most wisdom forms, they describe life situations that draw a connection between a particular manner of behavior and consequences that flow from such behavior. Most if not all of the sentiments expressed in the Beatitudes are found somewhere in ancient Jewish teaching. While the teachings of Jesus are all in some way directed toward the establishment of the reign of God, the values that he advocates are frequently the opposite of those espoused by society at large. This fact offers us a way of understanding the challenges set before us in the Beatitudes. They invite us to turn the standards of our world upside down and inside out.

❖ Reflecting on the Word

Holy Trinity Parish in Georgetown, Washington, D.C., recently inaugurated a one-day operation called "The Power of One." The goal was to engage as many parishioners as possible in various kinds of service in the community during one day. The "one" is not the one day or any one individual, but one community—a community working together for the good of the greater community. The power, of course, is rooted in the love God poured into their hearts to flow out into the world.

Today's feast celebrates the power of one that entered into the world through the dying and rising of Christ, and has been a presence in the world through all those who have been drawn into the one body of Christ through baptism. It is the power that comes when men and women are poor in spirit, mourn the world's sorrows, are meek, hunger and thirst for righteousness, are merciful, clean of heart, peacemakers, and withstand persecution for the sake of living in right relationship with God, others, and the world. They not only will receive heaven, they bring it into the world during their lives.

All Saints holds up a vision reminding us of our future when we will be fully joined with those who have gone before us, but with whom we are one even now in singing praise to our God, as we are reminded at every Eucharist. With them we cry: "Salvation comes from our God, who is seated on the throne, and from the Lamb."

❖ Consider/Discuss

- Have you known the power of belonging to a community doing good?
- Who are the saints who witnessed to you through their faith and now rest in the Lord?

❖ Responding to the Word

God and Father of all, thank you for the gift of your saints, especially those now forgotten men and women who embraced and incarnated the Beatitudes in their lives. May we join with them for all eternity to sing praise to your glory in the name of Jesus, your Son and our Savior.

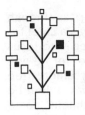

November 3, 2013

THIRTY-FIRST SUNDAY IN ORDINARY TIME

Today's Focus: Ripe for the Picking

The cosmic vision of Wisdom prepares us for the heart-warming story of one of Luke's most memorable characters. Answering an invitation to "Come down quickly" results in hosting the One through whom mercy blossoms into salvation. Indeed, "the LORD lifts up all who are falling and raises up all who are bowed down."

FIRST READING
Wisdom 11:22 — 12:2

Before the LORD the whole universe is as a grain
    from a balance
        or a drop of morning dew come down upon the earth.
But you have mercy on all, because you can do all things;
    and you overlook people's sins that they may repent.
For you love all things that are
    and loathe nothing that you have made;
        for what you hated, you would not have fashioned.
And how could a thing remain, unless you willed it;
    or be preserved, had it not been called forth by you?
But you spare all things, because they are yours,
    O LORD and lover of souls,
        for your imperishable spirit is in all things!
Therefore you rebuke offenders little by little,
    warn them and remind them of the sins
        they are committing,
    that they may abandon their wickedness
        and believe in you, O LORD!

PSALM RESPONSE
Psalm 145:1

I will praise your name for ever, my king and my God.

SECOND READING
2 Thessalonians 1:11 — 2:2

Brothers and sisters: We always pray for you, that our God may make you worthy of his calling and powerfully bring to fulfillment every good purpose and every effort of faith, that the name of our Lord Jesus may be glorified in you, and you in him, in accord with the grace of our God and Lord Jesus Christ.

We ask you, brothers and sisters, with regard to the coming of our Lord Jesus Christ and our assembling with him, not to be shaken out of your minds suddenly, or to be alarmed either by a "spirit," or by an oral statement, or by a letter allegedly from us to the effect that the day of the Lord is at hand.

GOSPEL
Luke 19:1–10

At that time, Jesus came to Jericho and intended to pass through the town. Now a man there named Zacchaeus, who was a chief tax collector and also a wealthy man, was seeking to see who Jesus was; but he could not see him because of the crowd, for he was short in stature. So he ran ahead and climbed a sycamore tree in order to see Jesus, who was about to pass that way. When he reached the place, Jesus looked up and said, "Zacchaeus, come down quickly, for today I must stay at your house." And he came down quickly and received him with joy. When they all saw this, they began to grumble, saying, "He has gone to stay at the house of a sinner." But Zacchaeus stood there and said to the Lord, "Behold, half of my possessions, Lord, I shall give to the poor, and if I have extorted anything from anyone I shall repay it four times over." And Jesus said to him, "Today salvation has come to this house because this man too is a descendant of Abraham. For the Son of Man has come to seek and to save what was lost."

❖ Understanding the Word

The universal love and providence of the Creator are celebrated in this most unusual reading. Unlike earlier traditions that envision creation as a kind of reordering of cosmic debris after the primordial battle, this passage depicts a Creator who is personally involved with every dimension of the natural world. We find here the same cosmic power, but it is coupled with love and mercy. Just as the power of the Creator is matched by the love of the Creator, so is this love manifested through mercy. God is merciful precisely because God is powerful. Finally, the author claims that the imperishable spirit of God is in all things.

Paul assures his people that though he has been the minister of the word, it is God who called them, and it is Paul's prayer that they remain worthy of that calling. He states that though they are obliged to live ethical lives, it is the prior grace of God and not their ethical behavior that saves them. He further teaches an "already-but-not-yet" form of eschatology (teachings about the end-times). Though the eschatological day of the Lord is imminent, it is not yet present. Believers must continue to live their lives in patient anticipation of Christ's coming, realizing that they do so in his presence, for he has already come.

The story of Zacchaeus demonstrates Jesus' mission to seek and to save what is lost. Not only did Zacchaeus belong to the hated class of tax collectors, he was chief among them. This means that he probably benefitted both from the taxes paid and from the fees that tax collectors themselves exacted from the people. The narrative draws bold lines of contrast between Jesus' attitude toward this man and the scorn of some of the bystanders. Jesus insisted that only those who are lost can be found; only those who are perishing can be saved. Those who revere themselves as righteous seldom understand this, and as a result, miss opportunities for their own salvation.

The beautiful opening words from the book of Wisdom slide easily from a poetic proclamation of the scale of creation before God ("Before the Lord the whole universe is as a grain from a balance or a drop of morning dew come down upon the earth") to a hopeful acknowledgment of the true strength of its creator ("But you have mercy on all, because you can do all things; and you overlook people's sins that they may repent.").

The story of Zacchaeus never fails to bring a smile. The man up a tree is plucked like a ripe apple to relieve God's hunger for lost souls. As the head tax collector, Zacchaeus was probably motivated to climb that tree more by fear than by his size. For a collaborator with Rome, any crowd was a dangerous place. But what went up came down a different person.

Jesus asks nothing of him. But he clearly communicated that God's prophet wanted to be with him, up close and personal. In Jesus Zacchaeus discovered that God truly was the Lover of souls and his response flowed easily and generously. Although the crowd grumbled, Jesus let them know that this was what he was all about: "The Son of Man has come to seek and to save what was lost."

You could imagine how it looked as they turned towards Zacchaeus' house, arms around each other's shoulders, going to spend the rest of the night eating, drinking, and rejoicing in how easily someone lost could be loved back into life.

❖❖ *Consider/Discuss*

- What makes Zacchaeus respond so generously to Jesus inviting himself to his house?
- How would you respond to Jesus coming to your house? What would you want him to say to you? What would you say to him?

❖❖ *Responding to the Word*

Lord, I am not worthy that you should enter under my roof but . . . (Complete this prayer in your own words, in light of where you find yourself at the moment—hopefully not "up a tree.")

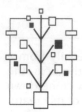

November 10, 2013

THIRTY-SECOND SUNDAY IN ORDINARY TIME

Today's Focus: Taking the Long View

In the days before Jesus was arrested, various groups, including the scribes, the Pharisees, and now the Sadducees, tried to trap Jesus in his words, so they would have a case to bring against him. Today's issue has to do with the belief in the resurrection of the body, which the Sadducees did not hold.

FIRST READING
2 Maccabees 7: 1–2, 9–14

It happened that seven brothers with their mother were arrested and tortured with whips and scourges by the king, to force them to eat pork in violation of God's law. One of the brothers, speaking for the others, said: "What do you expect to achieve by questioning us? We are ready to die rather than transgress the laws of our ancestors."

At the point of death he said: "You accursed fiend, you are depriving us of this present life, but the King of the world will raise us up to live again forever. It is for his laws that we are dying."

After him the third suffered their cruel sport. He put out his tongue at once when told to do so, and bravely held out his hands, as he spoke these noble words: "It was from Heaven that I received these; for the sake of his laws I disdain them; from him I hope to receive them again." Even the king and his attendants marveled at the young man's courage, because he regarded his sufferings as nothing.

After he had died, they tortured and maltreated the fourth brother in the same way. When he was near death, he said, "It is my choice to die at the hands of men with the hope God gives of being raised up by him; but for you, there will be no resurrection to life."

PSALM RESPONSE
Psalm 17:15b

Lord, when your glory appears, my joy will be full.

SECOND READING
2 Thessalonians 2:16 — 3:5

Brothers and sisters: May our Lord Jesus Christ himself and God our Father, who has loved us and given us everlasting encouragement and good hope through his grace, encourage your hearts and strengthen them in every good deed and word.

Finally, brothers and sisters, pray for us, so that the word of the Lord may speed forward and be glorified, as it did among you, and that we may be delivered from perverse and wicked people, for not all have faith. But the Lord is faithful; he will strengthen you and guard you from the evil one. We are confident of you in the Lord that what we instruct you, you are doing and will continue to do. May the Lord direct your hearts to the love of God and to the endurance of Christ.

GOSPEL
Luke 20:27–38
or 20:27, 34–38

Some Sadducees, those who deny that there is a resurrection, came forward [and put this question to Jesus, saying, "Teacher, Moses wrote for us,

> If someone's brother dies leaving a wife but no child,
> his brother must take the wife
> and raise up descendants for his brother.

Now there were seven brothers; the first married a woman but died childless. Then the second and the third married her, and likewise all the seven died childless. Finally the woman also died. Now at the resurrection whose wife will that woman be? For all seven had been married to her."] Jesus said to them, "The children of this age marry and remarry; but those who are deemed worthy to attain to the coming age and to the resurrection of the dead neither marry nor are given in marriage. They can no longer die, for they are like angels; and they are the children of God because they are the ones who will rise. That the dead will rise even Moses made known in the passage about the bush, when he called out 'Lord,' the God of Abraham, the God of Isaac, and the God of Jacob; and he is not God of the dead, but of the living, for to him all are alive."

❖ Understanding the Word

The reason given for the murders described in the first reading leaves no doubt in our minds that these are genuine martyrs, faithful Israelites who died for their faith. The real point of this narrative is the faith in resurrection. Early Israel believed that justice would be accomplished in this life, either during the time of those directly involved or in the time of their descendants. The idea of individual reward or punishment after death became a major issue after the experience of the Exile. This reading reflects the shift that took place in Israel's thinking around the time of the Maccabean revolt (c. 167 B.C.E.).

Paul prays for encouragement and strength for the Thessalonians. Though he asks that they pray for him, he is not concerned with his own personal needs, but with the progress of the gospel that he preaches. When he also asks them to pray for his own deliverance from opposition, he is less concerned with the consequences of the persecution in his life than with how it might set up obstacles for the progress of the gospel. He places his trust in the faithfulness of the Lord. It is Christ who will strengthen the believers, be their protection, and keep them on the path of righteousness.

The Sadducees, who claimed to be descendants of Zadok, the high priest at the time of David, were a conservative, aristocratic group who cooperated with the Romans and enjoyed a certain amount of privilege as a result. Unlike the Pharisees, they did not believe in the resurrection, and they used ridicule to demonstrate that the belief in it was foolish. In response to them, Jesus employs a very traditional Jewish method of argument. He points out that if one is in covenant with God, not even death can sever the bond of that union. His method of interpreting may be unfamiliar to us today, but Jesus employed it effectively to counter the challenge of the Sadducees.

To get the full impact of the first reading, I strongly suggest you go to your Bible and read Second Maccabees, Chapter 7. You wonder what the mother of the Maccabees would have said to the Sadducees trying to trap Jesus over belief in the resurrection of the body. How would this woman, who watched the thugs of a sadistic king cruelly torture with whips and scourges her seven sons over their refusal to eat pork, ever have been able to encourage her sons to remain faithful to God's law without a belief in the resurrection? This belief was her rock. It justified her taking the long view, that their death, in fidelity to God, gives way to a bodily resurrection.

For the Sadducees, however, faith was based on the Torah (the Pentateuch). Only what was written in the Torah had to be believed. Since there is no mention of resurrection, they rejected it. And they use a story of a woman marrying seven brothers to trap Jesus. Jesus says two things in response. First, what happens in the next life is going to be different, not the same old, same old. Second, when God spoke the divine Name to Moses, God did not say, "I was the God of your dead ancestors." Rather, God said, "I am the God of Abraham, Isaac, and Jacob." Implication: God is a God of the living—in God all are alive.

Couple that with Jesus' own resurrection and you have good reason for this hope we carry in our hearts.

✦ Consider/Discuss

- What does belief in the resurrection of the body tell you about God?
- What does it tell you about your own body? Does it have any implications for how you treat your body?

✦ *Responding to the Word*

God of the living, we thank you for the promise you have given us in the resurrection of our Lord Jesus. We thank you for the faith that tells us that those who die in him will rise in him. May this promise, rooted in our baptism, continue to give us hope in our difficulties.

November 17, 2013

THIRTY-THIRD SUNDAY IN ORDINARY TIME

Today's Focus: Prepare for the Day of the Lord

As we near the end of the church year, the prophet Malachi directs our attention to the end time, the "Day of the Lord." In the Gospel Jesus' final teaching before his passion advises how to be ready for it. Until that day arrives, St. Paul's advice to the Thessalonians holds for us: "Work quietly."

FIRST READING
Malachi 3: 19–20a

Lo, the day is coming, blazing like an oven,
when all the proud and all evildoers will be stubble,
and the day that is coming will set them on fire,
leaving them neither root nor branch,
says the LORD of hosts.
But for you who fear my name, there will arise
the sun of justice with its healing rays.

PSALM RESPONSE
Psalm 98:9

The Lord comes to rule the earth with justice.

SECOND READING
2 Thessalonians 3:7–12

Brothers and sisters: You know how one must imitate us. For we did not act in a disorderly way among you, nor did we eat food received free from anyone. On the contrary, in toil and drudgery, night and day we worked, so as not to burden any of you. Not that we do not have the right. Rather, we wanted to present ourselves as a model for you, so that you might imitate us. In fact, when we were with you, we instructed you that if anyone was unwilling to work, neither should that one eat. We hear that some are conducting themselves among you in a disorderly way, by not keeping busy but minding the business of others. Such people we instruct and urge in the Lord Jesus Christ to work quietly and to eat their own food.

GOSPEL
Luke 21:5–19

While some people were speaking about how the temple was adorned with costly stones and votive offerings, Jesus said, "All that you see here—the days will come when there will not be left a stone upon another stone that will not be thrown down."

Then they asked him, "Teacher, when will this happen? And what sign will there be when all these things are about to happen?" He answered, "See that you not be deceived, for many will come in my name, saying, 'I am he,' and 'The time has come.' Do not follow them! When you hear of wars and insurrections, do not be terrified; for such things must happen first, but it will not immediately be the end." Then he said to them, "Nation will rise against nation, and kingdom against kingdom. There will be powerful earthquakes, famines, and plagues from place to place; and awesome sights and mighty signs will come from the sky.

211

"Before all this happens, however, they will seize and persecute you, they will hand you over to the synagogues and to prisons, and they will have you led before kings and governors because of my name. It will lead to your giving testimony. Remember, you are not to prepare your defense beforehand, for I myself shall give you a wisdom in speaking that all your adversaries will be powerless to resist or refute. You will even be handed over by parents, brothers, relatives, and friends, and they will put some of you to death. You will be hated by all because of my name, but not a hair on your head will be destroyed. By your perseverance you will secure your lives."

❖ Understanding the Word

The day of the Lord is the time of the fulfillment. It is the time when justice will be realized, the scales of righteousness will be balanced, the good will be rewarded, and the evil will be punished. Israel believed that that day would be a time of vindication and rejoicing. On that day, the Lord will rise majestically for the upright, like the sun in the eastern sky that shines forth in righteousness. The healing flowing from this experience of God is the total reversal of the flaming destruction in store for the wicked.

Paul instructs the community to seek internal harmony and to strive for a positive reputation before those outside the community. Paul offers his own conduct as an example for them to follow. He reminds them that his own behavior has been beyond reproach. He has not presumed upon the hospitality of others; he is not a financial burden to them. This leads him to comment on a situation that he has been told exists within the community. Some have been acting like busybodies rather than actually being busy. Paul insists that if people want to eat, they must work like everyone else.

The Gospel reading addresses the signs that should alert the people to impending doom. These signs are demonstrations of upheaval. They include political unrest and violence as well as disturbances in the natural world, all experiences that people believed would precede the end of the age. They also portend the persecutions that the followers of Jesus will have to endure at the hands of governments, friends and acquaintances, and even family members. The persecutions they will be called upon to endure will be a witness to the name of Jesus. Though Jesus might be talking about the events that would precede the actual destruction of the glorious temple and the beloved city within which it stood, elements in his discourse suggest an end-of-time dimension to his teaching.

People say that 9/11 changed us irrevocably, that we have lost for good a sense of being invulnerable. That dreadful day revealed we were no longer secure from the kind of violence that could suddenly turn our world upside down, shattering our well-being, bringing death and destruction, and leaving us in a world of fear, insecurity, and anxiety. Unfortunately, such experiences characterize so much of human history.

The destruction of the temple in 70 A.D., an event that Jesus could see coming, was an "end of the world" experience for the people of Jerusalem. The temple was for them the heart of the city, the most sacred space for Israel, God's dwelling place among the Chosen People. Luke's own community also knew of the persecution and hardship Jesus speaks of today. What was important then and remains important now is a willingness to give witness to the Lord in all circumstances, even when doing so threatens our world. We too can take comfort in Jesus' words: "I myself shall give you a wisdom in speaking that all your adversaries will be powerless to resist or refute."

Consider Jesus' final words today: "By your perseverance you will secure your lives." We can take comfort knowing that if we persevere, when the Day of the Lord comes, we will counted among the just who will experience it as the arrival of "the sun of justice with its healing rays." In the meantime, as Paul advises, go about your lives, working quietly to bring about the kingdom of God.

❖❖ *Consider/Discuss*

- Don't we already know the "Day of the Lord" every Sunday when Christ comes to us in the Eucharist?
- How are you called to witness to the Lord in your life?

❖❖ *Responding to the Word*

God who comes, we ask that you give us the grace to persevere through whatever trials and upheavals come into our lives. Help us to live in the awareness that your Son is with us and continues to draw us more deeply into communion with you through the working of the Holy Spirit.

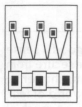

November 24, 2013

OUR LORD JESUS CHRIST, KING OF THE UNIVERSE

Today's Focus: Reigning from the Cross

"The Son of Man came to seek and save what was lost," Jesus said to Zacchaeus. Even from the cross Jesus continues to seek and save, promising Paradise to a criminal being crucified with him. He images the invisible God to the end, the good shepherd rescuing the one sheep.

FIRST READING
2 Samuel 5:1–3

In those days, all the tribes of Israel came to David in Hebron and said: "Here we are, your bone and your flesh. In days past, when Saul was our king, it was you who led the Israelites out and brought them back. And the LORD said to you, 'You shall shepherd my people Israel and shall be commander of Israel.' " When all the elders of Israel came to David in Hebron, King David made an agreement with them there before the LORD, and they anointed him king of Israel.

PSALM RESPONSE
Psalm 122:1

Let us go rejoicing to the house of the Lord.

SECOND READING
Colossians 1: 12–20

Brothers and sisters: Let us give thanks to the Father, who has made you fit to share in the inheritance of the holy ones in light. He delivered us from the power of darkness and transferred us to the kingdom of his beloved Son, in whom we have redemption, the forgiveness of sins.

He is the image of the invisible God,
    the firstborn of all creation.
For in him were created all things in heaven and on earth,
    the visible and the invisible,
    whether thrones or dominions or principalities or powers;
    all things were created through him and for him.
He is before all things,
    and in him all things hold together.
He is the head of the body, the church.
He is the beginning, the firstborn from the dead,
    that in all things he himself might be preeminent.
For in him all the fullness was pleased to dwell,
    and through him to reconcile all things for him,
    making peace by the blood of his cross
    through him, whether those on earth or those in heaven.

GOSPEL
Luke 23:35–43

The rulers sneered at Jesus and said, "He saved others, let him save himself if he is the chosen one, the Christ of God." Even the soldiers jeered at him. As they approached to offer him wine they called out, "If you are King of the Jews, save yourself." Above him there was an inscription that read, "This is the King of the Jews."

Now one of the criminals hanging there reviled Jesus, saying, "Are you not the Christ? Save yourself and us." The other, however, rebuking him, said in reply, "Have you no fear of God, for you are subject to the same condemnation? And indeed, we have been condemned justly, for the sentence we received corresponds to our crimes, but this man has done nothing criminal." Then he said, "Jesus, remember me when you come into your kingdom." He replied to him, "Amen, I say to you, today you will be with me in Paradise."

❖ Understanding the Word

Although it was the people who anointed David as their king, they believed that it was really God who had chosen him. They acknowledged the intimate bond that they shared with this new king. They were his bone and his flesh, his very kin. As king, David is characterized as a shepherd because shepherds were familiar with and personally concerned about their flocks. He is also seen as a commander or captain, one who leads the people. Both images represent the king as a leader for the people, not one who is removed from them, expecting only to be served by them.

The hymn from Colossians extols the divine character of Christ rather than his human nature. Paul characterizes Christ in several ways, each reference adding a significant dimension to our understanding of him. He is a visible manifestation of the invisible God. He enjoys priority in time and primacy in importance. He is the agent through whom all was created, and he is also the goal of all creation. He holds all things together. He is the agent of reconciliation. The sacrificial death of the human Jesus becomes the means through which the cosmic Christ reconciles all of creation with God.

Jesus claimed to be the chosen one, the Christ of God, the King of the Jews—all messianic titles. In the unsettling fashion that so often characterizes the gospel story, Jesus was ridiculed for being who he really was. What the people did not realize was that he was indeed the Messiah, the one for whom they longed; their error was in their messianic understandings and expectations. The inscription on the cross, "King of the Jews," is significant. Jesus was indeed the King of the Jews, even though his manner of ruling did not conform to the standard of the day. True to the paradox of the gospel, what was intended as a sign of derision actually became a proclamation of faith.

A good shepherd lays down his life for his sheep. For this reason the image of a shepherd become connected to the kingly role in the Old Testament. Good kings, like good shepherds, provided for and guarded their flock. As a boy David went from safeguarding sheep to defending his people, going up against Goliath. Later, as a king, he brought together all the tribes of Israel, uniting them as one people.

Jesus spoke of the good shepherd who left the ninety-nine to go out after the one lost sheep and bring it back. We see him do this even from the cross in his last moments. One criminal calls to Jesus to save himself and them, but the other recognizes Jesus is the innocent one who is passing over into his kingdom. When he asks that Jesus take him there, Jesus gently promises to do so.

As we approach the end of the year, we are reminded that our own end will come one day. Let us have the confidence of that criminal we commonly refer to as the "good thief" and make his request to the Lord our own. And whenever that day comes, we can learn from Jesus how to face it: by extending forgiveness to any who have hurt us, by being compassionate up to our final moment, and by handing over our spirit in trust to our Father in heaven. The king will then surely come, gather us up in his arms, and take us with great joy into the Kingdom.

❖ Consider/Discuss

- Does today's image of Jesus on the cross help you to appropriate the image of Christ as king?
- What does it mean when we hear that by baptism we are part of a royal people?

❖ Responding to the Word

Lord Jesus, remember us. Give us a share in the spirit of forgiveness you so generously expressed from the cross, the spirit of generosity that enabled you to turn from your own sufferings to comfort another, and the spirit of trust in your Father expressed in your last words.

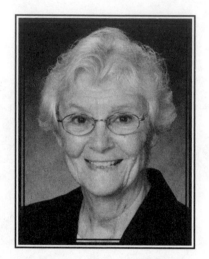

Dianne Bergant, C.S.A., is Professor of Biblical Studies at Catholic Theological Union in Chicago. She holds master's and doctoral degrees in scripture studies from St. Louis University. She was president of the Catholic Biblical Association of America (2000–2001) and has been an active member of the Chicago Catholic/Jewish Scholars Dialogue for the past twenty years. For more than fifteen years, she was the Old Testament book reviewer of *The Bible Today*. Bergant was a member of the editorial board of that magazine for twenty-five years, five of those years as the magazine's general editor. She is now on the editorial board of *Biblical Theology Bulletin* and *Chicago Studies*. From 2002 through 2005, she wrote the weekly column "The Word" for *America* magazine.

James A. Wallace, C.Ss.R., was professor of homiletics at the Washington Theological Union, Washington, D.C. for more than twenty-five years. He is the author of *Preaching to the Hungers of the Heart* (Liturgical Press, 2002) and co-author of three books of homilies, *Lift Up Your Hearts: Homilies for the A, B, and C Cycles* (Paulist Press 2004, 2005, and 2006). He has served as president of the Academy of Homiletics, the Catholic Association of Teachers of Homiletics, and the Religious Speech Communication Association. His articles have appeared in various journals, and he has lectured on preaching in this country, Europe, and Asia.

Notes

Notes

Notes

Notes